THE GENERAL WHO WORE SIX STARS

THE GENERAL WHO WORE SIX STARS

THE INSIDE STORY OF **JOHN C. H. LEE**

HANK H. COX

FOREWORD BY **CLARENCE E. MCKNIGHT JR.**

Potomac Books

AN IMPRINT OF THE UNIVERSITY OF NEBRASKA PRESS

∞

Library of Congress Cataloging-in-Publication Data
Names: Cox, Hank H., 1945– author.
Title: The general who wore six stars: the inside story of John C.
H. Lee / Hank H. Cox; foreword by Clarence E. McKnight Jr.
Description: Lincoln: Potomac Books, an imprint of the
University of Nebraska Press, 2018.
Includes bibliographical references.
Identifiers: LCCN 2017026965 (print)
LCCN 2017027214 (ebook)
ISBN 9781612349633 (cloth: alk. paper)
ISBN 9781640120105 (epub)
ISBN 9781640120112 (mobi)
ISBN 9781640120129 (pdf)
Subjects: LCSH: Lee, John Clifford Hodges, 1887–1958.
Generals—United States—Biography. | World War,
1939–1945—Biography. | United States. Army. Corps of
Engineers—Biography.
Classification: LCC E745.L377 (ebook)
LCC E745.L377 C69 2018 (print)
DDC 940.53/73092 [B]—dc23
LC record available at https://lccn.loc.gov/2017026965

Set in Scala by E. Cuddy.

To my dear friend
Lt. Gen. Clarence E. McKnight Jr.

CONTENTS

Foreword by Clarence E. McKnight Jr.   ix

Introduction   xiii

List of Abbreviations   xix

ONE. Slings and Arrows   1

TWO. A Woman Named John   8

THREE. Love and War   16

FOUR. The Great Flood of 1927   25

FIVE. Tragedy   33

SIX. War Clouds on the Horizon   42

SEVEN. Bolero   51

EIGHT. Lee's Darkest Hour   60

NINE. Torch   70

TEN. Back to Bolero   81

ELEVEN. Countdown to D-Day   94

TWELVE. The Overlord Logistical Plan   103

THIRTEEN. The Great Adventure Begins   115

FOURTEEN. The Great Breakout   127

FIFTEEN. Taking the City of Light   140

SIXTEEN. Lee in the Crosshairs   150

SEVENTEEN. Stalemate on the Western Front   163

EIGHTEEN. Lee's Finest Hour   176

NINETEEN. Lee's Advocacy of African Americans   189

TWENTY. Victory in Europe   201

TWENTY-ONE. Lee's Excellent Italian Adventure   213

TWENTY-TWO. An Unsung Hero   224

Notes   231

Bibliography   247

FOREWORD

CLARENCE E. MCKNIGHT JR.

The Germans have a term—*Materialschlacht*—that describes a battle fought by materials more than troops. War has always been dependent upon materials. Napoleon said an army travels on its stomach, and that is as true today as it was in his time—even more true, I would think, given the complexity of modern weapons and the sophistication of modern warriors.

World War II was a Materialschlacht of unprecedented proportions. The United States became truly the world's "arsenal of democracy" as we supplied arms, food, ammunition, medicine, vehicles—all the accoutrements of war for our own armies and those of our allies. But the production of war matériel is only part of the equation. An even bigger challenge is getting that matériel to where it is needed under wartime conditions. Invading Europe across the Normandy beaches called for an inventory of literally millions of items—spare parts and tires for vehicles, different kinds of ammunition, different kinds of food, clothing for all sorts of weather and conditions. The list was endless.

The United States had all of that stuff piled up in depots across Great Britain by early 1944, and on June 6 we began moving it across the English Channel and into France. The one guy primarily responsible for making this happen was Lt. Gen. John C. H. Lee, head of the Service of Supply (SOS), which later was renamed the Communications Zone, or ComZ. Getting it all across the channel was just the beginning of his challenge. When Patton's famed Third Army went on its end run around the Germans and across France, Lee suddenly had to throw all of the army's supply plans out the window and somehow figure out how to get fuel and ammo to the troops, who were farther away with each passing day. His supplies were coming slowly across Omaha Beach because it took a long time to capture and repair major ports. If that weren't challenge enough, he had to contend with recalcitrant combat generals who resented his authority and constantly sought to undercut him.

It is a little known fact that Lee commanded one in four American soldiers in the European theater of operations and was for a time General Eisenhower's deputy and thus second in command of the European theater. He contended with a host of problems that were exacerbated by his personal eccentricities, which made him a subject of widespread ridicule. When he first got to Great Britain, he demanded and got his own private train so he could travel around orchestrating the great buildup. When Paris was captured, he moved his entire command into the City of Light against Eisenhower's expressed wishes. He was more committed to protocol than most officers, as well as highly religious. Lee went to church every day, two or three times on Sunday, and made his staff go with him.

But perhaps his most "obnoxious" quality—and this was a sign of the times—was his advocacy of African Americans, whom he believed could contribute more to the war effort if the old racial attitudes could be discarded. About nine hundred thousand African Americans served in the U.S. Army in World War II, mostly in service and supply roles, which means many of them worked for Lee. When in December 1945 a troop shortage emerged and the War Department exhorted the field armies to move more men from service jobs into the infantry, Lee took it upon himself to issue an order permitting black men under his command to transfer to the infantry. That kicked up a firestorm, but he never backed down. And a few years later President Harry Truman made it official when he formally integrated the U.S. military.

Every military veteran who, like me, is steeped in our history knows stories about Lee. I came along too late for World War II, but I heard the stories. Lee's initials were J.C.H., so the wags said his initials stood for Jesus Christ Himself. As a younger officer he often volunteered to serve on court-martial boards, so some called him Courthouse Lee. He also had a peculiar habit of wearing three stars on the back of his helmet in addition to the three on his front. (I also made it to three stars, but it frankly never occurred to me to wear six.)

And yet I see many parallels between his career and his character and my own. Like Lee, I am a man of religious faith. Perhaps I do not wear my faith on my sleeve the way he did, but no one has ever had to ask me twice to share my faith with them. Like Lee, I was always a stickler for protocol. You get some rough characters in the army. Rigid discipline is a key component of keeping them focused on their jobs. Like Lee, I often served on court-martial panels. In Germany in the years after Vietnam we had serious discipline problems in the military. I tried to help young men in crisis as best I could, but when necessary I came down hard on them. I did not enjoy it, but that is the responsibility of senior officers.

What is most important is that I admire Lee's commitment to racial justice. He was far ahead of his time on this vital issue and much of the abuse he suffered was a result of it, but he had the power of conviction and never backed down. I like people like that.

Overall I think this book by my good friend Hank H. Cox, who incidentally helped me write my book, *From Pigeons to Tweets*, is a long overdue tribute to a maligned hero who played a decisive role in the defeat of Nazi Germany and who deserves to rank among the most distinguished officers to ever wear the uniform of the U.S. Army.

INTRODUCTION

In the late 1970s I subscribed to a series of books about World War II produced by Time-Life. They arrived in my mailbox like clockwork, once a month for forty months. They were slick, photo-heavy books, well researched and written. Each volume addressed a specific aspect of the war and offered insights into the key leaders of the major countries and of course the great battles. Lots and lots of battles. My library was rather thin in those days, so I gave these books my full attention, reading them more than once. In subsequent years I have acquired and read a variety of books about World War II, rereading the better ones. I began over time to acquire some expertise about that pivotal conflict of the last century.

In the 1970s we were only about three decades removed from the war. I had known many men who fought in it—teachers at our schools, deacons in our church, drunks in the local bars. As a boy, I lived in a small town in West Virginia that posted a prominent honor roll at our one main intersection. It listed the names of the locals who had fought, identifying those who had lost their lives. As I recall, it was near our one and only stoplight, directly across from the junior high school that is no longer there. I passed it countless times and always took note of it, wondering about the stories behind those names. The honor roll disappeared somewhere along the line and is now probably collecting dust in someone's garage.

The veterans who fought in that war are likewise disappearing at an accelerating rate as time takes its inexorable toll. But interest in the war does not appear to be on the wane. An issue of the *New York Review of Books* dated March 10, 2016, contains a review by Max Hastings of eleven new books about World War II. (I write book reviews for the *Washington Post*, but I have never covered more than two books in one review.)

"It is a publishing phenomenon, for which some of us who are authors have cause to be grateful, that seventy years after the conclusion of World War II, works about the conflict enjoy a popularity second only to cookbooks," Hastings writes. "This is unsurprising because it was the greatest human event in human history, a saga that offers narratives about a collision between the forces of good and evil much less nuanced—apparently so, at least, to unsophisticated readers—than the modern struggle between militant Islam and the West."

Great events and great heroes tend to generate many books. I have made my own modest contribution to the library of works on the Civil War and the life of Abraham Lincoln (*Lincoln and the Sioux Uprising of 1862*, Cumberland House, 2005). The publisher didn't really care about the specific topic. He said any book about Lincoln would sell, and it did. I figured if I could hitch a ride on the Civil War, I might as well try my luck with World War II as well, if only I could find the right topic—one that had somehow escaped the attention of the other writers plowing back and forth across the littered landscape of the war. And at long last I do believe I have found just such a topic—a big one just sitting there in plain sight awaiting a fresh look.

In reading about the war I was of course awed by the scale of the fighting, the chaos, the courage and carnage, but for some reason I was also taken by the importance of supplying the armies and the incredible production of U.S. industry that sprang almost overnight from the desuetude of the Great Depression into what would become the most explosive industrial expansion in history. I cite below a section from one of the Time-Life books: "The planes that rolled off the assembly line at Willow Run were only part of an avalanche of armaments produced by American industry during World War II. Before that conflict came to an end, American plants turned out 296,429 airplanes, 102,351 tanks and self-propelled guns, 372,431 artillery pieces, 47 million tons of artillery ammunition, 87,620 warships, 44 billion rounds of small-arms ammunition—in all $183 billion worth of war materials (in 1945 dollars). So impressive was this feat that even such a grudging admirer of American achievements as Russian Premier Josef Stalin proposed a toast at the Teheran Conference late in 1943 'to American production, without which this war would have been lost.'"[1]

Missing in that stupendous array of production are all of the other countless items that a military force depends on—food, gasoline, tires, uniforms, winter coats, underwear, sleeping bags, canteens, cigarettes, bulldozers, heavy-duty socks, trucks, Jeeps, locomotives (thousands of them) to pull the tens of thousands of railcars we sent over; the list goes on and on. It was reliably estimated that the Service of Supply (SOS), which provided the guns and food for the Americans, British, and Canadians who invaded Europe on D-Day in 1944, had to handle more than three million discrete items in its inventory, take care of it all, move it to the ever-shifting front lines, protect it from the enemy, and get it to the people who needed it to wage war and strive to survive.

It is that latter item that caught my attention and led to this book—the supplying of our forces in the European theater of operations (ETO) from D-Day, on June 6, 1944, until the surrender of Germany on May 7, 1945—a period of eleven months. The senior American officer in charge of that operation was the quartermaster, Lt. Gen. John C. H. Lee, head of the Service of Supply (SOS), commander of the Communications Zone (ComZ), and for a while deputy to the Supreme Allied Commander, Gen. Dwight D. Eisenhower. Lee arrived in Great Britain in 1942 to begin setting up his supply systems and two years later followed the troops across the English Channel to keep the vital supplies moving to our armies, which were themselves soon scurrying across the French countryside at breakneck speed.

Lee's assignment was an awesome one in the view of his boss. "With 36 divisions in action we were faced with the problem of delivering from beaches and ports to the front lines some 20,000 tons of supplies every day," Gen. Dwight D. Eisenhower recalled. "Our spearheads, moreover, were moving swiftly, frequently 75 miles per day. The supply service had to catch these with loaded trucks. Every mile of advance doubled the difficulty because the supply truck had always to make a two-way run to the beaches and back, in order to deliver another load to the marching troops. Other thousands of tons had to go into advanced airfields for construction and subsequent maintenance. Still additional amounts were required for repair of bridges and roads for which heavy equipment was necessary."[2]

It was actually a lot more complicated than that. Loading supplies from the beaches was woefully inefficient and subject to the weather, which could and did turn awful quickly. The army needed ports but was unable to capture them fast enough, and when they did they found the Germans had trashed them. And it was impossible to move all of the supplies needed to the front lines by truck—despite the valiant efforts of the celebrated Red Ball Express. Trains were needed, which meant Lee's people had to repair railroad lines and bridges destroyed in our preliminary bombings and then import trains from the United States. Every way Lee turned lay another seemingly insurmountable challenge.

There was never even a small chance that the senior officer in charge of supplies for all this activity would be popular. The quartermaster traditionally is the most despised individual in the military hierarchy simply because that is the officer who controls the cookie jar and has to say no to people. No battalion or division ever believes it is getting its fair share of supplies, and there are always shortages of critical items even under the best of circumstances, which reinforces the perception of being shortchanged. Such is the nature of warfare.

But Lee's reputation was greatly exacerbated by what can only be described as personal quirks in a male society intolerant of individuality. He was highly religious, attending services regularly and requiring his immediate staff to do the same. It was commonly said of him, not in fun, that the initials for his three given names—J.C.H.—stood for "Jesus Christ Himself." Lee also was a strong advocate of integration in the era of Jim Crow, when the U.S. Army was strictly segregated and most senior officers harbored racist attitudes. In addition he and his staff always found a way to live well in the midst of conflict and hardship, an option available to the men in charge of supplies but one that was understandably resented by the soldiers living in the cold and mud. And he was the only senior officer of his rank who wore three stars not only on the front of his helmet but also three more on the back—for a total of six. It is not uncommon for combat officers such as majors and lieutenant colonels to wear insignia on the backs of their helmets so troops following behind into battle will know their leader is ahead of them. But lieutenant generals do not lead troops in combat. To wear six stars was weird.

The bigger question is whether Lee performed his job well, and that is a matter of some dispute. Indeed it is safe to say that Lee has come down in history to us as one of the most controversial personalities of the great conflict, or perhaps any American conflict. Many of his colleagues in the senior American command were critical of his performance and personality, and several of them connived vigorously to have him removed. "Lee was a stuffed shirt," said Eisenhower's chief of staff, Gen. Walter Bedell "Beetle" Smith.[3] Gens. George Patton and Omar Bradley disliked him intensely and said so in no uncertain terms. Even those who expressed satisfaction with his performance did so half-heartedly, even apologetically. Few if any were able to get close to him personally.

For the most part the popular historians have been even harder on him. Stephen E. Ambrose writes in *Citizen Soldiers* that Lee was "the biggest jerk" in the European theater of operations.[4] Jonathan W. Jordan writes in *Brothers, Rivals, Victors* that Lee "was one senior general whom all field commanders could hold in quiet—and sometimes not so quiet—contempt."[5] Geoffrey Perret writes in *There's a War to Be Won* that "the theater was rife with Lee stories, and even the wildly implausible ones might be true."[6] D. K. R. Crosswell writes in *Beetle* that "the imperious Lee impressed fellow officers as a strange admixture of religiosity and pomposity."[7] Antony Beevor, author of *Ardennes 1944*, brands Lee "pompous and megalomaniac."[8] Rick Atkinson in *The Guns at Last Light* describes Lee as "a fussy martinet."[9]

But there is at least one credible historian who extols Lee's achievements if not his mannerisms: the prolific historian and biographer Jean Edward Smith, who gives him high marks in *Eisenhower in War and Peace* and other works related to World War II. "Despite his grandiose manner, indeed, perhaps because of it, Lee had no equal in amassing the supplies that an army needed to move forward—and crossing the Channel would pose an unprecedented logistical challenge," Smith writes, adding that Lee "proved to be a logistics virtuoso and in many ways was the unsung hero of the Allied victory in Europe."[10]

Certainly there was no shortage of "grandiose" generals in World War II. Gens. George Patton, Douglas MacArthur, and Bernard Montgomery come to mind. But though they offended many, they also excited admiration for their daring deeds on the battlefield. Lee, perhaps because his mission was supply instead of combat, never received that kind of fame and adulation. The question at issue in this book is whether General Lee warrants all of the opprobrium heaped upon him or whether the historian Smith was closer to the truth. Was Lee a jerk or a hero? Just who was this guy, and why do all those people say such terrible things about him?

ABBREVIATIONS

ADC	aide de camp
ADCSEC	Advance Section of ComZ
AEF	American Expeditionary Force
AGF	American Ground Forces
AIC	Army Industrial College
AWC	Army War College
CWA	Civil Works Administration
CCS	Combined Chiefs of Staff
ComZ	Communications Zone
DTC	Disciplinary Training Center
DUKW	Duck boat: amphibious transport craft
ETOUSA	European theater of operations, U.S. Army
LST	landing ship, tank
NRA	National Recovery Administration
PLUTO	pipeline under the ocean
POL	petroleum, oil, and lubricants
PWA	Public Works Administration
RAF	Royal Air Force
SHAEF	Supreme Headquarters, Allied Expeditionary Force
SOS	Service of Supply
SOLOC	supply system supporting Sixth Army Group
SS	Schutzstaffel: Nazi special security force

THE GENERAL WHO WORE SIX STARS

CHAPTER ONE

Slings and Arrows

They have sharpened their tongues like a serpent;
adders' poison is under their lips.
—Psalm 140:3

Any history of the European theater of operations during World War II not written by Jean Edward Smith will likely contain harsh words about Lt. Gen. John C. H. Lee, such as these by Geoffrey Perret in *There's a War to Be Won*:

Arriving in England, Lee demanded a train. The British were dumbstruck. The King had a private train, they conceded, but a small one. Not even Churchill had his own train. And Eisenhower never asked for a train. Lee insisted until he finally got one—two cars for his staff, two flatcars for vehicles, a dining car, a conference car, a private car for the general and several others. He liked the millionaire lifestyle, whatever the cost, submitting expense claims that might make an advertising vice president blush.

A stickler for ritual and a man whose memoirs refer to the author as "We," Lee expected dumb shows of deference wherever he went. He loved to hobnob with British aristocrats and aped their affectations. Lee expected to be noticed. He got Sam Goldwyn's former press agent assigned to sos to help keep track of his doings.[1]

Jonathan W. Jordan, author of *Brothers, Rivals, Victors*, describes an occasion when Patton met with Lee in London:

After a pea-soup flight to London, George [Patton] was greeted at the airfield by Harry Butcher and Lieutenant General John Clifford Hodges Lee. Cliff Lee, a fifty-six-year-old classmate of George's, had Patton's penchant for self-aggrandizement and an appetite for creature comforts that dwarfed George's living standards. He assigned himself a beautifully furnished personal train to move about the country, his helmet was decked with triple stars front and back, and he defended his perquisites like Rommel with his back to the sea.

Supply never gets good billing, but Lee's self-indulgences, his backroom politicking, his ostentation, and the natural inefficiency of a system supplying millions of men made him one senior general whom all field commanders could hold in quiet—and sometimes not-so-quiet—contempt. After working with Lee for a few months, George would subscribe to one officer's description of him as "a pompous little son-of-a-bitch only interested in self-advertisement," and it didn't help George's temperament when, on his arrival in London, Lee's sos men had quartered him in a hotel room that resembled a garish bordello, its boudoir featuring a white bear rug, nickel-plated furnishings, and a satin-sheeted bed perched low under a lewd ceiling mirror.[2]

Antony Beevor takes issue with Lee's move into Paris early in the ETO campaign:

> In Paris, Lieutenant John C. Lee, the Army supply supremo of the Communications Zone, known as "Com Z," took over 315 hotels and several thousand other buildings and apartments to house his senior officers in style. He also appropriated the Hôtel George V almost entirely for himself. The pompous and megalomaniac Lee even expected wounded soldiers to lie at attention in their hospital beds whenever he appeared on a tour of inspection in boots, spurs and riding whip, accompanied by a fawning staff.[3]

Eisenhower was reportedly enraged by Lee's takeover of Paris. Ike's naval aide, Capt. Harry C. Butcher, sometimes referred to as Eisenhower's Boswell, recounted his reaction:

> The Com Zone headquarters had been at Valognes, but when Paris fell, this center of transport, supply and personnel became the natural location for the large service organization. Ike felt that the combat troops who had taken Paris would look back over their shoulders from the front lines and see the supply people living in the luxury of Paris. He thought this very bad psychologically and

2

was in the process of ordering General Lee to abandon Paris completely but found the movement had proceeded so far that stopping it was impossible. So he had instructed General Lee to stop the entry of every individual who was not needed at that spot for essential duty. General Lee is to have an investigation of the American personnel in Paris and is to send away from there everyone whose presence is not necessary. He is to use every type of transport available to get them out, including empty trucks returning to base. He had also heard, as I had, that the dress, discipline, and conduct of American personnel in Paris left much to be desired. Paris was to be used as a recreation center for combat troops and space was to be retained for their comfort.[4]

(General Lee did not follow through on this order.)

Rick Atkinson chimes in on Lee and his Paris adventure:

In Paris, Lee kept a huge war room in the Hôtel Majestic basement, and three suites upstairs for his own use. (His personal baggage included a piano.) The adjacent Avenue Kléber became known as the "Avenue de Salute," and Lee dispatched officers to patrol the sidewalk and take the names of soldiers who failed to render proper courtesy. Additional suites were reserved for him in other grant hostels; denizens at one were advised, "The Hôtel George V is considered General Lee's personal residence, and assignments of accommodations carry the understanding that such persons are his guests." The front curb was to be kept clear for his own entourage; other cars "will be required to park around the corner or down on the next block."

"Why didn't someone tell me some of those things?" Eisenhower later asked after hearing of Lee's idiosyncrasies. The complaint said more about the supreme commander's inattention than about Lee. Not for two weeks did Eisenhower learn of the ComZ land rush in Paris, which he had intended to keep mostly free of Allied soldiers. He referred to Lee as "a modern Cromwell."[5]

"Lee was an unrepentant sinner," Atkinson writes. "'I have no regrets,' he said. 'One should be as far forward as possible.'"[6]

In his biography of Eisenhower's chief of staff, Gen. Walter Bedell Smith, D. K. R. Crosswell writes,

> Lee's friends called him Johnny or Cliff, but he carried a number of less flattering nicknames. Known as "Courthouse" because of his frequent volunteering to serve on courts-martial early in his career, the imperious Lee impressed fellow officers as a strange admixture. . . . Obsessed with preserving the outward signs of efficiency and military protocol, Lee rigorously enforced codes of discipline and dress, insisting that everything be "spit and polish." He had already taken to traveling around his domain in a private train. Although Lee capably shouldered an immense workload, his formidable manner and appearance, tactless exercise of authority, and jealous defense of his position made him a target of criticism. He produced results but also animosity.[7]

In his biography of Gen. Brehon Burke Somervell, the senior supply officer in Washington and Lee's boss, the historian John Kennedy Ohl has described Lee as a bald, fussy "oppressively religious" man. Lee was, he concedes, "an able, efficient, quick thinking, aggressive operator," but he projected the image of an empire builder. He had an exaggerated sense of his own importance, had eccentricities that wore badly on others, and was overly concerned with spit and polish. He also had a "supply sergeant's mentality" and doled out equipment to troops and generals alike "as if it were a personal gift."[8]

That J. C. H. Lee was the chief Allied logistician was detrimental to an effort that required the hand of someone far more skilled in the school of logistical support than the general sneeringly referred to as "Jesus Christ Himself," according to Carlo D'Este, who goes on to suggest that "Lee's narrow-mindedness, conventional peacetime quartermaster's mind, and his unwillingness to use every means at his disposal to improve a logistics system tailored to the needs of the combat armies (the Red Ball Express notwithstanding) produced what has aptly been called 'the tyranny of logistics' in the late summer and autumn of 1944. But instead of concentrating on the problems of resupply, Lee seemed more interested in winning the race with SHAEF to claim

4   SLINGS AND ARROWS

the best hotels and facilities in Paris, and in indulging his mania for creature comforts."[9]

But without doubt the most scathing indictment of Lee is offered by Stephen E. Ambrose:

> The biggest jerk in ETO was Lt. Gen. John C. H. Lee (USMA 1909), commander of Service of Supply (SOS). He had a most difficult job, to be sure. And of course it is in the nature of an army that everyone resents the quartermaster, and Lee was the head quartermaster for the whole of ETO. . . .
>
> He hated waste; once he was walking through a mess hall, reached into the garbage barrel, pulled out a half-eaten loaf of bread, started chomping on it, and gave the cooks hell for throwing away perfectly good food. He had what Bradley politely called "an unfortunate pomposity" and was cordially hated. . . .
>
> Lee's best-known excess came . . . at the height of the supply crisis. Eisenhower had frequently expressed his view that no major headquarters should be located in or near the temptations of a large city, and had specifically reserved the hotels of Paris for the use of combat troops on leave. Lee nevertheless, and without Eisenhower's knowledge, moved his headquarters to Paris. His people requisitioned all the hotels previously occupied by the Germans, and took over schools and other large buildings. More than 8,000 officers and 21,000 men in SOS descended on the city in less than a week with tens of thousands more to follow. Parisians began to mutter that the U.S. Army demands were in excess of those made by the Germans.
>
> The GIs and their generals were furious. They stated the obvious: at the height of the supply crisis, Lee had spent his precious time organizing the move, then used up precious gasoline, all so that he and his entourage could enjoy the hotels of Paris. It got worse. With 29,000 SOS troops in Paris, the great majority of them involved in some way in the flow of supplies from the beaches and ports to the front, and taking into account what Paris had to sell, from wine and girls to jewels and perfumes, a black market on a grand scale sprang up.[10]

Recounting Eisenhower's enraged reaction, Ambrose notes that Lee and his staff stayed put in Paris:

> And of course there was solid reason for so doing. And of course the combat veterans who got three-day passes into Paris could never get a hotel room, and had to sleep in a barracks-like Red Cross shelter, on cots. The rear-echelon sos got the beds and the private rooms. And their numbers grew rather than shrank. By March 1945, there were 160,000 sos troops in the Department of the Seine.
>
> The supply troops also got the girls, because they had the money, thanks to the black market. It flourished everywhere. Thousands of gallons of gasoline, tons of food and clothing, millions of cigarettes were being siphoned off each day. The gasoline pipeline running from the beaches to Chartres was tapped so many times only a trickle came out at the far end.
>
> Most of this was petty thievery. It was done at the expense of the front-line troops. As one example, the most popular brand of cigarettes was Lucky Strike, followed by Camel. In Paris, the sos troops and their dates smoked Lucky Strikes and Camels; in the foxholes the men got Pall Malls, Raleighs, or, worse, British cigarettes.[11]

Overall the historian's take on Lee is uncomplimentary to say the least. Even the official history compiled by Roland G. Ruppenthal and published in 1952 by the U.S. Army Center of Military History struggles to put a positive spin on Lee. "General Lee continued to be a controversial personality throughout the history of the theater, owing in part to the anomalous position which he held," Ruppenthal writes. He continues,

> But the controversy over the sos was heightened by his personal traits. Heavy on ceremony, somewhat forbidding in manner and appearance, and occasionally tactless in exercising authority which he regarded to be within the province of the sos, General Lee often aroused suspicions and created opposition where support might have been forthcoming.

It appears, however, that few of his subordinates and certainly fewer still of the persons with whom he dealt got to know him well. Those who did knew him to be kindly, unselfish, modest, extremely religious, and a man of simple tastes, however much this seemed to be contradicted by the picture of ostentation presented by the living arrangements of his staff and by his use of a special train for his comings and goings in the United Kingdom. General Lee has been aptly referred to as a "soldier of the old school," one who believed firmly in the dignity of his profession and wore the uniform with pride. He expected every other soldier, from general to private, to revere that uniform as he did. Many, without attempting to understand his rigid sense of discipline, were quick to label him pompous and a martinet. There can be no doubt that General Lee was motivated by a high sense of duty, and he expected others to measure up to his own concept of soldierly qualities.[12]

Even the estimable Jean Edward Smith, who has suggested Lee was the "unsung hero of World War II" in his biography of Eisenhower, was a bit more critical in his 1990 biography of Gen. Lucius D. Clay: "Lee's preparation for D-Day left little to be desired and the Allies crossed the Channel in fine shape—an achievement of enormous magnitude," he writes. "But over the long haul, Lee wore badly. A slightly pompous officer with the religious ardor of a Chautauqua evangelist . . . Lee doled out supplies with a supply sergeant's eye for rewarding past favors and punishing grievances."[13]

Not a fun guy, in other words. An unidentified officer privately offered that Lee was no one he would want to go fishing with for a week. But for the eleven months of the ETO campaign the head quartermaster's boss, Eisenhower, resisted intense pressure to dismiss Lee or at least limit his authority. In the end the Allies won the war. The question remains whether this was because of or in spite of the contributions of Lee.

CHAPTER TWO

A Woman Named John

There is many a boy here today who looks
on war as all glory, but boys, it is all hell.
—GEN. WILLIAM T. SHERMAN

John Clifford Hodges Lee was born August 1, 1887, in Junction City, Kansas, then and now a small city attached to the U.S. Army's Fort Riley, home of the storied First Division—known as the Big Red One. From his earliest days he was surrounded by military people and immersed in military culture. His maternal grandfather, Capt. John Noble Hodges, was killed in action as a supply service officer in the Confederate army—so that provides a connection, however tenuous, between Lee and the supply component of the military. Captain Hodges was married to Josephine Fredonia Hodges (nee Whitaker). Lee's grandmother Katherine's sister Sarah Katherine was married to John Hodges's older brother, Cooper Hodges.[1]

When Captain Hodges was killed in action, Josephine was pregnant with what she hoped would be a son, to be named after his father. She had a girl instead but still named her John. The middle name Clifford came from another kinsman. Thus the mother of John Clifford Hodges Lee was named John Clifford Lee. It is possible—even probable—that she was the only woman named John in Kansas, or indeed the nation.

The Hodges family was well off, but most of Captain Hodges's near male relatives had been killed in the war. His brother Cooper had survived but was partially paralyzed from his wounds. In the postwar years the widow Josephine Hodges was struggling to manage seven plantations in Mississippi. An old family friend from Vermont, James Streeter, came to visit and persuaded the widow to marry him and live with him in Kansas, where he and a partner had a bank, a general store, and a hotel, the Hale House. In those days westward-bound wagon trains plying the Santa Fe Trail depended on protection by troops at Fort Riley. Streeter died in 1896.

At the age of nineteen John Clifford Hodges married Charles Fenelon Lee, who his son described as an "insurance promoter" from Iowa. The teenaged John had met Charles Lee in Leadville, Colorado, where they both lived at the time. They later moved to Kansas City, Missouri, and spent much time riding the train back and forth to Junction City, where John's mother lived. John and Charles had three children: John C. H. Lee plus two sisters, one older and one younger than he. They were all born in Junction City. In 1892 Lee's mother left his father and moved with the children to Junction City to live with her mother and stepfather. Lee offers no explanation of this in his memoirs.

At one time James Streeter had owned substantial property, the last 550 acres of which were still held by Josephine when John C. H. was a boy. This farm lay along the Republican River just above its junction with the Smoky Hill River and across from Fort Riley. Many years later General Lee recalled that the family had a close relationship with local African Americans, some of whom had worked on the family plantations in Mississippi.

Grandmother Streeter was a devout Presbyterian, but the family somehow migrated into the Episcopal Church, where Lee would remain active for the rest of his life. His older sister, Katharine, died of meningitis in 1904. His younger sister, Josephine, he recalled, "was a great pal to me and took full part in all of our games. She was the best horse-woman in town, if not in the county. Lighter in pounds and hands than any of the men, she nevertheless could handle the best jumpers and accomplish their highest performance."[2]

Lee recalled that in the summer of 1893—the time of the World's Fair in Chicago—he suffered a broken arm, which was broken again about ten years later, and the injury left him with a crooked left elbow, "somewhat disfigured."[3] For some time he feared it would keep him out of military service, which suggests he was focused on a military career early in life.

Lee often traveled with his family to visit relatives in Montgomery, Alabama, and Denver, Colorado. They always took the train, and these trips young John clearly relished, setting a pattern for his later life. His mother never failed to thank the porters who helped them with their luggage. "She would give a generous silver coin to the porter if it were the last piece in her purse," Lee said. "She would try to have something for the conductor's children too—possibly special goodies from our lunch basket."[4]

In 1895 Grandmother Streeter's younger daughter, Jean Dodd Streeter, Lee's aunt, married Lt. George Foreman Landers, who was with the U.S. Army Fourth Artillery Regiment. He was posted to West Point as an instructor of chemistry and electricity. Knowing of Lee's interest in the military, Grandmother Streeter resolved to find a way to send him there to visit, which happened in the summer of 1899.

But the year before that young Lee had another accident that almost aborted his military ambitions. During the Spanish-American War, then much in the news, he constructed replicas of naval ships and relived the great battles of Havana and Manila Bay. In the quest to make his games more vivid, he constructed a cannon from iron pipe, using a baby carriage for a caisson. He acquired some black powder, which went off prematurely, blistering much of the skin of his face. "It was feared at first that I might lose my eyesight," he recalled. "For a week or more it was necessary to lie swabbed in linseed oil–soaked cotton bandages. When they were finally lifted and I could see, there was considerable rejoicing."[5]

The following year he was at West Point visiting his aunt and uncle. "With Uncle George [Landers] that early fall we had wonderful walks through the woods," Lee recalled. "A born teacher, he made mathematics so attractive and relatively easy. He was a thorough administrator and taught me much, consciously and unconsciously, about standards of the service."[6]

Not long after Lee returned to Junction City that autumn Grandmother Streeter passed away, and the family soon learned that much of her estate had been mismanaged, leaving the family virtually destitute. Their remaining income came primarily from a rental property in Clay Center, Kansas, and the structure burned down. "Sadly, the insurance had lapsed," Lee recalled.[7] The family made do the best they could. They obtained fresh vegetables from the farm, which was managed by tenants, and often provided lodging to those tenants during flood season. Lee took a job in a grocery store to help the family meet its obligations.

Through family connections Lee obtained an "alternate appointment" to West Point, and in 1905 he graduated from high school, number two in his class, which meant he was qualified to enter West Point without academic examinations. The family had trouble coming up with the money for his rail fare to the Point or the necessary deposit to his credit with the academy's treasurer, as required by regulations, but they managed it somehow. "It was impossible to send dear mother anything from my pay as a Cadet at West Point," Lee recalled. "Those lean years had a lasting effect upon my thinking and on my future planning."[8]

Lee recounted some advice he received from another cadet, who hailed from Manhattan, Kansas, and advised him to try to "stand well" in every subject but not worry about top standing: "Having the West Point summer of 1899 ambition revived in my heart, naturally I wanted to make good in the Military Department. Instead of getting into mischief, I worked at any chore that seemed to please the upper classmen."[9] The advice served him well. He finished twelfth out of 109 graduates in the class of 1909. His classmate George Patton finished forty-sixth. There is no record that he and Patton were chummy, then or later.

Religion continued to be a dominant theme in Lee's time at West Point: "The best influence of my four years at West Point was a God-given combination of Chapel services, including Episcopal Holy Communion once a month, singing in the choir as I had done in boyhood, attending the evening informal song and prayer meetings in the YMCA Hall over the West Sally Port and the Bible classes we tried to hold."[10]

Lee's high academic ranking earned him one of fifteen slots in the coveted Corps of Engineers that virtually all West Pointers aspired to because it was assumed they offered the best opportunity for advancement. After joining other classmates on tours of the Panama Canal (which was still under construction) for five months, he spent time on the upper Mississippi River development project and the Ohio

River lock and dam improvement before going to engineer school at the Washington Barracks. It apparently was a pleasant sojourn in the nation's capital. Every morning he rode a horse through Rock Creek Park, which was a favorite pastime for those who had access to horses. Just about every aspiring young officer in the U.S. Army in those days had access to a horse and knew how to ride it.

Lee was then assigned to Fort Leavenworth in Kansas to join the Third Battalion of Engineers. During this time in 1912 the fort was visited by Secretary of War Henry Lewis Stimson and his "relatively young" chief of staff, Gen. Leonard Wood. Lee was detailed as aide de camp for Stimson during the visit, making an important contact that would serve him well years later, as would his contact with Wood. He was making plans to have his mother come live with him when he got a command "request" to come to Washington to serve as aide to the chief of staff in his capacity as grand marshal for the upcoming inauguration of President-Elect Woodrow Wilson. So he had to tell his mother to postpone her trip, and then he was off again to the capital city. "In addition to this interesting work," he recalled, "I was permitted to ride each afternoon that the Secretary of War could get away. I was told by General Wood it was my duty to see that Mr. Stimson was reminded tactfully that his mount was saddled and waiting. He kept his riding clothes and boots in his office and seldom failed to break away."[11]

In the evenings Lee was permitted to accompany the secretary and his wife to official parties, where he often encountered fellow West Pointer Douglas MacArthur, with whom he developed a rapport. Lieutenant Lee was already working his way into an influential network. After the inaugural Secretary Stimson and General Wood offered him any station he wanted. He asked to rejoin his Leavenworth unit, which was then on the Mexican border in Texas. On his way out of office President Taft had ordered mobilization of the army's Second Division in and about Texas City in preparation for a campaign against the notorious bandit Pancho Villa, whose band of irregulars had been raiding across the border in Texas. Lee stopped off in Leavenworth to get his gear and had his horse sent ahead.

In Texas Lee and the other engineers were engaged mainly in map-

tain. "For my thesis, I submitted *The Manual for Topographers*. The Board examined me orally on engineering and strictly military subjects without any recalled embarrassment," Lee noted. "Apparently my ratings up until then had all been excellent or better. For my 'physical,' I was sent over to Governor's Island to ride ten miles—twenty times around a half mile track! Of course, I then called on dear General Wood who asked if the Stimsons knew of my being there. No? Well, he called the former Secretary who asked me to come to his office on Liberty Street and go out to Highhold for the night. We had time for a gallop that later afternoon, too!"[17]

Lee recorded that the happiest experience of his time in Wheeling District was meeting and getting to know Sarah Ann Row. Their budding relationship seemed to hinge on how well she got along with his mother: "But after I had brought lady-like Sarah, so perfectly gowned and gloved to have tea with dear little Muddie, we soon came to an understanding. They had so much in common, more than either realized, at first."[18] They agreed to be married but did not immediately set a date.

Sometime in the winter of 1916–17 Lee got a note from General Wood asking if he would be willing to serve as the general's aide de camp. "I believe that war is coming," Wood said to him. Both Lee's mother and his fiancée urged him to accept whatever came and to do his best. By April he and his mother were living in New York. "Thus ended my first real detail on so-called river and harbor duty," he recorded.[19]

Lee and his mother sent Jack Turner back to his children, who lived in Philadelphia. Turner later returned to Junction City, where the Lee-Hodge family helped support him until he passed on.

CHAPTER THREE

Love and War

Older men declare war. But it is
youth that must fight and die.
—HERBERT HOOVER

On September 24, 1917, John Lee and Sarah Row were married in St. Matthew's Church in Wheeling, West Virginia. The ceremony was performed by Rector R. E. L. Strider, who, Lee proudly noted, later became the Episcopal bishop of West Virginia. The pastor of the local Presbyterian church assisted. "All of dear Sarah's family were present, with her nieces serving as bride's maids and her sister, Emma, as Matron of Honor," Lee recalled. "My little mother was there to represent our family."[1]

After the ceremony the happy couple drove to Pittsburgh, where they caught the night train to New York so they could attend his sister Josephine's wedding the next day in Flemington, New Jersey, to Capt. Alfred Kenny Craven Palmer of the Sixth Field Artillery. Lee's mother discreetly traveled by a separate train to the second wedding. This one was also in an Episcopal church.

Soon Lee and his bride were on their way to Fort Riley back in Kansas. War was in the air, which is the sort of thing that lifts the spirits of young army officers. Lee was optimistic, as were many others, that his patron Gen. Leonard Wood would be the commander of the American forces in Europe.

Wood was a senior officer who had served as army chief of staff under President Taft; he was the only medical officer ever to hold that position. Wood was a strong advocate of military preparedness, which was favored by Republicans but not in accord with the agenda of the Democratic Wilson administration, which at the time was focused on staying out of the war in Europe. Wood became a focal point of those pressing for U.S. involvement. President Wilson ordered Wood to make no further public utterances, vocally or in writing, that might be construed to violate the administration's policy of strict neutrality. However, Lee's memoirs report that Wood had spoken privately and off the record to more than 250 dinner or luncheon meetings during the year Lee served as his aide de camp.

But war clouds were gathering. In January 1917 the infamous Zimmerman note, in which Germany offered to form a military alliance with Mexico should the United States enter the European war, was made public, stirring much indignation. On April 7 the United States declared war on Germany. In May 1917 Wood received word that the Selective Service legislation he had long advocated had at last been passed. "Aren't you happy, General?" asked Lt. Col. Charles E. Kilbourne, Wood's assistant chief of staff. "Yes," he replied, "but that's only half, the smaller half, really, of what we need. Nothing is being done for industrial mobilization. What are men without arms, ammunition, and equipment, including transportation?"[2]

Lee went with General Wood when the general was summoned to Washington. There he was instructed to go into the southern states and identify likely places where the army could establish training centers for recruits. "It seemed that every large community in those southern states wanted a training cantonment built nearby," Lee noted. "We inspected many sites and, when we were favorably impressed, we advised the General to visit the locality. This gave him many renewed contacts among friends he had made years before while serving at Fort McPherson just outside of Atlanta, Georgia."[3]

Lee recorded that by late summer Wood was offered the command of either a national army division for training in Kansas or one of the more important posts in Manila or Honolulu. "Obviously, President Wilson hoped that the General might be shifted to the other side of the globe," Lee wrote. "But not with the General's consent because he promptly chose the relatively humble job of training combat troops with the hope of leading them in battle."[4]

For several months Lee was part of that ambition. Wood was sent to Camp Funston, a training facility attached to Fort Riley, where he and his staff, including Lee, were engaged in training the newly formed Eighty-Ninth Division. Sarah went with Lee and was beginning to get acclimated to military life. When Wood was sent to conduct an inspection tour of the western front in France, Lee was left in Kansas as acting chief of staff under Brig. Gen. Frank L. Winn. "By that time we had a number of British and French officers on duty with us to help instruct in the most modern Western Front methods," Lee recalled. "We continued our training through the winter, day and night."[5]

It was too late for Wood to mend fences with President Wilson, who named Gen. John J. Pershing to command the American Expeditionary Force in Europe. Wood would never get his combat command. (In 1920 he sought the Republican nomination for the presidency without success.)

But Captain Lee would make it to the war. In January 1918 Lee and a few other officers in his command were summoned east to New York. Sarah went with him that far, and they had a few days to enjoy a second honeymoon, but she could not go with him onto the British liner *Oceanic* of the Cunard Line. "We knew then that another member of the family might be expected the following summer," Lee recalled. "She said goodbye to me at the hotel with brave if not smiling eyes."[6]

Lee was entering a raging conflagration that had begun in 1914 and had devolved into a stalemate as the opposing armies faced each other across a rugged, barbed-wire defaced no-man's-land stretching for hundreds of miles across central Europe. Periodically one side or the other launched massive infantry assaults that inevitably led to bloodbaths as tens of thousands, then hundreds of thousands, and eventually millions of men were mowed down like wheat. It should have been obvious that the machine guns and heavy artillery of modern industry had rendered obsolete the mass infantry tactics of the earlier century, but it was not—at least not to the generals in charge. By the time the United States entered the conflict both sides had pretty much bled themselves white. The entry of fresh U.S. troops into the struggle would turn the tide in the Allies' favor.

After landing at Le Havre, Lee went on to the American Staff College, where he received additional training as a G-2 (intelligence, not supply). But the curriculum was not too rigorous, or at least it did not interfere with Lee's afternoon horseback rides. "Because of my friendship with Douglas MacArthur," Lee recorded modestly, he was invited to go along for a weekend trip to the Forty-Second Division in the Vosges Mountains. "There we learned first-hand of MacArthur's stirring experiences to date, especially his courageous stand before General Pershing after the first review of the 42nd," he wrote.[7]

Lee graduated from the school in May and was sent to the Eighty-Second Division on the British front as G-2. The Eighty-Second was under the supervision of the British Seventy-Seventh London Division, based near Arras. "As our division's intelligence officer, it was my duty to go forward and learn all I could about the situation," Lee recalled, "including visits to the front line and one or two patrol operations."[8]

Not long afterward the Eighty-Second was shifted to relieve the Twenty-Sixth Division (New England National Guard) in the Lucey sector north of Toul under the French XXXII Corps. Lee recalled that it was a move from a hot zone to one less active. "Again, it became my duty as G-2 to know the situation and the terrain wherein we were serving," he noted.[9]

In July Lee learned that the Eighty-Ninth Division had landed in France, albeit without General Wood, who, according to Lee, "had been cruelly relieved after the Division had boarded its transports in New York harbor."[10] But Lee retained close ties to many senior officers of the division and soon found himself back with the Eighty-Ninth as G-3 (operations and training). That month he also learned that he and Sarah were the proud parents of a son, John Clifford Hodges Lee Jr. Lee did not record in his memoirs compiled many years later whether he took time to celebrate that news.

After a few weeks of maneuver training, the Eighty-Ninth was sent to relieve the Eighty-Second in the line. Lee was disturbed to learn the Eighty-Second had made no recent reconnaissance of the enemy. Just before pulling out, the Eighty-Second staged a heavy raid on enemy lines to capture prisoners. The Germans responded with a gas attack in which the incoming Eighty-Ninth experienced its first casualties from mustard gas.

"It proved most helpful to have known the terrain in which the 89th relieved the 82nd," Lee wrote. "As G-3, I not only knew the country, the French headquarters over us, but of course I knew the old division and was in position to perform my best work as an Assistant Chief of Staff. Just at this time we received the secret advance information of the coming offensive operations to be launched sometime in September as the Saint-Mihiel offensive."[11]

The Eighty-Ninth Division occupied about twelve kilometers of the front line. The front was shared with two other divisions that had already seen action, among them the Second Division, with its marine brigade, as well as its regular army brigade of the Ninth and Twenty-Third Infantry. On the Eighty-Ninth's left was the Forty-Second Division, "with our friend, MacArthur, now serving as brigade commander." (MacArthur had been promoted to brigadier general in June and was the youngest in the war.) The Eighty-Ninth was soon engaged with the enemy, moving forward on objectives and digging in to defend against counterattacks. "Throughout our front line service prior to, during and after the St. Mihiel operation, we patrolled the front line no man's land area vigorously every night," Lee recalled. "We also directed the four regiments in line that their patrols would not interfere with each other while trying to outsmart the enemy."[12]

Maj. Gen. William Mason Wright was sent forward to assume command of the Eighty-Ninth, a move Lee welcomed. "The Division felt from the start General Wright's strong command leadership," he wrote. "He was splendid also in dealing with other American commanders, especially those immediately over us."[13]

Apparently Wright also approved of Lee. At the close of the Saint-Mihiel operation Wright made Lee regular division chief of staff, and with that came promotion to colonel. "After we put the 12 kilometer front in good shape and the Argonne drive had been launched to the west, came word that we were to be relieved and assigned to General Summerall's V Corps in the Argonne," Lee noted. "The division that came over to relieve us was General Farnsworth's 37th Division. Unhappily for us, we were required to leave our Artillery Brigade in the line and told that in the Argonne we would be given another brigade of gunners to support us. Having seen a better practice carried on along the British front when the guns were actually left in position but the men and teams relieved, we so urged General Wright to appeal. He did strongly, but higher headquarters were adamant and we lost our wonderful gunners for the remainder of the fighting. It was a severe handicap."[14]

One evening Pershing stopped by the cabin that Lee shared with Wright. Pershing and Wright were old friends who had attended West Point together. "It was after dark and they sat at a candle-lighted table on which General Pershing would pound and the candles would fall," Lee remembered. "As I serviced them and replaced them I could see how deeply moved both generals were, Pershing grim and severe, Wright, usually sweating from every pore. Only fragments of their conversation were available to me who deemed it good manners to be working on staff papers at some distance."[15]

After the general's evening visit Wright told Lee that Pershing had exhorted him to push his troops forward regardless of cost and that they had to win the war that autumn or face defeat. Lee theorized that Pershing believed if he did not achieve such a victory in that time frame he would be relieved.

The Eighty-Ninth was engaged in bitter fighting in the Bantheville Woods before finally cleaning them out and establishing a jump-off line for a major offensive scheduled to begin November 1. It was at this time that Lee made a contact that would become a major factor in the rest of his career. Lt. Col. Brehon Somervell had been sent forward to become familiar with front-line division staff work. "Somervell was truly an answer to prayer," Lee wrote. "He learned with lightning-like rapidity, was fearless and brilliant."[16] Lee recommended to Wright that he make Somervell their G-3, which was accomplished. A bond between Somervell and Lee was established that would echo in Lee's favor in World War II.

Lee also recalled a story he indicated was told to him by Col. George C. Marshall, another vital contact for Lee, describing the reaction of France's Marshal Foch on learning that the Eighty-Ninth Division had seized the wooded heights of Barricourt: "La guerre est finie."[17]

But not quite yet. "The next day's advance was tedious in that the infantry had advanced beyond direct support of our artillery," Lee recalled. "We suffered from National Guard inefficiency in the brigades attached to us and of course the long range corps and Army support which had given us such a splendid start were no longer available. However, the 353rd Infantry under the inspired leadership of Dr. [Capt.] Paul Withington reached its objective well before midnight. Thus the reputation of the division was saved."[18]

Rumors were rife that the Germans were finished and the war would soon end, but to officers on the line it was business as usual. On the night of November 5–6 Lee took Somervell with him on a front-line reconnaissance opposite Pouilly, where it had been reported that the Germans had failed to blow a key bridge over the Meuse River, which was six hundred yards beyond American lines. "We took a patrol forward to the canal that ran alongside the river and reached the bridge approach," Lee noted. "It had been damaged but we could not tell in the darkness how badly. It being midnight and apparent that no operation could be attempted without a detailed reconnaissance, I let Somervell take the patrol across the wreckage in order to obtain the information we needed."[19]

Lee returned to division headquarters in order to issue orders for the following day. Somervell and his detail encountered enemy troops, fought them off, and returned without losing a man. For that he was awarded the Distinguished Service Cross. Somervell was one of only nine American officers—another being Douglas MacArthur—to be awarded both the Distinguished Service Cross and the Distinguished Service Medal in World War I.

The point of the exercise was to get American troops across the river and moving toward the German homeland. Hoping to reduce civilian casualties, Lee's troops dropped messages to the villages across the Meuse warning that an attack was coming. For three nights the artillery blasted the area. On the night of November 10 Lee's troops crossed the river with seven battalions, losing fewer than twenty men. To their right the 353rd Infantry crossed the remains of the bridges to Stenay.

"Unfortunately, on our extreme left our liaison battalion commanded by recently promoted Major Hanna (nephew of Mark Hanna, the Ohio political kingmaker) had to serve under a Second Division U.S. Marine Battalion commanded by a Lt. Colonel," Lee noted. "This liaison combination was to assure our maintaining contact. In that one battalion we lost 256 casualties including young Major Hanna, killed in action."[20]

The very next day the war came to an end—at the eleventh hour of the eleventh day of the eleventh month.

Following Germany's capitulation, the Eighty-Ninth Division moved by stages into the Rhineland through Luxembourg. "We had to maintain law and order throughout a wide area while making our men as healthfully comfortable as possible," Lee stated. "In working on our reconstruction problem of roads and bridges, we soon employed all available German manpower, feeling that our soldiers should not be working for the German inhabitants' ease of transportation. Moreover, we saw to it that able-bodied Germans were not more comfortably bedded down than our American soldiers."[21]

The Eighty-Ninth spent several months in Germany keeping the peace, assisting with reconstruction, and keeping the soldiers physically fit. It was clear even then that Lee was a stickler for healthy, wholesome living. "At division headquarters we followed our old practice of getting up early for exercises which we shared with our fellow officers and men," Lee recalled. "To meet the entertainment program, we were blessed in having a wonderful woman from Chicago, Miss Anne Purnell, who wore the uniform of the Young Women's Christian Association. She became a strong as well as most charming member of the G-1 staff."[22] There were football games and other sports to keep the men occupied and busy. The Eighty-Ninth football team traveled to Paris for a championship game with the Thirty-Sixth Division, which until then was unbeaten. The Eighty-Ninth won.

"As we prepared for our leaving, the division strove to have a clean getaway, all occupied areas being in better condition than we had found them as fully policed up," Lee recalled. "Less vigorous outfits teasingly referred to the 89th as the best saluting-policing outfit in Germany. At subsequent reunions our men seemed to enjoy this— typical of the American soldier who later boasts about his hard service and perhaps hard commanders."[23]

The Eighty-Ninth Division returned to the United States in May 1919. Lee's new friend Somervell remained behind as assistant chief of staff, G-4, in charge of supply for the U.S. Third Army and the

American forces in Germany, as it was redesignated on July 2, 1919. He was posted to the Office of the Chief of Engineers in Washington DC. Like Lee, Somervell had graduated near the top of his class at West Point and had distinguished himself in battle in the Great War, as World War I was known at the time.

Lee also had done very well indeed for an ambitious young officer. He rose to colonel and served on the staffs of two divisions, first as the intelligence and operations officer and then as acting chief of staff. In the process he won the Distinguished Service Medal and a Silver Star. What was more important was that he had made a reputation for himself and developed several friendships that would serve him well in years to come. When Lee's ship arrived in New York Harbor he was welcomed by his wife, Sarah, and his now ten-month old son, John Jr.

CHAPTER FOUR

The Great Flood of 1927

How high's the water, mama?
Five feet high and rising.
—JOHNNY CASH

At the close of the Great War the U.S. Congress dismantled most of the army. The war was over, and with no clear and present threats to national security there was no need to maintain a large military. But Congress recognized there was always the chance the country would need to raise an army in a hurry, as it did in 1917. It thus passed a bill that became the National Defense Act of 1920, which created structural change without a fundamental alteration in the concept of defense requirements. The basic idea was to create an expansible army. It kept a core force of officers sufficient to form the first twenty-seven divisions (546,000 men) to be put into action within a year after the outbreak of hostilities.[1]

Even so there was naturally a postwar surplus of officers, many of whom left the service to pursue peacetime careers elsewhere. Those who remained would face a prolonged period of desuetude when their responsibilities were unchallenging and promotions hard to come by. But officers like Lee were never in danger of being mustered out, and he never had a backup plan if his military role ended. As a career officer in the Corps of Engineers, on the other hand, he had excellent prospects of useful employment, if only because the corps was eternally engaged in maintenance of rivers, dams, and other waterways and structures. The advent of the New Deal during the Great Depression in the 1930s would create even more opportunities for the corps.

Lee initially returned to Camp Fulton near Fort Riley, where he closed out his divisional duties and turned in all pertinent records. He then had three possibilities on his plate: the Office of the Chief of Engineers in Washington, an assignment to West Point at MacArthur's request, or General Wood's Central Department headquarters in Chicago. He went first to West Point, where MacArthur had said he had two openings, but by the time he got there those slots were filled. So he was off to a reunion with Wood in Chicago, where he took a position on the general's staff. But that was the summer of the Republican National Convention, when Wood failed in his quest for a presidential nomination. Wood was subsequently dispatched as governor to the Philippines, where in Lee's assessment Wood performed excellent work, a view not shared by everyone. To Lee it was a matter of religious faith. "The country suffered in not having him [as] President instead of Warren Harding," Lee wrote. "But our country could take and overcome those troubles whereas our Christian frontier in the Philippines would have probably gone down into a collapse from which it might not have recovered. As an outstanding doctor, as a kindly friend of the Filipino people with their Spanish and Mestizo backgrounds, as an unsurpassed administrator as well as a soldier and a statesman, Leonard Wood filled all needs in that vital Far Eastern post."[2]

Lee had firsthand knowledge of Wood's work in the Philippines because he and his family were there from 1921 to 1923. Serving on Wood's staff as G-2, Lee had made several trips to Japan, China, and the Dutch East Indies. On one trip Lee attended the Imperial Japanese Maneuvers. "For the first time, we Americans had been invited to attend the Japanese maneuvers along with the British commander from Hong Kong," Lee recalled. "With the dissolving of the Anglo-Japanese alliance and after the famous Washington Conference wherein naval ratios were re-established on the 5-5-3 basis, we were then supposed to be allied with the British and Japanese [so] our invitation to attend the maneuvers was logically accepted."[3]

Back in the Philippines Lee and Sarah took up golf, and Lee also spent time playing polo. MacArthur loomed large in the Lee ambit once again when he was given command of the American Brigade in the Philippine Department, with quarters in Manila. MacArthur came with his first wife, Louise, and her two children. (In World War II MacArthur was there with his second wife, Jean.)

By the summer of 1923 Lee and his family were back in Washington. Lee was working on aerial navigation maps "for the new airways," as the fledgling air industry was first finding its wings, and other random assignments as they came up. In 1926, with that work well in hand, he was offered one of two assignments: the upper Mississippi valley and the "less desirable" station of Vicksburg, Mississippi. "Instinctively, I asked for the least desirable post," he noted.[4]

It would prove a fateful decision. He had been warned of excessive "paternalism" among corps personnel and also that there was a serious drinking problem. "At each of the levee camps and even aboard the ships the foreman in charge or the master would bring in a bottle for us," Lee said. "I had decided to ride the water wagon and did so for those five years—much to the amazement of the southerners. Our employees, however, soon took the hint and accepted gladly my ruling that we would enforce the proper regulations banning liquor from government camps and all government equipment."[5]

Lee got to Vicksburg just in time for the greatest Mississippi River flood in recorded history. He recalled "the warning we got in the fall of 1926 when the Vicksburg gauge not only passed 30 feet but touched 40 feet."[6] That gauge lay at the foot of the delta and roughly halfway between the Ohio River confluence at Cairo, Illinois, and the Gulf of Mexico. In October the Vicksburg gauge usually hovered not far above zero. Only six times in history had the river exceeded thirty feet on that gauge in October. Each time the following spring brought record high water. Lee knew serious trouble was coming.

The rains abated and everyone sighed in relief, but Lee and other experts knew they were not done with it. The Mississippi River drains much of Middle America. As recorded by John M. Barry, "six weeks later unusually violent storms carrying heavy precipitation began pelting the Mississippi Valley again. On December 13, in South Dakota the temperature fell 66 degrees in 18 hours, followed by an intense snowstorm. Helena, Montana, received 29.42 inches of snow. Minnesota snowdrifts of 10 feet were reported. As the storm swept south and east, 5.8 inches of rain fell on Little Rock in one day, with Memphis reporting 4.11 inches and Johnson City, Tennessee, near the Virginia line, 6.3 inches. By Christmas 1926, heavy flooding had begun."[7]

On New Year's Day, 1927, the Mississippi River reached flood stage at Cairo, the earliest it had done so for any year on record.

"From Cairo to the Gulf, the 1,100 miles where the river was mightiest and angriest, people readied themselves," Barry writes. As he describes it,

> Major Lee had taken charge of the Vicksburg district only the preceding July and had no experience with the Mississippi. Still, he was a man of order and discipline (attending Episcopal services daily and as often as three times on Sunday) and was an outstanding organizer. He had been preparing for months for what he considered the equivalent of war. Already engineers under him had walked each foot of the 800 miles of levees in the district—400 miles on each bank—and mapped weak areas so he could deploy resources.
>
> His army numbered 1,500 full-time levee workers, including six levee contractors who each operated camps where one or two white men worked 100 to 200 black laborers. These were isolated, violent and brutal places. (One camp operator named Charlie Silas may have been the original 'Mr. Charlie,' slang for a white boss in blues songs, who was reputed to routinely murder black workers and throw their bodies into the river.) But the levee contractors moved earth. Ten modern levee machines, each one looking like a giant dinosaur, also moved mountains of earth in a few days. Quarter boats served as highly mobile levee camps. Ten separate groups of men were working on reverting the riverbank, protecting it from the currents by covering it with willow mattresses much like the ones Eads used for the jetties.[8] The Corps had begun experiments laying asphalt and concrete over the riverbank as well. And in an emergency, Lee and the local levee boards could call upon virtually all the plantation labor within miles of the river, a total labor force—and army—approaching 30,000.
>
> On April 1, Lee mobilized nearly all of these forces and put them to work on the levees. He also summoned Navy seaplanes and Army observation planes to inspect miles of levee quickly, and communicate to men on the levee out of reach of telephones.[9]

"I first used a U.S. Department of Agriculture airplane that had been stationed in Tallulah, Louisiana, for cotton dusting," Lee recalled. "It was piloted by an Army Air Corps sergeant who was skillful, dependable and quite willing to fly me during the emergency. . . . With that plane I could in a single morning reconnoiter our 400 miles of front line—verify the presence of levee guards, all main items of plant (dredges, quarter boats, tow boats) and even the automobiles of our Area Engineers. On the top of each such vehicle we had painted boldly their key symbol, as were the vessels' names on their pilot houses.[10]

"Airplane use was still rather unusual in those parts," Lee wrote. "Also 'twas helpful to our field men who were pleased to see our daily interest—and receive their mail including newspapers which we'd drop—in old inner tubes for the boats. We bought the high test gasoline used for us and also set up a maintenance service in our Vicksburg harbor machine shop that became a more important factor when the Navy came in with their sea planes from Pensacola."[11] Lee's levee guards wore broad white bands on their hats, which they would wave as the planes flew over them.

Lee had armed guards all along the levees, and with reason: "As the flood crests approached, we took all possible precautions to prevent sabotage by overly anxious cotton farmers who might, at night, try to blow out the levee opposite their plantations and thus reduce pressure on their own side. No such attempt was made in 1927."[12]

Despite Lee's assertion, Barry reports there was violence aplenty. "Marked Tree, Arkansas, was a rough lumber town on the St. Francis River, surrounded by rich alluvial lands," he writes in *Rising Tide*. "In early February, a 4-foot-deep cut in the top of the levee was discovered. Armed men [Lee's men] began patrols there. On April 6, the guards shot four men trying to plant 105 sticks of dynamite."[13] It seems unlikely that Lee would have been unaware of that, or of subsequent acts of violence confirmed by others, but ever and always Lee was attuned to the importance of public—and political—relations. In later years his fellow officers would complain that he always insisted everything was just fine when they all knew otherwise. He simply preferred to look on the bright side of things.

Thus at a critical juncture of the crisis Lee stated publicly that all was under control: "It is not believed that the new rise in sight will necessitate emergency topping at any point. The organization is functioning perfectly in all sectors."[14] Privately he was less sanguine, asking for reports of broken levees. Already tributary streams and backwater flooding had made thousands of people homeless.

The rising tide was awesome, relentless, and not just the Mississippi—it was all the rivers and streams feeding the Father of Waters—some of them mighty conduits in their own right. The White River is 720 miles long, and the Arkansas is 1,459 miles long. Together they drain 189,000 square miles and flow into the Mississippi a few miles apart. At their mouths the greatest pressure on the levees began. More rain fell on Good Friday, but even before that the White and Arkansas had burst through their levees and reached record levels.

"The rains loosed unimaginable power," Barry writes. "In Little Rock, a Missouri Pacific Railroad bridge trembled as the current of the Arkansas tore at its pillars. To steady it engineers packed an engine and twenty-one coal cars on it. The trembling continued; the vibration ignited the coal. Just as the fire started, the bridge crumbled into the river. Great clouds of steam burst forth. In the roar of the river itself the tremendous hissing was barely audible. No trace of the spans or the cars could be found later."[15]

"When we realized that our levee heights were doomed to be overtopped, and 'twas only the location of the first break that would come and reduce the strain, most people expected the levee near Lake Village in Arkansas to fail," Lee recalled. "There I had put our best high water fighter, Kenneth (Cy) Young."[16] Lee afforded all possible effort to save the city of Greenville, but it had to be mostly evacuated.

Lee and his troops did all that was humanly possible to stanch the rising water, but in the end all they could do was wait for it to make its way to the Gulf of Mexico, by which time vast amounts of land had been inundated, millions of acres of crops ruined, and countless towns and villages swamped. The administration of President Calvin Coolidge offered no assistance because the conservative president from Vermont did not believe that was the proper function of the federal government. Local problems, he believed, should be handled on the local level. He did dispatch to the scene Secretary of Commerce Herbert Hoover, who, working with the American Red Cross, managed to summon substantial assistance to the region. Hoover was all over the place and spent much of his time with Lee surveying the damage and identifying priorities for action and relief of people who had been effectively bankrupted by the river. Hoover gained much positive news coverage with this work, which helped him successfully win the presidency the following year.

The great flood's devastation affected seven states, but Mississippi, Louisiana, and Arkansas were hardest hit. More than 16 million acres were flooded, 162,000 homes damaged, and 9,000 homes destroyed. The total death toll will never be known.

There was a congressional response of sorts in the Flood Control Act of 1928, known as the Jadwin Plan, named after Lt. Gen. Edgar Jadwin of the Corps of Engineers, Lee's boss. The basic thrust of the plan was the assumption that the Mississippi River itself could never handle the volume of water it was sometimes obliged to accommodate, so the solution was to build a series of spillways and other diversions to funnel the water away from the river channel. "As we had recommended, the small Vicksburg District was consolidated with the Third Mississippi River Commission District," Lee wrote. "Moreover, all engineer department activities within the limits of my district, including surveying and dredging, became my responsibility. Prior to that time, such activities were directed from St. Louis, then the headquarters of the Mississippi River Commission."[17]

It was also decided to move the Mississippi River Commission headquarters from St. Louis to Vicksburg, the center of the overflow area but located high above the river itself. It fell to Lee to supervise design of the new facility. He was also charged with locating and constructing the new U.S. Corps of Engineers Waterways Experiment Station. Lee described it as "the important hydraulic laboratory that has done so well for the Corps of Engineers not only in Mississippi River work but for numerous other projects elsewhere in the United States and indeed abroad."[18] (As of 2016, the experiment station is still in operation.)

In his memoirs Lee is at pains to point out that during his time in Vicksburg he did not accept any special favors or gifts of monetary value from either corps employees or contractors. "The cagey contractors I found prompt in their offers of kindliness, first in a brace of ducks or a basket of quail which they had personally shot and offered to the new District Engineer," he recalled. "Later came cases of Florida fruit which they had picked up on vacation. Had I encouraged them, they would have doubtless sent contraband liquors. In every case, however, I sent the gift to the local hospital for use in the charity wards and in the name of the contract giver. And in each case I wrote personally to the giver, thanking him for his personal thought and kindliness." Lee noted that "these dispositions were not misunderstood. It is my feeling that such practice should be not only recognized as SOP [standard operating procedure] among our more thoughtful Engineer Officers but should be laid down in regulations. I have seen departing District Engineers accept gifts of golf clubs and even sets of silverware for their wives—a practice I deplore and would forbid."[19]

Lee spent five years in Vicksburg. His next stop would be the U.S. Army War College, then located in Washington DC.[20]

CHAPTER FIVE

Tragedy

But O for the touch of a vanished hand,
and the sound of a voice that is still.
—ALFRED LORD TENNYSON

While in Germany Lee and his friend Somervell, in the manner of bright young officers, had come up with some great ideas for "improving" General Staff organization and procedures. Having secured a posting to the Army War College in Washington DC at the conclusion of his Vicksburg tour, Lee thought his new position would be an excellent opportunity to articulate their ideas, especially when he was given chairmanship of the First Committee, which was tasked with reviewing General Staff organization and procedure.[1]

"Our Committee reviewed staff and especially General Staff organization and procedure of all then known armies," Lee recalled. "No one of my Committee agreed with its chairman [Lee] that we should change what had been established in the War Department. Therefore, I felt that it would be unwise if not unfair to submit a minority report."[2]

Lee and Somervell (who had attended the War College in 1925) believed staff organization should be based on clear responsibility and not implied functional responsibility, which was the prevailing wisdom. Many years later Lee still regretted his failure to stand up for what he believed in. "We were expected in a few weeks' time to study the Army staff history not only of our U.S.A. but of Britain, France, Germany, Italy and Japan, and to recommend changes in the American War Department and Staff if we so agreed," he wrote. "Personally I wrestled with my beliefs that we might improve our General Staff procedure, such as Bill Somervell and I had agreed on by the time we parted company in Germany in June 1919. But I could not convince any of my fellow committeemen who, being Command and General Staff College graduates, all felt we should hold to the doctrine of functional coordination, in the name of the Commander (as long taught at Ft. Leavenworth) rather than direct responsibility and authority."[3]

As chair of the First Committee, Lee presented the report outlining its findings and recommending no change. "In retrospect, I regret that we could not bring before the entire class the discussion we had in our committee. In this, I failed," he noted. "Maybe I should have submitted a minority report. But I did not."[4]

Judging by the space Lee accords to this event in his memoirs, it is clear it stayed with him as major personal failing. "We were spending a year at the AWC [Army War College] to qualify for future command responsibility," he wrote. It was "not expedient to tangle with the Commandant who had to sign my final rating." Lee knew he had to make a superior rating to keep his name on the "eligibility for promotion" list. "Having been about the youngest officer on the initial General Staff eligibility list and the youngest Colonel Chief of Staff of a combat division, one may be pardoned for desiring to hold his good standing in the Army." But it does seem clear he had trouble pardoning himself.[5]

After concluding his year at the War College, Lee was detailed as assistant commandant and engineer instructor to the relatively new Army Industrial College (AIC). Established in 1924 to focus on wartime procurement and mobilization procedures, the college had an initial class of only nine students, but by the early 1930s forty to fifty students were graduating in each class. During the first three years of its existence the college provided a five-month course of study. In 1927 the program was expanded to ten months, with one graduating class each year. Maj. Dwight D. Eisenhower graduated from the college in 1933 and later served on the faculty.

This was clearly an excellent opportunity for a man destined to be responsible for supplying huge armies, though Lee had no way of knowing that such a responsibility lay in his future. "In those days, the Assistant Commandant of an Army College or School was the most active officer who was expected to do most of the planning and supervision for the Commandant," Lee wrote. "The responsibility was a challenge and the experience gained was providentially helpful in later years during World War II."[6]

The time in Washington was happy for Lee and his family. He and Sarah refined their golf games at the Army-Navy Country Club and did their share of entertaining, including one or possibly two events for the West Point class of 1909. They renewed their friendship with Douglas MacArthur, who by then was divorced from his first wife and was living at Fort Myer with his mother and widowed sister-in-law, Mary. The secretary of war, Patrick J. Hurley, had been a houseguest of the Lees in Vicksburg when inspecting Corps of Engineers work. They also spent some time with President Herbert Hoover, who "remembered our trips together in the lower valley," and Secretary of State Henry Lewis Stimson, a longtime Lee friend.[7]

"My second year [1933] as Assistant Commandant of the AIC was lighter in work because we had the courses well organized and staffed," Lee recalled. This was the first year of the first term of President Franklin D. Roosevelt, who, unlike Hoover, was not on Lee's social list. But it did not take him long to ingratiate himself with the new administration: "By winter I was able to take on some extra duty which came first as adviser to President F. D. Roosevelt's Civil Works Administrator Harry Hopkins. He had no adequate organization nor experienced administrators to take effective responsible charge of his staff functions or the regional offices that we recommended. He was trying personally to deal directly with Governors of 48 states. They were crowding the halls and stairways of his N.Y. office."[8]

It was a time of great confusion and disorder. By then the country was immersed in the Great Depression, with millions of workers unemployed in a time when there was virtually no social safety net. Unemployed workers translated into families without food or medical care and often without shelter. It was a desperate time. The FDR administration and a compliant Congress had created agencies to provide relief, most notably the National Recovery Administration (NRA) and the Public Works Administration (PWA), but for various reasons they were having trouble getting off the ground. In desperation Roosevelt created the Civil Works Administration (CWA) with an executive order and turned to his aide, a political operative named Harry Hopkins, to run it.[9]

Lee would get caught up in that scramble, as would everyone in the Corps of Engineers, which was historically preeminent among branches of the peacetime army. The chief of the corps ranked second only to the chief of staff in terms of power and prestige. In 1933 the post of corps chief was held by Maj. Gen. Lytle Brown, an aloof West Pointer of the class of 1898. The big thing for the corps, at least in peacetime, was its responsibility for rivers and harbors, which gave it easy access to Congress and its politicians, who were ever eager to bring to their districts water projects such as dams and locks. As funding for the corps moved through Congress, it always got bigger and bigger. President Chester A. Arthur was the only chief executive to veto a corps appropriations bill, in 1882, and that veto was promptly overridden.

Naturally the Roosevelt administration called upon the Corps of Engineers to play a leadership role in the PWA and CWA simply because it was the only federal government entity with hands-on experience in such things. But the new political order caught the corps off guard. "Accustomed to the careful, leisurely consideration of congressional projects, often years in maturing, to time-honored cost-benefit ratios, and to the Army's ancient red-tape bureaucracy, the Corps soon found itself seriously out of step with the new administration," Jean Edward Smith writes. While FDR sought immediate remedies for the nation's jobless, the corps remained "wedded to its rigid patterns of no make-work, no emergency undertakings, no federal involvement in areas previously reserved for the private sector."[10]

Fortunately Brown retired and was replaced by Maj. Gen. Edward M. "Joe" Markham, who got along famously with the president and was ready to put the corps to work. "When the New Deal began I don't think the Army had any real interest [in it] one way or the other," stated Maj. Gen. Lucius Clay, who, as a colonel, had worked closely with Markham. "But it soon became very clear, when the government went into a large public works program," he continued, "that the Corps of Engineers was going to have to expand and take on a great deal of this work, because we were the only ones, except for the reclamation service, that had programs and projects on the drawing board. And so we were immediately put under pressure to increase the pace of our public works program."[11]

Like Clay, Lee was soon caught up in the New Deal "make-work" projects like those overseen by the CWA. "In the Corps of Engineers, the Corps was the club," Clay said. "It was a very proud group of people. And it was relatively small. There were only a couple hundred of us. Everybody knew everybody, and it was quite an elite organization. Everyone had his idiosyncrasies, but beneath those idiosyncrasies was a sharp, intelligent mind. And you couldn't help but learn working in that atmosphere."[12]

Unlike traditional relief programs, the CWA created jobs. Within ten days Hopkins had put more than 800,000 people to work, 2.6 million by mid-December, and by early January the figure had passed the 4 million mark. The CWA did useful things. It laid 12 million feet of sewer pipe and built or upgraded 500,000 miles of secondary roads, 40,000 schools, 3,700 recreation areas, and nearly 1,000 airports. It employed 50,000 teachers to keep rural schools open and to provide adult education in cities. It even provided paid work for artists and writers. By the time it closed in April 1934—a short lifespan for a government agency—it had pumped close to $1 billion into an ailing economy. (A billion was a lot of money back then.)[13]

The army assigned Lee to study the CWA, and by his own account he was astonished to see Hopkins put people to work in every county in the country in under two months. But Lee had a hand in the CWA's success. "It was my strong recommendation that he [Hopkins] group the states into about 10 regions, as I recall," Lee recalled. "Meanwhile, he had sent me to New York City and Dan Sultan to Chicago to see what could be done in untangling the CWA at those two largest centers."[14]

Lee noted that in the Great War it had taken the army a year and a half to muster as many men, and unlike the army Hopkins managed to pay his people each week. Lee also confessed admiration for Hopkins's casual management style, which contrasted sharply with that of the military. "These assistants address Mr. Hopkins fondly as 'Harry,'" he noted. "There is no rigidity or formality, yet he holds their respect, confidence, and whole-souled cooperation."[15]

That winter Sarah and John Jr. were off on a trip to France with family friends. By midsummer 1934 Lee was district engineer in Philadelphia, where his family joined him upon their return. The Philadelphia District had recently absorbed the Wilmington and Delaware District, along with its Chesapeake and Delaware Canal, which connects the Delaware River with the Chesapeake Bay. It was a good time to propose public works projects when the Roosevelt administration was actively looking for anything that would put people to work. "Having seen something of our CWA projects, many of which were of doubtful value, I felt that all of our Engineer Department projects were relatively worthy," he stated. "We were merely advancing them on the priority list."[16]

Lee reported that Hopkins finally came around to his regional organization plan and put him in charge of the region encompassing New Jersey, Pennsylvania, Maryland, and the District of Columbia. "General Markham approved this duty in addition to my other responsibilities," Lee noted.[17] Lee resisted suggestions that firing a few staff might be beneficial: "My reply was that we were trying to keep men at work and that unless gross incompetence or dishonesty were evident, I would try to utilize existing personnel more efficiently."[18]

In 1936 Lee received word that his surviving sister Josephine was seriously ill. Her marriage to A. K. C. Palmer had ended in divorce years earlier. Lee went to his sister's bedside and promised her he would look after her three children. Although Palmer had remarried, he agreed to a plan proposed by Lee to provide for the children's education. It was an extremely awkward time in the Lee family, which was unable to develop a good relationship with the children's stepmother.

In 1937 Lee invited General Markham to address a meeting of corps engineers in Philadelphia. He drafted an address and took it to the general in Washington. Markham read it, approved it, told Lee to go back to Philadelphia and present it in his stead, and then to proceed to the Mississippi valley, where another serious flood threat was pending. Lee complied and took a group of young engineers with him, instructing them in flood fighting along the way.

That was the same year that John Lee Jr.'s appointment to West Point came through. John Jr. had been attending the Massachusetts Institute of Technology but chose to complete his education at the United States Military Academy, following in his father's footsteps.

In 1938 Lee Sr. was sent to Portland, Oregon, to become the corps's North Pacific Division engineer. "That was an important assignment, especially in view of the huge power development possibilities in the Columbia Basin where some 40 percent of the total potential hydroelectric power of North America awaited development," Lee wrote. "About the same time came a plea from Col. James H. Burns in the Office of the Assistant Secretary asking me to become the Commandant of the Army Industrial College. I urged him to take the job himself, expressing the hope that it would carry the rank of General Officer which he deserved."[19]

Lee and Sarah had to make this trip west alone, as John Jr. was at West Point. They went by train and stopped off in Junction City, where Lee was honored by locals for his achievements. Since their son could not leave school so soon, they decided to go north to take a look at Alaska, a trip they took by ship. As division engineer, he would end up making several trips to Alaska. On one of them he had reconnoitered a location for an air base near Anchorage. By Christmas their son was able to visit them in their Portland residence.

In the spring of 1939 Lee got a visit from two luminaries—the chief of the Army Air Corps, Gen. H. H. "Hap" Arnold, who flew out to visit Lee and was accompanied by Gen. George C. Marshall, who had become assistant chief of staff for war plans. After the obligatory ceremonies Arnold asked Lee to accept a temporary detail with the air corps. "He wanted an experienced Engineer Officer to fly on an inspection of his principal construction projects which were behind schedule," Lee recalled. "He wanted to report actual conditions along with recommendations for improvement."[20]

By that time, Lee noted, he had his office well in hand, with qualified people at every post. "Construction work was going well, channels were being maintained and our 308 Survey Reports under Principal Engineer Grimm in full progress," he wrote. "Therefore, I could recommend to the Chief of Engineers approval of General Arnold's request."[21] Lee spent several weeks on an inspection tour of Caribbean points of interest, including British Honduras, Panama, Maracaibo, Trinidad, and Puerto Rico. Lee and Arnold were accompanied by Gen. George Strong, G-2 of the War Department.

When the trip was completed, Arnold asked Lee to go to Alaska to help his staff locate several new air force installations, one of which was to be near Anchorage, where Lee had already done some initial surveys. Lee was accompanied by several high-ranking officers.

When John Jr. had visited at Christmas, Lee had promised him a visit to Alaska. He offered his son the job of cadet recorder for the group of officers he was to guide there. "This he accepted with his dear mother's kind consent provided he would fly in one of the two planes and I in the other," Lee noted. "We had two amphibian [sic] ships similar to the one used by General Arnold on the tour around the Caribbean."[22]

Lee reported that the group was able to visit all of the sites on its itinerary, obtain the information they were seeking, and keep on schedule. He also noted that the attitude of the air corps personnel was not that of the army engineers in terms of work. "It became my sometimes painful duty to insist upon adhering to our schedule rather than taking time off for delightful fishing jaunts," he recalled.[23]

Lee and Sarah got to spend a few happy days with their son before he had to head back to the Point. After seeing him off, they headed south on a trip Lee wanted to make in connection with the Los Angeles army engineers' district flood control plans. "We took both our own Buick and an official convertible, more useful on inspection trips," Lee noted.[24] They visited a cherished aunt and on their return trip north drove through Yosemite.

On the way back to Oregon they stopped off in Oakland for the convention of the Association of Port Authorities. They encountered many old friends there and attended a banquet that evening. "We did not feel we had to go to the ball with the subsequent drinking parties that always followed," Lee wrote. "Rather we strolled out in the moonlight overlooking the artificial lake in front of the hotel."[25]

"The next day we started back to Portland driving in the open Chrysler with our official chauffeur following in our own Buick," Lee recalled. "Near Woodlawn we turned off of the main highway for a short cut and ran into the fatal crash caused by migrant grape-pickers coming in from the left and rolling us over. Dear Sarah was pinned under the car which probably broke her back. She never regained consciousness and actually died in my arms there on the crossroad. An ambulance came and although the nurse with it said Dear Sarah's pulse had stopped[,] I would not accept that decision but went to the hospital with her where the doctors confirmed the sad news."[26]

Lee was devoted to his wife. His heart was broken but not shattered. His faith did not protect him from calamity but steeled him against it. He took a long, lonely final ride with Sarah across the country to Wheeling, where she was buried against the day when they would lie side by side in Arlington National Cemetery. General Marshall made arrangements to facilitate his lonely journey. Lee instructed John Jr. to stay at West Point and to remember his mother when she was at her best. After the funeral and burial, he did the only thing he could do. He went back to work.

CHAPTER SIX

War Clouds on the Horizon

I have said this before, but I shall say it again and again and again: your boys are not going to be sent to any foreign wars.

—PRESIDENT FRANKLIN D. ROOSEVELT, October 30, 1940

Military people know when war is coming. They follow the news, they talk to their friends, but mostly they feel it in their bones. A generation of officers had spent years spinning their wheels in a time of prolonged peace, when promotions were few and far between. But with another war on the horizon all of a sudden promotions were coming thick and fast.

The military knew war was coming, but many Americans were determined that it should not. Many believed the previous engagement in Europe had been a mistake that cost the nation many lives and much wealth to no discernible advantage. Given subsequent events in Europe, that opinion had more than a little credibility. There was an active antiwar movement afoot in the country, as well as a substantial pro-German cohort, which included the famous pilot Charles Lindbergh, the first to fly solo across the Atlantic Ocean. Lindbergh visited Germany, appeared in public with Nazi leaders, and insistently campaigned against U.S. involvement in the war.

Meanwhile the British prime minister, Winston Churchill, was making a strong case that his country was the last bulwark of Western civilization against an encroaching new dark age of Nazism and that without U.S. aid that bulwark could not long survive. President Roosevelt was sympathetic to Great Britain and shared Churchill's worldview, but he had to tread carefully to accommodate antiwar sentiment. FDR always had his ear to the ground, which was why he was able to be elected president four times.

In the fall of 1939 the U.S. Army numbered 190,000 men. It maintained three square infantry divisions at half strength—instead of

28,000 men each they had 15,000. The only division near its authorized strength was the First Cavalry Division at Fort Bliss in Texas; it
had 12,000 men and 6,000 horses. The U.S. Army was a long time
relinquishing its love affair with horses.[1]

But when France fell to the Germans in 1940, the army suddenly had plenty of money. Marshall, now the army chief of staff,
wanted to increase the army's ranks to a million men by October
1941 and two million by January 1942. To do that the nation needed
a draft. On September 16, 1940, FDR signed the Selective Service
Act authorizing induction of 900,000 men for a year, federalizing
the 270,000 men in the National Guard, and raising regular army
strength to 500,000. Congress appropriated $9 billion for the army,
more than all the money spent by the War Department since 1920.
The buildup for World War II was under way, though the United
States was not yet at war.

In 1940 Lee received notice that he had been promoted to brigadier general, which, like most promotions in that time, was officially temporary. He was given command of the San Francisco port
of embarkation at Fort Mason in California. "I found urgent need for
changing port plans in the San Francisco area as well as provisions
for port facilities in Southern California, at Portland and Seattle," Lee
noted. During his year at Fort Mason he received a visit from Marshall, who suggested Lee identify a replacement because he was destined for other things. "I promptly obtained the assignment of Col.
Frederick Gilbreath whom I broke in as deputy," Lee recalled.[2] That
freed Lee to attend the army's summer maneuvers in Texas and Louisiana with the Second Infantry Division—at Marshall's suggestion.

"During those maneuvers, the performance of the 2nd Infantry
Division had left much to be desired," Lee wrote. "For example, one
Regimental Combat Team was 'captured' by enterprising scouts of
the 45th Oklahoma Division who had imitated the insignia of the
2nd Division's Military Police, had misguided the column into a pas-
ture as its bivouac area, closed the gate and then gave word for the
surrounding 'enemy' to call for surrender." To make matters worse,
a raiding party of Patton's tanks broke into Second Division headquarters and captured the division commander and his staff. "As a

visiting observer I was released," Lee recalled, "but the others were out of the maneuver for some time."[3] In addition to the experience with the maneuvers Lee was given a refresher course at Fort Benning, Georgia, to familiarize him with modern infantry training and the latest types of transportation. It did appear the senior army leadership had Lee in mind for a combat command.

Soon Lee received orders to report to Fort Sam Houston to assume command of the Second Infantry Division—a stimulating challenge for a freshly minted brigadier. "I found it in a low state of morale," he recalled. "Two of the Infantry Regiments were actually well commanded, but the 38th Infantry, that one that had been 'captured' by the 45th, was recognized as trailing in nearly every respect."[4]

Lee brought in an officer he had known at West Point, Col. William G. Weaver, who had earned an excellent fighting record in the war. "He was my answer to prayer for the 38th Infantry," Lee noted. "He promptly brought it back to a high standard of performance and gave the old 9th and 23rd Infantry Regiments full competition."[5]

Lee held no reviews or parades, of which he was unduly fond, at Fort Sam Houston, preferring to devote time to field and range training. "I kept our regimental combat teams under canvas most of the time," he wrote. By systematic training and coaching he was able to earn high marks from his superiors. He took the division's artillery brigade to Fort Sill in Oklahoma for special training. "I was anxious that we expedite the ability of the artillery to respond when requested by the infantry for supporting fire. The system of transmitting messages and fire information seemed unnecessarily prolonged." He was driving to Fort Sill on Sunday, December 7, 1941, when he heard over the radio of the Japanese attack on Pearl Harbor. "It was difficult to believe but soon confirmed," he recalled. He knew then, if there had ever been any doubt, that war was imminent.[6]

In the meantime he had the routine challenges of an infantry division to attend to. Lee discovered that many of his men suffered from athlete's foot, which can keep men out of action. (When the war came, the problem would be trench foot, caused by prolonged exposure to cold and wet conditions.) "After consulting our Division Surgeon, Colonel Hurley, we conducted a cleanup campaign, isolating all active cases of athlete's foot in special barracks where intensive treatment was given," Lee wrote. "Quite as important was the strict enforcement of foot and sock washing daily, and the use of antiseptic food powder such as Quinsana. Personally, I have used cotton socks within woolen ever since Sergeant Billy Wilmot taught us the trick in 1911. If a soldier keeps a pair of clean cotton sox with him, washes his feet and soiled sox daily, and uses Quinsana, he need not fear athlete's foot."[7]

Another problem, and one that likely was of more interest to his troops, was the poor quality of food in the mess hall. "I had difficulty in obtaining volunteers to attend the cooks and bakers school," Lee remembered. "There seemed to be a feeling among Texans that cooking was beneath their dignity. I tried to get the Army Commander to approve my request for the detail of Negro soldiers whom I knew to be generally good cooks and happy in such work. However, my request was denied. By patient, thorough attention and inspection before reveille until after the evening mess, we got the kitchens and messes of the 2nd Infantry Division in good shape." Lee made it a habit to get up before reveille and visit the various messes in rotation, but not in a regular rotation that could be predicted. "Later, I let the regimental commanders know that I was coming—that is, after they had of their own accord been getting up early as I had done."[8]

Of course after reveille Lee would stop at the post chapel, where the division chaplain, at that time a Roman Catholic priest, said an early mass each day. Lee was dismayed to learn that of his thirteen division chaplains, there were no Episcopalians. He also sensed a lack of spirit among the "God squad." He personally held a chaplains' school to let the chaplains know what he expected of them, that he was a general who took religion seriously, and he warned them that if any chaplain was found guilty of "unbrotherly behavior with or toward a fellow chaplain" he would be promptly relieved of duty. "We had only one such case," he recalled. "When I called his spiritual superior by long distance, I was thanked and promised an immediate replacement." When President Roosevelt declared a national day of prayer, Lee made certain all men of the division attended a service of their choice. "I had a Rabbi come out from San Antonio for the Jewish soldiers," he noted.[9]

Gen. Lesley McNair came by to review the Second Division troops, was favorably impressed by the job Lee was doing, and happened to mention to Lee that his second star had come through. He was now a major general.[10]

"Without warning I was called long distance the first Sunday in May [1942] by Brehon Somervell from Washington who said in effect, 'How long will it take you to turn over your command and report for duty in Washington?' I told him I could get going the following day. He said, 'Waste no time and come prepared for prolonged duty in a cool climate.'"[11]

Lee's friend Somervell had become a major force in the rearmament effort. From 1936 to 1940 he served as head of the Work Projects Administration in New York City, where he was responsible for a series of Great Depression relief projects, including the construction of LaGuardia Airport. There he earned a reputation as a man who could handle major projects. In December 1940 he became head of the Construction Division of the Quartermaster Corps and was responsible for building a variety of military facilities, including the Pentagon, where he was the driving force plowing through ranks of opposition from local citizens and members of Congress objecting to the cost. Somervell did not care what it cost. By May 1942 Somervell had some thirteen thousand workers going at it around the clock. The complex was completed early the following year.

All of which was mere prelude to what was to come. By that time Somervell had a formidable reputation. A rigid disciplinarian consumed by ambition, he was feared. He boasted that he never had a subordinate who made the same mistake twice. By the time he called Lee, Somervell was wearing a new hat. Marshall had made sweeping changes to the War Department intended to reduce the number of people reporting to him so he could focus on planning a global war. Three huge new commands were created, putting the Army Air Forces under Lt. Gen. Hap Arnold, the Army Ground Forces under Lt. Gen. Lesley McNair, and the Services of Supply under Somervell, who was promoted to lieutenant general. In that role Somervell was responsible for making sure the U.S. Army got everything it needed to win the war. Somervell was ambitious, aggressive, and driven. The creation of an independent unit of supply was the conscious reaction to a perceived supply inadequacy in World War I, when individual units were responsible for their own supplies and chaos often resulted.

Supply has always been the orphan child of the military. It is a given that soldiers cannot win battles if they don't have bullets for their guns, food for their stomachs, and boots for their feet. Their tanks and trucks and aircraft cannot run without fuel. Providing requisite supplies for an active infantry division involves thousands of tons each day. But supplying the troops rarely makes for vivid headlines or provides rapid career advancement for ambitious officers. Thus the battlefield luminaries of World War II tended to give scant attention to the supply component—until their artillery began running out of ammunition and their tanks rode to a stop for lack of fuel.

Somervell was responsible for providing essential supplies to Allied forces all over the world, not only the U.S. forces in the Atlantic and Pacific but for the British, Soviets, and other allies as well. The United States was to become the supply depot for the world, but it was a challenging task and the production of guns and planes was only part of it. The other part was getting all those items produced to where they were needed. The Allied governments had determined that Germany would be their top priority. After Germany was defeated, they would make Japan their primary focus. But conquering Germany meant it would be necessary to invade Europe, and that would require an amphibious assault across the English Channel. Thus a matériel buildup in Great Britain of vast proportions would be the first essential step to wresting the continent from Germany's grip.

To manage a buildup and subsequent supply of that magnitude in Europe, Somervell needed his best man—someone with proven ability that he could trust. Somervell achieved big things because he selected men who knew what they were doing and were determined to get it done. Somervell recommended to Marshall that he name Lee as commander of the European theater Service of Supply. "Others also passed Lee's name to Marshall," John Kennedy Ohl writes.

"Stimson, who had known Lee for decades, thought highly of him as did Major General Mark Clark of the AGF (Army Ground Forces), who later claimed he convinced Lesley McNair to suggest Lee's name to Marshall. Having come across Lee in the late 1930s while serving on the west coast, Marshall was likewise impressed by Lee. If Marshall had any doubts about Lee's fitness, he overcame them in light of the recommendation of Somervell, whose judgment in personnel matters carried great weight with him."[12]

When Lee and Somervell met subsequently in Washington, the latter assured Lee, "First, that I am not inflicting this job on you. You were selected by my superiors, General Marshall and Secretary Stimson." He added, according to Lee, "I wouldn't wish such a job on such a good friend."[13]

"Initially, Lee balked," writes D. K. R. Crosswell in *Beetle*, "but he backed down when Marshall and Stimson insisted he take the new assignment in London. Marshall granted Lee a mandate 'to take all measures . . . necessary and appropriate to expedite and prosecute the procurement, reception, processing, forwarding and delivery of personnel, equipment and supplies' for the buildup in Europe."[14]

Lee recalled that in Washington he was given "inspiring" interviews with Secretary of War Stimson and General Marshall. They both "emphasized the importance of good relations with our British partners," he noted. "They said my ability to get along with people was one factor in my selection. General Marshall told me to spare no effort in dealing fairly with the British and had me given a discretionary fund of $20,000,000 to use in any way I felt that he and Secretary Stimson would approve. I did not use all of that money[,] but it was comforting to have it in reserve."[15]

At the time, General Eisenhower was chief of the War Plans Division. Eisenhower "gave me a good orientation of what lay ahead," Lee recalled, "namely the main American effort to defeat Germany first and before going 'all out' against Japan. He had made the overall plan for a combined landing against 'the fortress of Europe' with the British Isles as our base. He told me of the skepticism held in some British senior officials' minds about the practicability of our plan. We emphasized when we realized that, having been knocked out of the ring recently, the British wanted to be sure they could remain in it when [they] climbed back to fight it out with Hitler."[16]

Lee was given a free hand to select his staff and set about finding people who had worked with him in the past and earned his respect. He chose as his chief of staff Col. Thomas B. Larkin, who at the time was serving in Panama. When Larkin arrived in Washington, Lee arranged to have him promoted to brigadier general.

Before leaving the United States, Lee and Larkin flew to New York to discuss shipping issues with Gen. Homer M. Groninger, commanding general of the port that would handle millions of tons of supplies going to Great Britain in the years ahead. Lee knew he would need a good rapport with Groninger.

Also mindful of the difficulties faced by the sos during World War I, Lee took Larkin with him to interview Gen. James G. Harbord, who had been Pershing's last supply commander in the European theater in World War I. That earlier effort had been compromised because the sos had to adopt an organizational structure that did not parallel that of the War Department. As a result there were no clearly defined command and technical channels between the two, leading to poor organizational control and inefficient movement and distribution of the supplies needed by combat units. Somervell and Lee were determined not to repeat that experience.[17]

According to Lee, "Harbord said he was sorry for me, a fellow Kansan who, like he, had given up command of the 2nd Infantry Division to take such a thankless job! He cautioned us that our job would be more difficult because of increasing demands and the fact that we could not draw on the Continent of Europe as he had for many of his needs. He also urged our having an inspection train made available, recalling that he had used his inspection train fully half the time while he was General Pershing's sos commander."[18]

Lee assembled his staff for a final dinner at a restaurant in Baltimore. One of their guests was a British liaison officer, Brigadier General Kerr, whose family had long been involved in shipping. "He later became Chief of the Royal Army Supply Corps who's [sic] Academy we then inspected in England," Lee noted. "He was invaluable when we landed and got us in touch with all the British officials as well as our own American headquarters at Number 20 Grosvenor Square."[19]

Lee arrived in Great Britain with a heavy agenda. As commanding general of the sos, Lee held responsibilities equivalent to a corps area commander in the zone of the interior. Marshall's reorganization had left Lee's authority outside the strategic and operational loop. Somervell had instructed Lee to forge a functionally organized, semi-autonomous sos command inside the theater's highest headquarters. He reasoned that whatever headquarters structure emerged in the ETO would influence staff organizations in other theaters.

Soon Lee and his staff were on a transatlantic flight in a British Overseas Air Corporation airplane headed for the British Isles. When he arrived in London on May 24, 1942, Lee had with him the sos organizational setup, complete with a control division and a chief of administrative services. He would find that this broad-based authority, unprecedented in the history of the U.S. military, evoked intense resentment and opposition from other senior officers who were not in on the plan. But initially Lee was mostly on his own.

CHAPTER SEVEN

Bolero

> You will not find it hard to prove that battles,
> campaigns, and even wars have been won
> and lost primarily because of logistics.
>
> —DWIGHT D. EISENHOWER

One senior officer who was not in on the new organizational plan was Maj. Gen. James E. Chaney, commanding general of the U.S. Army forces in the United Kingdom. He had devised his own sos plan and just one month earlier had suggested his own candidate to run it. Chaney had been sent to lay the groundwork for a buildup that Washington knew was coming. He was in the U.S. Army Air Corps, which made sense in that the first action against Germany would clearly come in the air. But Chaney was not merely out of the loop when the supply plans were being made in Washington; the intent to limit the senior leadership of the army in Europe to a minimum of administrative and supply functions constituted a dramatic departure from traditional military doctrine. This departure from tradition was the basis of a fissure that would generate friction and lead to several reorganizations over the next two years, without ever resolving the issue.

Chaney and his staff were not up to date on the new organizational structure creating three great commands for air, ground, and service forces. Lee, his chief of staff (Larkin), and eight other members of Lee's staff arrived in Great Britain on May 24, 1942. Four days later Lee issued a general order outlining the functions and responsibilities of the sos as he saw them. He believed that virtually all supply and administrative functions of the theater should be taken over by his sos and placed under his command. Chaney and his staff were virulently opposed to Lee's order. In particular some of Chaney's staff took issue with the very concept of three commands, but they did not realize that the issue had already been decided in Washington.[1]

In asserting the parameters of his power, Lee conceded that the air wing was a special case because of the uniqueness of its supply requirements. Before leaving the United States, Lee had met with leaders of the U.S. Army Air Forces and agreed to a division of supply functions. The Air Service Command would assume complete responsibility for supplies peculiar to air forces but would leave to Lee's SOS all construction and handling of supplies common to both ground and air forces.[2]

The buildup of U.S. forces in Great Britain was code-named Bolero, and it was intended to prepare for an invasion of Europe tentatively scheduled for 1943. The code name for the actual invasion, then in its initial planning stages, was Sledgehammer (which the British had already been planning under the code name Roundup). There was much communication among Lee, Chaney, and headquarters in Washington in the first few weeks as they tried to resolve the differences of opinion regarding ultimate authority over the supply chain. Chaney was trying to exercise influence as the commander on the spot, but Lee was a master of this kind of inside politicking. In early May Eisenhower came to Great Britain, met with Chaney and Lee, and returned to Washington to confer with Marshall. Eisenhower was back in Britain by May 26.

With him came Somervell, who met with Chaney and his staff in an effort to sell Washington's reorganization plan. In this he was clearly not successful. He and Eisenhower met with British leaders to discuss the facilities that might be placed at the disposition of the Americans. After an additional day of conferences and a weekend stay at the prime minister's estate at Chequers, Somervell and Lee undertook a whirlwind tour of U.S. installations via a special train provided by Gen. Sir Bernard Paget, commander of the British Home Forces.

That train apparently rang a bell with Lee. "When we talked with the Secretary of British Transport, Lord Leathers, and he asked how he best could help us, I told him of our need for train transportation, how the French had made two trains available, one for General Pershing and one for General Harbord, whereupon Lord Leathers said substantially, 'Well, of course, the King keeps a small train and we have a small one for the Commander of the Home Forces. We hope that you will keep your requests small because of the strain in our railway system,'" Lee recalled years later. "Exchanging glances, I knew that Somervell would support my request for a minimum of 'one small American train' of such size as would meet our needs. That is what we got and used much more than half the time. Yes, we were criticized both in England and at home by people who did not understand what we were doing," Lee wrote, "but that is part of one's service task: to take the blame and say nothing. And when success finally crowns one's effort, we give the credit to the Commander and his gallant troops[,] including, if we can, the service lads who worked their hearts out day and night both in the months of preparation and throughout the campaign."[3]

Work hard they did, and some of the hardest work Lee's people performed was on that train, which some of them described as an instrument of torture. To be sure, it was a serious train. It included two cars for Lee's staff, two flatcars for vehicles, a dining car, a conference car, a private car for the general, and at times other cars. But it was a work train. Lee set a grueling pace on his inspection trips, and it was rare for a meal to be served on the train in daylight hours, for most runs were made at night. The day's work consisted of inspections and conferences without end, normally beginning at five in the morning and lasting until dark. "Most of the staff members who accompanied the sos commander considered the trips agonizing ordeals and would have avoided them if possible," Roland Ruppenthal notes.[4]

"On our trip together to the ports of England, Scotland and Northern Ireland, Somervell and I with our senior staff advisers were able to learn what would be our capacities and limitations in receiving and caring for men, equipment and supplies," Lee wrote. "By June 5, we had a fairly clear estimate of the situation."[5]

Hap Arnold, the senior air force general who was with Somervell on his May visit, was pressuring Lee and the British to have enough large airfields ready to receive the U.S. heavy bombers on schedule. "As at home, the program had been lagging," Lee wrote. "Although at first most of the work had to be done by the British, we would take over with our engineers as soon as possible and meanwhile do all we could to help speed up results. We found many ways in which time could be saved and utilized. 'Twas a fairly touchy task[,] but Arnold's initial presence with Somervell too, proved invaluable to us."[6]

By June 8 Somervell was back in Washington, meeting with Marshall and Stimson to discuss what was needed to convert the island nation into an American military base. On the basis of his survey Somervell told Marshall the administration and supply arrangements for the reception and accommodation of U.S. troops could be worked out satisfactorily, though he foresaw tremendous problems for the sos and particular difficulties in rail transportation and airfield construction.

A major concern of Somervell was the shortage of sos troops on the ground in the United Kingdom. They would be needed to unload, sort, and organize a flood of supplies that would soon be coming across the Atlantic. Earlier Somervell and his planners had estimated Lee would need 350,000 service troops. But already other senior army officers were nibbling away at that total in favor of more men in combat units—a situation that would be a continuing problem throughout the war.[7]

"Our most serious handicap was in not having Americans trained in receiving, sorting, storing[,] and reissuing equipment and supplies," Lee wrote. "Such lack of personnel we tried to meet with British civilians who were willing but who did not know or understand our terms—our names for equipment. Nor was the equipment, nor were the supplies, adequately marked until we developed a sound system and got it adopted. All that took time."[8]

A key decision made when Somervell was in Britain was for the United States and Britain to share the British ports and rail system. "At first, some of our people felt we must insist upon having ports and even rail facilities turned over to us as had been done in France in 1917–1919," Lee noted. "We wisely accepted the British offer to share everything, only taking over such definite storage space as would be necessary to sort out and reissue our equipment and supplies."[9]

On June 4 Col. Everett Hughes, whom Lee had requested, arrived at sos to serve as Lee's chief ordnance officer. He was immediately caught up in the confused command structure, as well as confusion back in the States. Hughes soon realized that the sos in Great Britain had little say over what supplies came from the United States. Prewar army regulations dictated that the momentum of supplies must come from the rear of the army in the field. The doctrine of supplies from the rear was misunderstood or misconstrued throughout the war, Hughes later reported, adding that "the sos shipped what it thought the theater commander should have," not what the commander requested.[10]

Upon Somervell's return to the United States, Marshall issued a directive creating the ETOUSA (European theater of operations, U.S. Army) and instructed Chaney to cooperate with the other allies but to maintain the U.S. contingent as a separate entity. It left little doubt that Chaney was in charge, at least on paper, but a subsequent circular on June 13 gave Lee far-reaching powers, including those of a corps area commander, an unprecedented role for a supply officer.[11]

The June 13 circular fostered confusion, leaving it unclear who was in charge of what. Within a few days Eisenhower was formally chosen as commander of ETOUSA, replacing Chaney, who was sent back to the United States. He never did get on board with the new program, and his career paid the price.

By then Lee was busy moving his headquarters from London to Cheltenham, which created a certain amount of chaos. "Our first task was to get settled and squared away so that we might undertake our great task," Lee wrote. "In crowded London we were hampered by the British custom of getting to work late in the morning albeit they worked late into the night. We knew that Americans did better on our own schedule, and therefore asked for accommodations out of London."[12]

Cheltenham was a fairly modern city of about fifty thousand located about ninety miles northwest of London. A group of temporary one-story blocks of offices had been erected by the British War Office. This building complex had the advantage of already being there. It offered about five hundred thousand square feet of office space and was the hub of an adequate road and rail network. It had hotels where the officers could be based but no barracks for enlisted men. Most of the enlisted ranks would be lodged in tents, at least initially, until huts could be erected. This facility would be sos headquarters until after the D-Day invasion, when it moved to France.

The move to Cheltenham led Eisenhower to issue a new order "clarifying" the roles of sos and ETOUSA, an order that actually broadened Lee's authority but did not resolve the continuing dispute. There were many in the upper echelons who resented Lee, or anyone in supply, having as much power as he did. Lee was now assigned the additional function of administration and supply planning, and he was authorized to communicate directly with the War Department in Washington, as well as with British officials, on supply matters without reference to ETO headquarters.[13]

Ruppenthal reports that the changes fostered even greater confusion. "The administrative services were those in which counterparts were named at Headquarters, ETOUSA, and in which the division of authority became very troublesome," he writes. "Even those staff sections which General Eisenhower had decreed should be placed under ETOUSA—that of the provost marshal for example—were split when the sos moved to Cheltenham. ETOUSA and sos each established its own adjutant general, provost marshal and other special staff officers. The inevitable result was an overlapping of function and conflict over jurisdiction. In varying degrees this tendency also carried over into the supply services, where the senior representatives at theater headquarters were inclined to develop separate sections and encroach on the functions of the sos."[14]

U.S. and British planners were trying to decide how much force was needed for Bolero. Predictably ground, air, and service branches were competing for personnel. It was realized that up until then the army had been allocating only 11.8 percent of the 1942 troop basis to services, well below what Lee, Somervell, and everyone else familiar with the challenge believed would be necessary. The earliest breakdown of the Bolero force basis suggested about 26 percent of the troops should be in supply units.

The army was busy training combat troops, but few trained service troops were available and most of them were busy stateside. But to prepare for the arrival of combat troops in Britain, Lee needed service troops there first to receive equipment and supplies, prepare depots and other accommodations, and make ready essential services for the units to follow. In desperation Lee agreed to accept partially trained service units, intending to provide them with on-the-job training.

At this juncture there was a serious shortage of shipping to transfer equipment, supplies, and personnel across the Atlantic. The United States was even then commencing its peacetime mobilization, which would eventually transform a nation, only recently moribund by the Great Depression, into the free world's arsenal. Ships were a priority, but so were tanks, airplanes, artillery, and a host of other things. Also problematic were the German submarines that were busy sinking U.S. and British ships almost as fast as new ones could be built.

This was the beginning of the U.S. mobilization. At the end of June 1942 there were only 54,845 U.S. troops in Great Britain, and almost all of them were in Northern Ireland. Fewer than 2,000 members of the Eighth Air Force had arrived.[15] General Chaney had done little to lay the groundwork for a major infusion of U.S. forces, and most of what he had done was of little use because he was not privy to the plans being made in Washington.

The basic Bolero plan envisioned three main phases: a preparatory period, the cross-channel invasion and seizure of beachheads, and the beginning of a general advance. The preparatory phase included a buildup of air forces to begin preliminary bombardment of the enemy's positions. The planners imagined a decisive offensive, to take place in the spring of 1943 with combined U.S.-British forces of fifty-eight hundred combat aircraft and forty-eight divisions of infantry and armor. By far the biggest challenge the Bolero planners initially faced was the construction of camps, hospitals, and training facilities in anticipation of an enormous influx of people from the United States.

At the height of the U.S. buildup in Britain the U.S. uniform was everywhere to be seen, American ammunition and other supplies and equipment were stacked along the roads, and U.S. troops were lodged in more than one hundred thousand buildings, either newly built or requisitioned, ranging from small Nissen huts and cottages to sprawling hangars, workshops, and assembly plants in more than eleven hundred cities and villages. But in 1942 there was little of that visible.

The three major tasks faced by Lee in the early days were to organize the reception of troops and cargo in the ports, establish a depot system for the storage and distribution of supplies, and launch a construction program, especially for airfields, for which sos was responsible. During the first several weeks Lee spent much of his time inspecting ports, depots, and other accommodations offered by the British.

On July 8 Hughes returned to the United States to meet with Somervell and other supply officers to try to improve the supply situation. Hughes argued that requests for supplies should come from the theater and not from Washington. "The trouble was," Hughes argued, "that equipment came to the Port from all over the U.S. without much regard being paid to priorities and space. It had to be shipped and we had to take it whether we wanted it or not."[16] Hughes reported that Somervell and his staff were persuaded by his arguments. When he returned to Great Britain, he was appointed Lee's chief of staff.

As if Lee did not have enough on his plate, he was also made responsible for the operation of training centers and officer candidate schools. sos had established both officer candidate and specialist schools at Shrivenham, southwest of Oxford, in August. Later in the year the two schools were combined to form the American School Center and opened to all students from all commands under a quota system.[17]

Things got even more interesting in July, when Marshall, Adm. Ernest J. King, and presidential advisor Harry Hopkins came to London. "There was a fairly complete discussion of likely ability to effect a sufficiently large landing on the Continent that could be held against the forces Hitler would throw at us," Lee wrote. "The plan was called Sledgehammer. I recall one conference presided over by General Marshall when he asked me how many divisions I felt could be supplied through Cherbourg [the nearest French port to Normandy, the projected landing site]. My answer was 'Fifteen,' as I recall, provided the port had not been destroyed. At best, it was an optimistic estimate."[18]

Another key issue that came up, and would resurface often, was that of landing craft—the famous landing ship, tank (LST)—that would be needed to transport and land equipment and troops on the coast of France. It was a British design displacing on average four thousand tons. It could carry dozens of tanks and trucks plus troops. It was the size of a light cruiser yet had a flat bottom so it could beach itself at low tide and float off at high tide.[19] "It was soon realized that we could not expect to have on hand sufficient landing craft to assure a proper landing on Normandy shores in November 1942," Lee wrote. "Moreover, by that time it had become the combined policy that landing craft must be commanded by naval personnel, not by amphibious engineers. In Washington during May it had been argued and tentatively decided that . . . the Navy could not guarantee sufficient personnel to command cross channel landing craft." Instead, Lee noted, "the Army Engineers under General Charles Gross and later his Transportation Corps, would supply such commanders and crews. During the summer conferences in London, Admiral Stark and Lord Louis Mountbatten both protested that 'no self-respecting Allied soldier would want to risk his channel crossing to a land lubber boat captain.' They made it very clear that all landing craft, large and small, must be commanded by naval personnel, either Royal Navy or U.S. Navy. To this the Prime Minister apparently agreed and General Marshall concurred, albeit perhaps amusedly."[20]

It was at this meeting that Lee first became acquainted with another major campaign afoot. Called Torch, it would present a major challenge to his fledgling command.

CHAPTER EIGHT

Lee's Darkest Hour

I don't know what this logistics is that Marshall
is always talking about, but I want some of it.
—ADM. ERNEST J. KING

By midsummer Lee's sos was beginning to receive the large quantities of war equipment and personnel pouring into ports in Britain and Northern Ireland in the Bolero buildup. By the end of June there were growing mounds of supplies scattered about the countryside. Lee was building his organization and organizing his operation as best he could, given his staffing shortages. He was taking soldiers from other units and as quickly as possible training them to be supply technicians. They had to learn a lot about identifying different components and organizing stock, but overall the training of a service technician took about half as much time as training an infantryman. Lee established four base sections to control his operation, which initially relied on the British for many services. In that regard he attempted to avoid duplication with the British efforts because he was shorthanded as it was.[1]

Lee was focused on Sledgehammer, the proposed invasion of Europe. By the summer of 1942 it had acquired the code name Roundup and was expected to transpire in 1943, or at least Lee and his staff thought it was. There was much to be done, but he figured he had at least a year to get everything organized and operating smoothly.

Except all of a sudden he had little time. The war had its own schedule. The German army was marching through the Soviet Union, and the Soviet dictator Joseph Stalin was exhorting the United States and Great Britain to take some of the pressure off of his beleaguered armies. It was evident to President Roosevelt and Prime Minister Churchill and their advisors that an invasion of Europe was out of the question in 1942 because the Allies simply did not have the requisite forces available. Yet 1943 seemed a long way off, and they believed they had to do something to put pressure on the Germans. Their solution was an invasion of North Africa, where British forces under Lt. Gen. Bernard Montgomery were locked in mortal combat with German forces under Gen. Erwin Rommel, the famed "Desert Fox."[2]

Lee wrote that "during July, as I recall, it was decided that although an effective landing could not be made in Normandy that year, a British-American effort must be made in North Africa in order to establish what the Russians insisted upon, a 'Second Front.'" The decision to face the Germans in North Africa "was so secret that some of the British Cabinet were not informed. It was during this strained interim that the Lord Mayor of London held his banquet in the newly re-roofed Guild Hall in honor of the American forces. General Eisenhower, of course, was invited with a large number of his Americans, there to meet the senior officials of the British Government. General Eisenhower delegated to me the task of representing him and of making his apologies along with a few appropriate remarks," Lee recalled. "I had short notice. In fact, I came up on our train from Cheltenham and wrote out en route what seemed best to say. Those words and others spoken on the occasion were printed in a small pamphlet, thanks to Jim Franey [a member of Lee's staff], entitled 'Two United Nations.' However pleasantly that record may read, I was not unconscious of the underlying resentment that many of the senior British officials seemed to feel over General Eisenhower's absence. They did not know then that he had been chosen to command the combined operation in North Africa."[3]

They indeed did not know about Eisenhower's appointment, and it had not yet dawned on Lee how much trouble the North Africa operation, code-named Torch, would mean for him. The decision had been made when Marshall, King, and Hopkins were in London a few days earlier. All thought of an early cross-channel invasion was abandoned in favor of an immediate invasion of North Africa. The plan did not negate Bolero, but the senior command made it clear the more immediate task was Torch.

When the Allied powers embraced this plan, it was clear at least to more senior planners in the United States and Great Britain that

Roundup would not happen in 1942 or 1943 either. There was only so much they could do at one time. Roundup was in effect put on a back burner for several months, and Bolero was held in abeyance. By this time Eisenhower had three stars—a lieutenant general. (Lee was still a two star.) Eisenhower's deputy was Maj. Gen. Mark Clark, who had arrived in Great Britain in July as commander of the II Corps. Clark was in charge of planning for Torch.

The final scheme for the African campaign was complex, and a final agreement did not appear until September 5. The Western Task Force, comprised almost totally of U.S. ground, naval, and air forces, would sail directly from the United States to land near Casablanca on the Atlantic coast of Morocco. The Center Task Force, also mainly U.S. forces, would sail from Great Britain with British naval support to land at Oran. And the Eastern Assault Force, consisting mainly of British but also some U.S. troops and escorted by the Royal Navy, was to land at Algiers.

At the outset Lee's sos was designated to supply the Center Task Force, but the plan specified that responsibility for supply of the entire U.S. commitment in North Africa was to be gradually and fully assumed by Somervell's organization in the United States. But it became clear almost immediately that Lee's sos was not prepared to supply the Center Task Force, at least not right away. Lee's sos had been organizing seriously for only a few months, setting up a supply operation of unprecedented scope in a foreign country a long way from home. The system was not ready for prime time. To make matters worse there was at first no tactical plan they could use to assess what was needed for the Center Task Force.

The shortage of personnel was the biggest problem. Not only was Lee shorthanded but right off the bat he lost many of his best people to the Torch command. Somervell had attempted to provide Lee with enough supply troops, but the War Department was more focused on combat troops. By the end of September service troops in the sos accounted for only 21 percent of the overall force, well below the projected 35 percent envisioned by Somervell, and many of them—both officers and enlisted men—were learning their new craft by trial and error. The receiving, inventorying, and storing of war matériel was not rocket science, but neither was it simple, if only because of the unprecedented volume involved. For much of the summer confusion reigned.

Even worse there was little communication between Washington and London, and much of the communication that did transpire was garbled. The people responsible for supplying Lee's organization were unclear what the military priorities were, in part because there was no tactical plan of action. No one was responsible for synchronizing movement of men and logistics. The War Department was soon rushing inadequately trained troops to Great Britain while their equipment lagged far behind. An army without its equipment is basically an orderly mob.

Somervell was at least partially responsible for this dissonance. In the early summer he had been loading ships "full and down" with whatever was available without regard for what Lee's sos was requesting.[4] The goal was to get "stuff" to Great Britain, and with shipping in short supply Somervell's people wanted every inch of cargo space filled with something, simply to avoid wasting the ships' capacity.

With the announcement of Torch in July the traffic accelerated but without adjustment of the "full and down" technique, which was based on automatic supply tables, not Lee's requests. The people in New York loading the ships thought they were doing great work, but at the other end where the ships were unloaded there was mass confusion. There was little paperwork arriving with the shiploads to distinguish among different types of materials. Ship manifests arrived late if ever and often bore no relation to the actual content of the ships. Because of the critical shipping shortage, the vessels stayed in port only long enough to offload their cargoes before heading back to the United States. Lee's people were deluged with boxes and crates they did not know what to do with. They ended up with huge stockpiles of who knows what stashed hither and yon. Lee did not know what they had, in what quantities, or where anything was. It was one huge, chaotic mess. Lee reported on September 4 to senior command that sos simply could not supply the fifty-five thousand U.S. troops assigned to the Central Task Force from the goods on hand, largely because he had no idea exactly what he did have on hand. On September 6 he added that a shortage of ships might require cutbacks in both numbers of troops and supplies.

But the supplies, or at least most of what was needed, were actually there. "Most of the equipment that was needed was available in the United Kingdom, but it had been randomly scattered among the makeshift depots by British workers without records or box or crate markings," Ohl writes. "Finding the necessary equipment and delivering it to the combat troops was now out of the question."[5]

To add to the disarray, a month before the target date some of the units slated for action in North Africa had only about half of their required signal equipment. A military unit unable to communicate with its leadership is virtually useless and inevitably in peril. Other units had too much stuff. The First Armored Division disembarked in Scotland with many more vehicles than it had use for and had to leave them behind when it eventually sailed to North Africa.

The famous First Division, known as the Big Red One, showed up in Great Britain without its equipment. It might as well have been on a tourist excursion. Eisenhower wired Marshall that the Big Red One's equipment was still somewhere out in the Atlantic—no one seemed to know exactly where—and that as a result the target date for the landings in North Africa might have to be set back.[6] While it waited, the division began training with borrowed British equipment, which did not exactly inspire British confidence in their allies.

It was mass confusion, and the guy in charge of Torch, General Clark, held Lee personally responsible, as did Eisenhower's chief of staff, Lt. Gen. Walter "Beetle" Smith. They both wanted Lee's head on a platter, but Eisenhower then and later proved to be reluctant to sack senior leadership. As a rule Eisenhower paid little attention to logistics, but he could not ignore this snafu and he was not shy about chewing people out. Ike signed a message to Lee drafted by Beetle Smith, who often played the bad cop to Eisenhower's good cop. "He instructed the sos commander to spare no effort or expense to accomplish the task of sorting and cataloguing supplies that had already been received," Roland Ruppenthal writes, "and he urged Lee to utilize to the utmost the proffered assistance of British organizations and to exploit every possible means of avoiding unnecessary shipments from the United States. Eisenhower asked Lee to devote full personal attention to this task, authorizing him to delegate responsibility for the normal routine functions of the SOS to a subordinate."[7]

The fact was that Eisenhower was heavily invested in Lee. It was understood among the hierarchy that Lee was Somervell's man, which was reason enough to leave him alone. Somervell sat at the top of the military totem pole and had Marshall's ear. As ultimate arbiter of U.S. military supplies the world over, Somervell was not to be trifled with.[8] But more than that Eisenhower had been impressed by Lee's bearing and efficiency.[9] When he first arrived in London, Eisenhower noted that the headquarters staff there lacked confidence. The one officer who stood out for Eisenhower was Lee, who had "his whole gang going at top speed." Eisenhower told Somervell he was fortunate to have an officer of Lee's ability. In July he said Lee was one of the finest officers in the army. In mid-August he nominated Lee as his deputy at ETO and authorized him "to handle matters in his own name."[10] He told the War Department that Lee was by far the best qualified to be his successor as ETO commander. It would have been a stretch at this juncture to suddenly cashier Lee for the supply conundrum, which, like most disasters, had many parents.

Like Somervell and Lee, Eisenhower was well aware of the problems that had beset the supply situation for U.S. forces in World War I and that the same set of difficulties had recurred. In a conversation with his naval aide, Harry Butcher, Eisenhower noted that "the same issue kept coming up throughout the last war and remains a tough one. There is no perfect solution."[11]

Butcher was something of a court gossip, spending his days with Eisenhower and recording notes every night in his personal log. "In General Lee, Ike felt he had one of the finest officers in the Army and a man who had the best possible qualifications for a job that requires a high degree of human understanding," Butcher recorded at the time.[12]

September 14 brought a bombshell from Everett Hughes, Lee's

former chief of staff for sos, who was by now working on Eisenhower's staff and enjoying a close rapport with him. Eisenhower sent Hughes, who became known as Eisenhower's troubleshooter, to check up on the situation at sos. Hughes went to sos headquarters in Cheltenham and met with the section heads individually, asking each what his branch needed.

Hughes identified a multitude of problems with the sos and summarized his findings in a September 8 cable that ran eleven pages. Assigned the number 1949, this cable requested a long, detailed list of items, from four hundred life preservers to carrier pigeons with feed. Hughes also requested that forty-five days' worth of combat supplies be shipped to England. Hughes concluded that Torch as then contemplated could not be supported and maintained within the projected time. Noting that all supplies were supposed to be well in hand by then, Hughes recommended a six-week delay in launching Torch, until December 15.[13]

Somervell was taken aback. Message 1949 was a frank admission that things were not going well. Somervell had Gen. Leroy Lutes of his staff draft a letter to Lee expressing concern about the mess and urging him to have his staff "swarm on the British ports and depots and find out where these people have put our supplies and equipment."[14] All of this activity got Eisenhower's undivided attention. He called an emergency meeting the next day during which he laid into Lee and other senior officers, telling them their careers depended on them solving the problem. (D. K. R. Crosswell notes in *Beetle* that Eisenhower could have added his own career to that list.) Eisenhower was blowing smoke. There was no way he could sack all of those senior people. He was, however, firing a warning shot across Lee's bow, and Lee got the message loud and clear.

In his memoirs Lee recorded this as his darkest period—more stressful than the lead-up to D-Day—probably because his neck was clearly on the block. "Our greatest difficulty continued to be a shortage of Service personnel," he wrote. "We were urged to provide as many Service troops as we possibly could in support of the ground and air forces that would leave the UK with General Ike. This meant a still further depletion of the service personnel available to sort and issue, pack and ship the equipment and supplies we had already received and continued to receive. This period of weeks was the most difficult of all my war service. Not even the driving pressure of the 1944 summer campaign was as hard on my nervous system as the fall of 1942."[15]

Lee returned to Cheltenham, assembled his staff, and lit a fire under their bottoms. Acknowledging that the job looked hopeless, he challenged them to pull out all the stops and give it their best shot. Eisenhower's deputy, Clark, demanded an updated inventory of sos stocks, and Lee provided him with one on September 18. "While Col Hughes indicated it is difficult for the sos to meet the date now set for the operation," Lee wrote to Clark, "I believe they can be met with fair efficiency." Lee was ever and always an optimist, one of many traits that aggravated his detractors to no end. "The campaign should succeed although the logistical prearrangements be far from perfect," he said to Clark.[16]

It was all part of the Lee persona. "I am up against Clark who does not want any bad news," Hughes stated, "and Lee who says he can support any operation."[17] Brig. Gen. Thomas Larkin, Lee's former deputy and by now the officer assigned to command sos units in Algeria, complained to Clark in person that Lee's attitude was not helpful, and he then stormed out of Clark's office. Clark reported the incident to Eisenhower, whose reaction is not recorded.

Eisenhower's aide Butcher noted there were repeated criticisms of Lee "riding around the Island on his special train, handsomely equipped, while the supply situation has been so difficult."[18] On September 19 Eisenhower withdrew his recommendation that Lee succeed him as ETO commander.

The First Division may have shown up without its equipment, but that did not deter Lee from welcoming his old friend, one of the U.S. Army's legendary officers, Gen. Terry de la Mesa Allen, "an old friend, with Brigadier General Theodore Roosevelt, Jr., as second in command. For that occasion, a number of British officials were on hand as a greeting party[,] including, as I recall, the Secretary of State for War. I then realized what a good impression the American troops could make and how much they needed strong leadership."[19]

In this as in all things Lee attributed his survival to the benevolence of the deity whom he continued to honor each morning, rain or shine, along with his immediate staff, who were required to go with him unless they had a valid excuse. "For this I was blessed in always having available Anglican Churches which our American chaplains shared with the British clergy. The practice of attending the daily celebration which I had begun in the Pacific Northwest in 1939 and had been able to continue at Fort Mason and Fort Sam Houston became my greatest source of strength and clear decision."[20]

It would appear—at least to Lee—that all of that praying had paid off. By the third week of September it had become clear that the supply situation was turning around. Lee's staff was working all out, running about the countryside day and night, identifying what was where and taking inventory. Somervell's people back home were doing their part, transferring equipment from units in training to the forces in Great Britain preparing to join the fight. Special efforts were made to have the crates marked before they were sent across the sea. Marshall even suggested—a suggestion from Marshall was like a mandate from heaven—that a detachment of three or four men familiar with the cargo and loading plan be placed on each ship to follow through on the discharge and keep track of priority freight so that it would be properly dispatched and the people who received it would know what it was.

On September 24 Lee produced a much improved status report. As he informed Leroy Lutes of Somervell's staff, who was in Britain to help bring order to the chaos, "speaking in baseball vernacular, we lost only vendor supplies—pop, chewing gum—but no bats and balls."[21] In the first half of September sos had unloaded two hundred thousand long tons, with more on the way. By November the invasion of North Africa would be under way.[22]

The five months between the activation of the theater and the launching of Torch had been traumatic for Lee and sos, and the responsibility for much of their difficulty lay with others. But in war excuses do not count for much. Lee and his people got the system working reasonably well in time to support the invasion, and that was what mattered. Lee said later that one of the principal lessons he learned from Torch was that supply planning and operations must be closely coordinated with tactical planning and operations. That lesson would serve him and sos well in 1944—right up until Eisenhower sent Patton's Third Army on a wild run across France, when all supply plans went out the window.

CHAPTER NINE

Torch

There is no greater pacifist than the regular officer.
Any man who is forced to turn his attention to the horrors
of the battlefield, to the grotesque shapes that are left
there for the burying squads—he doesn't want war.
—GEN. DWIGHT D. EISENHOWER

Lee's group may have finally got a fix on what supplies they had in Great Britain, but there was still a major challenge in getting ready for an invasion several hundred miles away that he had not anticipated and for which preparations had to be completed in great haste. Lee basically had only three months to do it. The original British plan for Torch allowed for a force of ten to twelve divisions, half of them British and half American, to be put ashore on the northeastern African coastline. Eisenhower was determined that he would make a massive commitment, even if it required drawing down all of the resources in Britain committed to Bolero. Early in September he estimated that about 102,000 troops would be taken from the United Kingdom, and that total eventually rose to 150,000. The core of that force consisted of the First Armored and the First and Thirty-Fourth Infantry Divisions, which were already in Britain and available. The Torch plan was to seize three port cities—Casablanca, Algiers, and Oran—and to do that the Allies would land troops at nine coastal sites scattered across nine hundred miles.

A major portion of this invasion force was to come not from Britain but from Hampton Roads, Virginia, where the United States was mounting a huge armada consisting of nearly four hundred transport and cargo vessels under the command of Rear Adm. Henry Kent Hewitt. The force included about thirty-four thousand ground troops under the command of Patton. The armada was to sail across the Atlantic under tight security and to mesh with forces coming south from the United Kingdom. It was a highly complex undertaking and vulnerable not only to the vagaries of weather but also to attacks from German U-boats and aircraft. "Some believed it would be the greatest amphibious gamble since Xerxes crossed the Hellespont in the fifth century B.C.," Rick Atkinson writes. "The only modern precedent for landing on a hostile shore after a long sea voyage through perilous waters was the British disaster at Gallipoli in 1915, which cost a quarter of a million Allied casualties."[1]

Supplying material and personnel for the African campaign drained the repository of equipment and supplies Lee and the U.S. Army Air Forces had been accumulating for Bolero. The Eighth Air Force, for example, lost nearly eleven hundred of its aircraft and 75 percent of its supplies. The diversion was such that the Eighth had to virtually cease its operations against Germany for a time, and afterward its activity was severely curtailed for several months. The ground combat forces took an even bigger hit. The Twenty-Ninth Division and the 156th Infantry Regiment were just about all that was left on the ground in Great Britain after the drawdown. Withdrawals of U.S. troops from Great Britain were not completed until February 1943, when total ground troops remaining there numbered about one hundred thousand, including Lee's diminished supply force. Not until the following May was Lee able to begin replenishing his depleted forces. Lee also lost some of his senior officers, including General Larkin, his chief of staff, who had proven to be one of his most able assistants.

The drawdown of supplies and equipment was even more draconian. In the period from October 1942 through April 1943 more than four hundred thousand long tons of U.S. supplies were dispatched from the United Kingdom to North Africa. The burden of supplying the North Africa operation gradually shifted back to the United States, but the drain on supplies in Great Britain was much higher than anticipated. Lee's cupboard was almost bare.

Predictably Lee was short of supply troops during this period— having about thirty-two thousand in his command. He warned his superiors that this force would be inadequate to operate essential installations in Britain. Even worse it was an unbalanced force in which many key skills were absent. He asked for ten thousand more personnel and suggested they not be withheld for lack of training—they could get their training on the job. The British were a major source of both supplies and services for Lee throughout the year. In particular the British army was feeding about fifty thousand American troops, which was not only embarrassing but the Yanks had trouble adjusting to British food. After a couple of months Lee got some more personnel, but the War Department insisted supply troops were at a premium and the forces in combat, which included both the North Africa and the Pacific theaters, took precedence over Lee's operation.

All the while Lee was gathering as much staff as he could from among whatever people in uniform got off the transports from the United States—regardless of whether they were trained in supply. One such group was B Company of the Thirty-First Division, from Louisiana. 1st Lt. Van R. Mayhall found himself in England looking around at his new surroundings and wondering what would happen next. He reported to a Lieutenant Colonel Gent, who offered him a cigar. "You and your company have a week to learn how to run this Quartermaster Depot," Gent said.[2]

Mayhall was nonplussed. "My people had been trained to be infantry soldiers," he recalled years later.

> All we had to do was turn some riflemen and machine gunners into typists, checkers, warehousemen, and a few other specialists we didn't know anything about yet. In the States, spend two years in the field, sun, rain, heat, cold, sand. Overseas, lay down rifles to pick up pencils and typewriters! We had to take bills of lading and load trucks with rations to go to the different outfits that we had to supply, but we didn't know where the outfits were. My motor corporal normally had two Jeeps to take care of; now he had twenty-five 2½ ton trucks to oil, gas, repair, and keep on the road.[3]

Mayhall's people were not complaining about the change of occupation. "They could see that working inside beat the hell out of long marches in the mud," Mayhall notes. "In addition, we were all eating better. The men found that if they put an elbow in the right place a crate of special food would fall off a stack, break open, and couldn't be shipped. So this food would have to be turned over to our kitchen crew instead of letting it spoil."[4]

With no preparation or briefing Mayhall's platoon had moved into a situation that had been suddenly vacated by a British unit. "Considering that some of the infantrymen hadn't been old enough to drive before they came into the service, it was a fast-training program to get them into condition to handle large trucks on the 'wrong' side of the road," Mayhall recalls. "I never knew how many fender benders there were, but no one was broken up, thank goodness."[5]

Mayhall's people were soon busy unloading trucks from boxcars and unloading the trucks into storage. "One of the things that this platoon had to learn about warehousing was to be able to find what they unloaded when it was called for," Mayhall writes. "If ten days of rations have been put in front of fifty cases of rifles and rifles are ordered, the rifles can't be loaded without moving ten days of rations."[6]

This was the supply organization Lee was pulling together on the run from whatever resources he could find. Supply procedures were not highly complicated, but the army had found that it took a lot more time to train a rifleman than a supply soldier, so the use of riflemen to move supplies did not seem an efficient use of human resources. But the work still had to be done, and riflemen were what Lee had at his disposal at that time.

Predictably there was much confusion in the supply operation for North Africa. Somervell had directed that supply requisitions be sent directly from the task forces in North Africa to the port in New York, where his people could control disbursement. But for as long as Torch was also drawing men and supplies from Great Britain, there was frequent duplication and confusion, largely due to poor communication. The combat units in the field did not really care where their supplies came from as long as they got there. If on some occasions they got double what they asked for, with deliveries from both New York and Great Britain, that was fine with them.

But the flow of supplies from the United States to Great Britain almost ceased entirely for several months. The War Department decreed that supplies sent to Great Britain during this period would be merely enough to sustain the U.S. troops that were already in country. But Marshall made it clear that Bolero was still an active plan and that a cross-channel invasion was still in the works, and he exhorted the War Department to "make superhuman efforts to build up U.S. strength in the United Kingdom after the Torch requirements have been satisfied."[7]

Eisenhower and Lee were also of one mind that the preparation for accommodating U.S. troops and supplies in Britain should continue.[8] Even though most of the troops had been sent to North Africa, Eisenhower decreed that all storage and hospital facilities previously planned for Great Britain be built "without interruption or modification."[9] The actual construction was mostly performed by British firms under SOS supervision. With regard to the air force, planning was done by the Eighth Air Force subject to the approval of Lee's SOS, which actually supervised the work. The SOS controlled all engineering units, including those in aviation. The air force did not like this system, and its grievances came to a head during Torch when British ports were unable to keep pace with all of the materials coming into the country, prompting Lee to divert forty-five hundred engineer troops to help with the unloading. Among these were some aviation engineers allegedly taken off other projects.

Lee pointed out that these aviation engineers had yet to even begin work on air force construction because their equipment had not yet arrived. In late November they were returned to the air force projects, but they remained under Lee's command, which continued to be a thorn in his relations with the air force.[10]

It was agreed by Washington and London that a target number of 427,000 troops would be gathered on the island, the first step toward an eventual total of more than a million men. In essence the powers that be had resolved that the diversion of troops and resources from Britain to North Africa was a temporary expedient that would be reversed as soon as the enterprise in the Mediterranean area was brought under control.

But that did not happen quickly. The invasion of North Africa is generally given short shrift in most history books, treated as a prelude to the real battle for Europe to come later, and so it was. But for those who fought it the conflict was brutal and bloody enough and then some. It began with some ugly business with French naval and ground forces whose loyalty was in question. The Germans had over-run France early in the war, forced its surrender, and set up a pup-pet French government based in Vichy. The French forces in North Africa were ostensibly controlled by the Vichy government, which was in turn controlled by Germany. Many of the French forces, includ-ing much of its naval capacity, were in Algeria, which was then part of the French empire. It was hoped the French would not fight the British and American invaders, but most of the French did fight for their honor, if not the Germans. It was a great challenge figuring out which French leaders to work with. Thousands of lives were lost before the French folded the tricolor, after which most of the French military began rallying to the Allied cause. But in the early stages German U-boats were raising havoc among the ships ferrying troops and supplies to the beaches defended by the French. Several ships were torpedoed and sunk. Many American and British soldiers and sailors died under French guns.

But the real fight ensued when the Germans staked out their ground in Tunis and put up a stiff fight for several months, giving the Americans a taste of what the British and Soviets had been deal-ing with for years. "The Wehrmacht's entrenchment in Tunis set the stage for a confrontation between German and Anglo-American armies that was to scorch two continents the next two and a half years and cost several million lives," Atkinson writes. "Here began the struggle for possession of the earth itself, or at least the western earth, an unremitting series of titanic land battles that would sweep across Salerno and Anzio, Normandy and the Bulge, broken only by brief interludes to cart away the dead and revivify the living."[11]

The American troops and most of their leaders, especially the junior officers, were green and untested. They felt they were in a strange land filled with strange people, the climate was harsh and the land forbidding, and the horrors of combat came as a shock. The supply operation was also unprepared for the chaos of the battle-field. The Allies were counting on mounting a mobile force, but for that you need motor vehicles. By November 12 the plan was calling for some eighty-seven hundred vehicles to be ashore in Oran. The actual number put ashore was eighteen hundred. Inability to bring fuel to the aircraft left the skies to the Germans, whose infamous Stuka dive bombers—actually pretty much obsolete by then—had a field day pouncing on Allied soldiers milling about on the ground. Thousands of young men rudely jerked from their families only weeks before found themselves living in filth, hugging the ground, watching their friends be blown to bits, and being ordered to run through machine-gun fire by inept officers who had little idea what they were doing, all to claim some desolate hills.

The Allies were afflicted with inadequate port facilities (which would also be a problem in Europe), underdeveloped base sections, and a lack of locomotives, rolling stock, and trained operators. In North Africa and later in Europe the most important means of supply would be railroads simply because of the volume involved, and in North Africa the Allies had exactly one—a single-track affair running east-west. They were contending with six hundred miles of bad road from Algiers to Tunis and another four hundred to the American base in Oran. "In the rush forward, using every conceivable kind of transportation including air, naval, railway and all types of nondescript vehicles on roads, we have outrun present possibilities of minimum supply, of immediate reinforcement and, what is even more important, of reasonable air support," Eisenhower said in early December.[12] With the exception of air support, he would encounter the same situation in Europe, mostly as a result of his own decisions.

The end result in North Africa may have been inevitable, but it did not seem that way at the time, at least not to the men on the ground who were being shot and blown up left and right. The Germans had even worse supply problems. They were at the lonely end of a fifteen-hundred-mile supply line that ran across the Mediterranean Sea and was relentlessly hounded by Allied naval and air forces. They could not replace the planes and soldiers who fell before the Allied onslaught. But they still displayed a robust determination to fight to the death for Germany and for Hitler. The German military was an awesome force, well disciplined and led, and it would remain so until its final days.

Despite their inexperience the Allies made rapid progress at first against a handful of German forces allied with unreliable Vichy troops. Rommel's famed Afrika Korps to the east was locked in combat with British forces under Montgomery and could offer little help against the Americans. But Hitler, after denying Rommel reinforcements for twenty months, made an abrupt decision to send in more support. By air and sea seventeen thousand German troops with armor under the command of Gen. Hans-Jürgen von Arnim, a seasoned veteran who had fought in the Soviet Union, moved from Italy into Tunisia. The Allies still had more men and matériel, but they were inexperienced. Also during this period the German Luftwaffe had control of the skies.

In the winter rain and mud the Germans held off the Allied rush to Tunis and held open a supply line to Rommel's forces farther east. In February they punished the Americans, virtually destroying two tank, two infantry, and two artillery battalions in one forty-eight-hour operation. Rommel then launched an armored attack through the Kasserine Pass and drove Eisenhower's troops back several miles. Many of the green American troops panicked and fled before the German onslaught, giving rise to disdain among veteran British troops who said the Americans simply could not fight. But the Germans were outnumbered and outgunned and were gradually worn down by the inadequacy of their supplies. A last push by Rommel was thrown back, and on March 6 he was summoned back to Germany. It just wouldn't do in the Nazi scheme of things to have a national hero defeated. The Allies tightened their grip on German supply lines, and the tide began to turn.

By this time Eisenhower's forces were being supplied directly from the United States, and it was time to follow through on the plan to relieve Lee's sos from responsibility for supplying Torch forces in North Africa. A complete break was decreed between the two theaters. In August Eisenhower had been given command of both Torch and the ETOUSA, but he was spending most of his time in North Africa in a frantic effort to keep the French happy, mollify the British (who frequently expressed contempt for both him and his command), and forge his green troops into an effective fighting force. Gradually he managed all of these three tasks, but it took time, effort, sweat, and a lot of blood. By the time victory was won the French were joining the fight and the British were beginning to develop confidence in the fighting qualities of their American cousins.

Meanwhile Eisenhower could not spend time in Great Britain while he had all this on his plate, so he appointed Lee as his executive deputy to handle affairs there, reserving for himself the right to intervene if necessary.[13] He suggested that the North Africa operation be separated from ETOUSA and that Lee be given command of the ETO. Marshall agreed to this plan as a temporary measure. However, at Lee's suggestion the appointment as deputy went to Gen. Russell Hartle, the senior commander in the United Kingdom.[14] In February the ETO received a new commander, Lt. Gen. Frank M. Andrews, who had commanded forces in the Middle East. This left Lee free to focus on supply.

In January 1943 Lee went to North Africa to observe firsthand Eisenhower's supply system and learn whatever he could from it, as well as that of Britain's Gen. Bernard Montgomery. "With General Hartle's permission I planned the trip which was later approved by General Frank M. Andrews who became our new theater commander," Lee wrote. Lee took training as an air force gunner so he would not be a useless passenger en route to the war zone. He went to Gibraltar, Algiers, and Casablanca and met with Generals Patton and Montgomery. He recorded the importance that Montgomery placed on supply. According to Lee, Montgomery said that in the British campaign for Tripoli "unloading ships became the critical battle."[15]

Lee mercifully declined to offer his opinion of the overall supply situation in North Africa in his memoirs, but it must have at least to some extent relieved his concerns about his own performance in Great Britain. It was clear his colleagues were not doing well without him in North Africa. The rush into Tunisia was ad hoc and chaotic, especially with regard to supplies, and the top guy was aware of it. Eisenhower told Brig. Gen. Thomas Handy that "our operations to date . . . have violated every recognized principle of war, are in conflict with all operational and logistical methods laid down in text-books, and will be condemned in their entirety by all Leavenworth and War College classes for the next twenty-five years."[16]

While in North Africa Lee attended the Casablanca conference on January 14, 1943, where President Roosevelt met with Prime Minister Churchill.[17] Stalin, as marshal of the Soviet Union, had been invited, but the battles in his country had reached a fever pitch and he was unable to attend. General Marshall was present, however, as were Gen. Hap Arnold and Adm. Ernest King. It was at this meeting that FDR and Churchill proclaimed the "unconditional surrender" demand that ruled out any sort of negotiated settlement with Germany. Some critics were concerned it would inspire the Germans to fight to the finish, but in retrospect the thought of Hitler negotiating a surrender does not seem credible.

At that meeting Lee surely noted that Eisenhower had troubles of his own. Eisenhower sought to put a positive spin on things, but the British were not impressed. The British general Sir Alan Brooke contended Eisenhower's forces were at risk of being squeezed between the German Fifth Panzer Army in the north, which had eighty-five thousand troops, and Rommel's Afrika Korps, which had an estimated eighty thousand. Eisenhower spoke without notes and was clearly not ready to respond to the British critique at a time when his forces were struggling. Brooke said that Eisenhower's plan of action "was a real bad one." Later, after Eisenhower had met with FDR, the president told his aide Hopkins that "Ike seems jittery." Eisenhower's aide Butcher concurred in a note in his log, writing that "his neck is in a noose and he knows it."[18]

As if to underscore Eisenhower's delicate position at this juncture, Roosevelt denied a suggestion from Marshall that Eisenhower be made a four-star general, which would put him at the same level as his British colleagues. "The President told Marshall that he would not promote Eisenhower until there was some damn good reason to do it," Hopkins stated. "The President said he was going to make it a rule that promotions should go to people who had done some fighting, and that while Eisenhower had done a good job, he hasn't knocked the Germans out of Tunisia."[19]

But one critical decision of the Casablanca conference was a reaffirmation of commitment to Bolero, which must have rejuvenated Lee. He swung into action. Before leaving for North Africa, he had instructed his staff to draw up a plan for supply and accommodation for a projected 427,000 troops, which was already being planned, and another one for upwards of a million men, which was pure conjecture. On January 28, while still in North Africa, he wrote to Maj. Gen. Wilhelm D. Styer, chief of staff of the War Department sos, giving him advance notice that he would be making requests for more service troops when he got back to Great Britain. He asked for 30 port battalions, 30 engineer regiments, 15 quartermaster service battalions, and about 30 depot companies.[20] Lee anticipated they would be unloading 120 to 150 ships per month when the focus returned to Bolero. He insisted that the United States would not be able to handle all of that with British workers the way they had done for Torch. "With the experience of August and September 1942 fresh in his memory, General Lee noted that the sos had learned the hard way in the past seven months and he was determined that there should not be a repetition of the frantic efforts of the previous summer," Roland Ruppenthal writes.[21]

Lee called into action his current chief of staff, Gen. Robert Littlejohn, and the new theater commander, Gen. Frank Andrews, to make a forceful case to the Pentagon, which had been urging him to work with fewer service people. Lee and his staff made the case that during World War I the portion of the American Expeditionary Force allotted to sos had been 33.1 percent. Based on a proposed buildup to 1,118,000 men by December 1943, the sos should have 370,000 troops, of whom 67,000 should be engineer troops. In World War I the aef component of engineers was 99,500. By mid-February Littlejohn had massaged the numbers to show Lee needed 358,312 men.[22]

On February 19 Marshall punched a hole in Lee's balloon. Marshall said the decision to resume the Bolero buildup was not firm and there would be no shipping for the months of March and April because of the continuing demands of Torch.[23]

CHAPTER TEN

Back to Bolero

Logistics is the ball and chain of armored warfare.
—GEN. HEINZ GUDERIAN

After months of intense, bloody fighting the Allies had suffered more than 70,000 casualties in North Africa. The Germans suffered even more and yielded roughly 250,000 prisoners. After the German capitulation the Allies rousted the Germans from Sicily after hard fighting and then on September 3 launched an invasion of Italy that would continue for the duration of the war. But even amid the hard fighting in North Africa, Sicily, and the Italian peninsula, the Allied leaders knew the Mediterranean was a sideshow. By mid-1943 the attention had returned to Great Britain, Bolero, and the inevitable invasion of the European continent. And Maj. Gen. John C. H. Lee was responsible for making sure the Allies had what they needed to do it.[1]

Somervell had emphasized to Lee the need for him to assert control of administration and supply matters in the ETO within the SOS, such that authority would not be shared with the generals of the major armies that would be in the field when Europe was invaded.[2] This was essential, Somervell said, for logistical planning to be fully coordinated. It would not be accepted by the generals of the armies, however.

Lee had his marching orders. In March he proposed to Andrews, the ETO commander, that he be named deputy theater commander for supply and administration and that the theater G-4, the senior officer in charge of supply, be placed under him. This proposal would have given Lee a regional command similar to what Somervell had exercised in Washington, where he had virtually taken over the War Department's G-4 role. Andrews turned thumbs down on this idea, contending it was unsound to put the chief of a general staff under a subordinate headquarters and that as far as he was concerned Lee already had more than enough authority to carry out his mission without being made deputy commander.

Like many senior officers, Andrews bristled at the elevated role of the sos that Somervell was attempting to impose on the army, and he also disliked Lee intensely. He thought Lee had an exaggerated sense of his own importance, as reflected in his private train and the retinue that followed him everywhere he went. By February Andrews was fed up with Lee and had decided to ask Marshall to relieve Lee and send him back to the States. If Lee was aware of Andrews's animosity toward him, he left no record of it. Throughout his career and later in his memoirs Lee seemed curiously oblivious to the negative reaction he evoked from his colleagues. Soon Lee was off to the United States to confer with his superiors.[3]

"In the spring of 1943, I felt it necessary to confer with General Somervell and his senior staff officers regarding our build-up plans," Lee recalled. "Our shortage at that time was in ship tonnage. Naturally, we wanted to take full advantage of whatever tonnage could be available. Also, by that time we had fairly definite build-up plans for the arrival of our troops, their equipment, and necessary supplies for the operation Overlord."[4]

Lee visited the port of embarkation in New York from which most of the supplies for the sos were being shipped to Great Britain, and then he went on to Washington, where he stayed with Somervell at his residence in Fort Myer. Lee suggested while in New York that the supply situation would be greatly improved if he could keep members of his staff at the port. "There they would assist in selecting the most needed items for shipment in the limited tonnage," he wrote. "To this, the Port Commander and also General Gross, Chief of Transportation, objected. They felt it would mean interference and delay in loading out ships. Perhaps they were right. At any rate, General Somervell decided in their favor and was adamant. I was able, however, to develop a number of other procedures such as the marking and invoicing of shipments and also plans for eventual pre-loading of ships which would be unloaded in Cherbourg or other Normandy ports after the landing. This practice had been developed in England and had proved valuable in the Torch operation."[5]

While Lee was stateside General Andrews was killed on May 3 when a transport aircraft in which he was flying chanced an instrument landing in Iceland and crashed into the side of a mountain. "When I landed in Scotland on my return trip I was shocked to learn of General Andrews' death from a fatal crash in Iceland where he had flown with his brilliant young Chief of Staff Brigadier General Charles H. Barth, and also a Bishop of the Methodist church," Lee recalled. He noted that Andrews, thanks to "Barth's insight and understanding," had "accepted rather fully our organizational plans to coordinate the operational and support organizations for Overlord."[6]

That statement contradicts what Andrews had told others and belies his intention to ask Marshall to relieve Lee, but now there was no one to challenge Lee's version of events and he was apparently unaware of Andrews's opinion of him. Andrews was replaced by Maj. Gen. Jacob Devers, who had been a classmate of Lee. Devers was a fighting general. He had been appointed chief of the armored forces in August 1941 and was an articulate proponent of the emerging tactical doctrine of combined arms—as opposed to the traditional American view that tanks were for rapid exploitation, not for fighting other tanks. He wanted bigger, more powerful tanks but was overruled. As a result, the American Sherman tanks often found themselves outclassed by the German Tigers and Panthers. When they encountered German armor, U.S. troops had to rely on antitank guns, which were not always available when needed.

Although Lee and Devers had been classmates at West Point, they had never been close friends. When Devers took over, he bluntly told Lee he had heard critical reports about his "private train." Lee replied that Devers was theater commander, so it was actually *his* train. "We of the sos use it habitually, but it is always available to you on a priority basis," Lee said. "I suggest you use it soon to see how helpful it is." Lee took Devers on a tour of the Eastern Base Section of England, where the sos had many construction projects under way. "This permitted General Devers to see our work on depots, hospitals and airfields, where he made timely inspections of the Air Force units under General Ira Eaker."[7]

According to Lee, that trip sold Devers on the train. "From then on, he called me 'Cliff,' as had General Ike from the first," Lee noted.[8]

Devers was a rising power in the army, and his favorable opinion of Lee was a coin in Lee's pocket as Devers went on to bigger things. In 1944 he was sent to the Mediterranean as commander of North Africa theater of operations, then focused mainly on Italy. Devers helped plan the invasion of southern France in 1944 and later successfully led the Sixth Army Group in France and Germany. But his immediate task in 1943 was to organize Bolero and preparations for Overlord.

Devers recorded his positive impression of Lee and sos in a report to Marshall: "The S.O.S. has accomplished much. It has been able to keep ahead of the peak loads, has worked well with the British, has a fine organization and is well-disciplined. . . . Lee has been particularly aggressive and efficient and is responsible for the fine condition of his organization."[9]

Lee records being "blessed" by the arrival of Col. Royal B. Lord, a young engineer officer about whom he had heard good things. He put Lord in charge of engineer supply. "That job had practically killed two older Engineer Officers," he noted. "Roy Lord took it on and not only put Engineer Supply in splendid condition, guaranteeing its support of all other operations, but then offered to take on and was given the coordination of all supply as our sos G-4."[10]

Lee lamented his inability to keep a chief of staff, which was due at least in part to the dynamic situation he was in, one that was characterized by rapid shifts of key personnel from one position to another and often from one theater to another. He had already had several chiefs of staff—Thomas Larkin, Robert Littlejohn, Claude Thiel, Everett Hughes, Paul Baker, and Charles Saltzman. "Finally," Lee wrote, "I was delighted to hear that I might obtain the detail of Col. William G. Weaver who had done so splendidly for us in the Second Infantry Division when he commanded its 38th Infantry and brought it up to high competence."[11] At the time Lee had recommended Weaver for promotion to brigadier general but was told Weaver was too old.

Weaver got the star as Lee's chief of staff and eventually became deputy commander of the sos. "He was splendid and carried on admirably while I was in North Africa," Lee recalled. "Upon my return I found conditions better in many respects than when I had left. That was a source of great comfort as it should always be to an under-standing commander." Weaver was eventually taken away from Lee and ended up commanding a combat division. "By that time, Roy Lord had earned promotion to Chief of Staff and Deputy sos Com-mander," Lee noted.[12]

By this time Lieutenant Mayhall from Louisiana and his platoon had shifted from the supply depot they were managing to Lee's headquarters in Cheltenham. "We were to be General John C. H. Lee's Security Company," Mayhall recalls. "Some people called him 'Court House Lee'; we called him 'Church House' Lee. . . . but General Lee was always good to B Company. . . . War changes things so fast that it is rather hard to keep up," Mayhall notes. "General Lee was a Division Commander in 1940, and he had a Regimen-tal Commander by the name of Colonel William G. Weaver. Over the years they must have developed considerable respect for each other's ability to do their jobs."[13]

Mayhall records that General Weaver became field coordinator, Lee's G-4. Weaver spent much of his time motoring around Great Britain in a fancy Packard when he wasn't on Lee's famous train. "It was not a Cadillac, but with the pecking order being what it was, not a lot of Cadillacs were being handed out," Mayhall writes. Weaver told Mayhall the Packard rode considerably better than a Jeep: "The General told me that he planned on riding down the main street of Berlin in his Packard just as soon as the shooting stopped. I thought this was fine."[14]

As for Mayhall, he was perfectly happy to have a Jeep at his dis-posal. "I was like all infantry people: we loved the Jeep," he writes. "The little truck could take us just about anywhere a mule could go. It was about as tough as one, too. It saved a lot of soldiers from a lot of long, hard miles of walking, and infantry never suffers from a shortage of walking."[15]

Mayhall reports that Lee ran a tight ship—everyone was expected to look sharp every day, never knowing when an inspection would happen. He also noted Lee's particular concern about wasted food. "General Lee put out orders that there would be no waste of food," he said.

When you went through the mess lines at meal time you took all you wanted, and you ate it—and there was an officer or non-com at the Mess Hall door to see that there was nothing edible left on your tray. If there were food left over on the serving line, the Mess Sergeant better have something good to make with left-overs. One day General Lee and some of his officers came over for inspection of his new Security Company B. Naturally he looked in the garbage can where Mess Sergeant Landry had emptied a box of raisins. The General asked, "What are these raisins doing in the garbage can?"

Mess Sergeant Landry said right away, "They're rancid, General," never expecting what happened next. The general reached down into the garbage can, picked up some raisins, put them in his mouth, and started chewing. He said, "They don't taste rancid."

Sergeant Landry said, "I'll get them out of there right away, wash them and have them served." And out they came.[16]

This was one of the stories that contributed to Lee's reputation in the ranks, but Mayhall did not intend his account to be mockery. "The big concern in this food business was shipping space. If each man dumped one-third of a pound of food in the garbage each meal, by the end of each day he would have thrown away one pound of food. At the end of the month, that would be thirty pounds," May-hall writes. "Now you may notice this guy is not by himself in Chel-tenham; there were maybe twenty thousand soldiers going to a mess hall somewhere every day. If all of them had eating habits like the first soldier, that would be about twenty thousand pounds of waste per day. At the end of the month, 20,000 times 30 days is room on a boat for several tanks, trucks, or airplanes."[17]

And in fact quite a few American soldiers had eating habits like that first soldier. The U.S. military in World War II earned a rep-utation for conspicuous waste that sparked both envy and resent-ment among soldiers from less prosperous countries, friend and foe alike. Of course many if not most of these young men had just come through the Great Depression, when food was often hard to come by, and they were now caught up in a dire situation in which violent death lay just over the horizon. They were understandably careless about their eating habits.

Mayhall insists, however, it was exactly that waste that motivated Lee to crack down. "General Lee was in charge of every bit of equipment and personnel that needed transportation from and to the Department of the Interior, that is, the United States," Mayhall notes, adding that "leftovers weren't the only waste we had to account for." U.S. troops in Great Britain used "honeydew buckets" for collecting their excrement, which was distributed to local farmers for use as fertilizer.[18]

Mayhall reports that B Company worked hard to provide security for Lee's headquarters and also to stay in good physical condition. "For, as we had already found out, we never knew what they might decide to use us for next. We had run a G-4 depot, an overflow depot, motor pool and now we were providing security for a large headquarters. This headquarters was responsible for everything that moved," Mayhall states. "The first question was where the storage area would be located for thousands of trucks, tanks, airplanes, many different kinds of boats, and training grounds for troops. This was only in the planning stage, and had to be coordinated with the British. British landowners were brought into the planning, for many civilians had to house both British and American troops, to say nothing of changing some of their land into shooting ranges."[19]

Mayhall notes that 1943 was a year of planning and building, at least for the troops in Great Britain if not for those in North Africa.

Troops were being trained in the United States, and there were combat divisions being bloodied in Africa. Some of them would come back to England when the African campaign was over, to say nothing of the British troops that would come home for R&R, refitting and replacements. New equipment was being developed— larger, faster tanks and better long-range airplanes.

One other thing was needed: larger and faster ships to transport this better equipment and all these troops being trained in the United States and Canada. German submarines were giving hell to the shipments. The Germans were sinking our ships right at the mouth of the Mississippi River. Some of my company, including Mess Sergeant Landry, lived in Morgan City, close to the Gulf of Mexico. They were not seeing any fighting in England. They thought they could do more at home.[20]

The salient factor in Mayhall's recollections is not that Lee had to convert combat troops into supply troops but that they were able to make the adjustment rather easily. The flexibility and mechanical know-how of U.S. troops was a major asset in the war, and more of these versatile fellows were on the way. At the Trident Conference in Washington in May 1943 the commitment to a cross-channel attack by May 1, 1944, was confirmed. Twenty-nine divisions were to be in the United Kingdom by the spring of 1944, and there were to be no further diversions of resources to the Mediterranean theater. In fact four U.S. and three British divisions in the Mediterranean area were to be held in readiness after November 1 for movement to the United Kingdom.

Another positive omen for Lee's SOS was the decline in losses of ships from attacks by German U-boats.[21] After near record losses in March 1943 the Battle of the Atlantic began to turn in the Allies' favor due to improved detection technologies and more efficient use of convoys. The U-boats were now on the run, being sunk by the dozens. Thus the potential for a major buildup of forces and matériel in the United Kingdom was suddenly much brighter.

The Trident planners projected that by June 1, 1944, there would be 1,415,300 troops in Britain. The rate of buildup was not based on troops available but rather the ability of British ports to accept the cargo, the maximum practical limit being 150 shiploads a month. Lee's people had been busy in early 1943 assembling a vast trove of logistical data covering all aspects of the buildup—labor, storage and housing, transportation, construction, and supply. But they lacked the critical information they really needed—the overall allotment among air, ground, and service forces needed to create a balanced force. For several months they were operating by guesswork. Devers and Lee were counting on more supply troops, but Washington was dragging its feet. This was to be a recurrent theme during the buildup—a conflict of opinion between Lee's SOS and the planners at the Pentagon about how many people he really needed for his supply operation. For its part the War Department was looking at a shortage of personnel all over the world and was eager to trim requirements anywhere and everywhere it could.

"There was no formula for economy which could fit all the varied circumstances of a global war, and it was difficult at best to prove that logistical support would be jeopardized by eliminating one or two depot companies or port battalions," Roland Ruppenthal writes. "In general, the view persisted in the War Department that the ratio of service to combat troops was excessive, and it had become normal to regard the demands of the service forces with a certain suspicion, at times with some justification."[22]

Lee's people had come up with a request for 490,000 service personnel, a figure that they insisted was the minimum number needed to do the job. Devers had chopped that down to 375,000 based on 25 percent of the projected overall troop commitment, which was eventually accepted by the War Department with minor changes.

But the number was a goal, not a reality. From June through August Lee's SOS received only forty-six thousand troops.[23] Despite the earlier decision at the Trident Conference, the Allies' quick victory in Sicily teased out a decision to invade Italy. So once again troops and resources intended for Great Britain were being diverted to the Mediterranean. Lee protested this diversion, making a strong case that it would inevitably impair his ability to prepare for the invasion of Europe, but the combat troops in action in Italy took priority over service troops in Britain. Once again Lee was forced to accept partially trained troops.

But by September the picture had improved.[24] In the last four months of the year the SOS almost tripled its strength in the United Kingdom, with the number of personnel rising from 79,000 to 220,200. By this time the war was clearly going in the Allies' favor. Italy was on the brink of collapse, and the Germans were being pushed back from their early conquests in the Soviet Union. By the end of the year ETOUSA had an overall total strength of 773,753. It was an encouraging number but less than projected. It was clear the influx of military personnel would have to be stepped up in early 1944.

There was also a hotly debated issue of who would control training and replacements, which had been a major problem in North Africa. In April Marshall issued a directive calling for formation of a command "with no other responsibilities than that of handling replacement procedures" in conformance with War Department policy.[25] Lee objected vigorously to losing his control over staffing. Eisenhower promised Marshall he would follow through on the directive, but Lee dug in his heels and it never happened. (The issue would arise again after the Battle of the Bulge, when a shortage of personnel became critical.)

By May the focus had shifted to a controversy over management of supplies in yet another internal command campaign to loosen Lee's tight grip on SOS. "I am so certain that a command problem of major proportions will confront US forces in ETO before many weeks," Gen. Everett Hughes wrote in a memo to Eisenhower, that "I am constrained to outline the problem and prepare a solution for it."[26] Hughes had served briefly as Lee's chief of staff and had subsequently become one of Lee's most strident critics. But he touched a sensitive nerve when he suggested that the existing command structure left it unclear who was in charge. Brig. Gen. Raymond Moses, the First Army quartermaster, was another Cassandra who was forecasting disaster. He wrote a memo to "Beetle" Smith saying, "It is a definite mistake to have the Deputy Theater Commander for administration also the Communications Zone Commander." (It was planned that after the invasion of France Lee's SOS would become the Communications Zone or ComZ.) Moses said there would be a conflict between ComZ and the First Army over supply issues. He also said that Lee had too much authority, adding that there was an "inherent conflict of interest" that would have Lee defending his interests at the expense of the field commands. "In any case," he concluded, "I emphasize my belief that the Communications Zone Commander and the ETO or Deputy ETO Commander should not be the same person."[27]

Lee had other enemies. Bradley and Patton exhibited field commanders' traditional disdain for logisticians and resented Lee's theoretically superior position over them as deputy theater commander. They did not look forward to going into battle beholden to Lee for supplies and replacements. To them that meant the logisticians would dictate the pace of battle to the battlefield commanders. They wanted none of it. They leaned on Eisenhower to get rid of Lee. Hughes predicted that would never happen. "John Lee is Somervell's great hero," he said, "and do you think Ike is going to be stupid enough to fire him just before the invasion?"[28]

As if to underscore the Lee-Somervell link, in January Somervell suggested to Eisenhower that Lee be promoted to lieutenant general, giving him that coveted third star. Eisenhower saw no good reason for the promotion other than Somervell's own wish to be elevated to full general—four stars—so he would outrank his subordinate Lee. Eisenhower refused to do it. But a few weeks later Marshall promoted Lee to lieutenant general without consulting Eisenhower.[29]

Eisenhower was irritated when he learned about Lee's promotion, assuming Somervell had pulled it off behind his back. As it happened Marshall was carried along on a wave of promotions. Beetle Smith had been promoted to lieutenant general, as had MacArthur's chief of staff, Gen. Richard K. Sutherland, in the Pacific theater. Not wanting to submit only one name for promotion—at this level promotions needed congressional approval—Marshall put together a list of likely candidates and simply assumed Eisenhower would want Lee's name on it. Eisenhower forgave Marshall of course. He had little choice. He said later he had no objection to promoting Lee but that the way it was handled upset him, as well it should have. Marshall apologized to Eisenhower for the miscue.

The record is not clear as to when Lee began his curious habit of putting his stars on both the front and back of his helmet, but it seems likely that began when he got the third one. Soon he was wearing three stars on the front and three on the back—six in all. Nor is there any record of any of Lee's colleagues or superiors challenging him on this curious affectation. But soon people began to notice and comment, always behind Lee's back. Another feature of the Lee legend was born.

Beneath all the rancor there remained a grudging respect for Lee. Devers had assumed command of the ETO intending to lower the boom on Lee, but after reviewing the organization Lee had set up and observing it in action, including a few rides on Lee's famous train, he changed his mind. Eisenhower felt the same way. It became clear that Lee would remain in the saddle, at least until the invasion took place. Later on, in a possible moment of relative equanimity, Patton tipped his hat to Lee. "Gen. Lee is certainly doing a good job in getting us what we need," he said.[30] For now, the important thing was to get the troops and their gear ashore in bad weather under enemy fire. A lot of careers were hanging in the balance on that one.

The mountains of supplies that had begun to arrive in British ports in 1943 put a tremendous burden on Lee's organization, but Lee and his people had learned a lot from their unhappy experience with Torch the year before. The sos by this time was much better versed in receiving and storing vital supplies, as well as keeping track of where they were. Lee and his senior staff spent a good bit of their time running back and forth in his special train, which may have seemed luxurious to Lee's critics, but was for him strictly a work venue, enabling him to get around a countryside in which the few narrow roads were overloaded with military traffic.[31]

Because of the continuing traffic jam, U.S. supplies could not be easily moved about the countryside in trucks. Lee relied on trains as much as he could, to move supplies as well as his staff, because the narrow and winding British roads were not designed to handle large vehicles or military convoys. The British train system had limited rolling stock, limited head space, and inadequate tunnel clearances, which made it difficult to move tanks and other large equipment. But working closely with the British, Lee's sos squeezed every possible ounce of traffic out of the British system. By 1943 the United States was shipping hundreds of locomotives and freight cars to Britain to handle the increased loads.

Another problem was that while many of the vehicles, including trucks and Jeeps, sent to Great Britain were ready to roll, others came in boxes with assembly instructions—like furniture from Ikea. Some required more assembly than others. General Motors and Studebaker trucks, for example, were shipped in twin-unit packs with two vehicles in four cases. Diamond T cargo trucks and wreckers and 1½ ton trucks were packed two vehicles in three cases, and Jeeps came in single-unit packs. Lee was struggling to set up assembly lines and find men with enough mechanical aptitude to assemble a variety of vehicles. But one Jeep at a time and bit by bit, it was getting done.[32]

CHAPTER ELEVEN

Countdown to D-Day

An army marches on its stomach.
—NAPOLEON BONAPARTE (also attributed
to Frederick the Great)

While the senior command of U.S. military forces under Eisenhower at the Supreme Headquarters of the Allied Expeditionary Force (SHAEF) planned the pending invasion of Europe, tentatively scheduled for May or June, Lee went about his business, moving around Britain on his special train and directing his supply operation, which would make or break the great adventure. On the ground he was leaning heavily on his new chief of staff, his old friend General Weaver, who in turn sought the assistance of able officers, one of them being Lieutenant Mayhall. "I think General Weaver asked for me because, being an infantry officer himself, he liked having infantry people around him," Mayhall recalls. "He had been to inspect my Company many times to watch our training exercises."[1] Mayhall was made G-1 liaison to the field commander.

SHAEF was at the center of a chaotic madhouse with more than a million personnel and vast stores of matériel stacked up all over the place, with more coming in constantly. "I was to help General Weaver plan trips here and there for his job as Field Coordinator to General Lee," Mayhall writes. "He was what we would call a troubleshooter. When there was a supply stoppage anywhere in England, General Weaver would show up to get that line of supply unstopped. This didn't mean a half pound of ham for supper, but tons of food, ammunition, tanks, trucks, halftracks, airplanes, airplane parts, artillery and men."[2]

The sniping at Lee—and even more at the command structure dictated by Somervell—continued unabated in the final months leading up to the invasion.[3] Somervell was hearing complaints about Lee and the new organization from senior officers in the

United Kingdom. Gen. Leroy Lutes, Somervell's chief of operations, was sent to Great Britain to survey the logistics situation. Lutes found things to be generally satisfactory. He reported the assault forces would receive adequate equipment and supplies, there were plans for forty-one days' worth of supplies after the initial landings, and new plans were being developed to cover the first ninety days. But he also detected problems. He told Somervell and also Beetle Smith that the main problem was confused command chains and deep-seated personal antagonisms that "boded ill for the future."[4] Lee was the focus of most of those personal antagonisms.

This came as no surprise to Smith, who disapproved of Lee acting as titular deputy theater commander and also commanding general of the Communications Zone. Lee defended his position and ignored Smith, taking his problems directly to Eisenhower.[5] Smith in turn became furious at Lee for going around him to the supreme commander, who always acted the peacemaker. But Eisenhower was becoming increasingly disenchanted with the controversy. Smith records that he persuaded Eisenhower to dump Lee in favor of Larkin, his former chief of staff, or Everett Hughes, another of Lee's former chiefs of staff. Another name that came up was Lt. Gen. Lucius Clay, a man of extraordinary ability, whose name would come up yet again a few months later in France in yet another effort to unseat Lee. Lutes himself came under consideration for the job, but Somervell nixed that. He needed his own people in Washington. As D-Day loomed closer, Lee remained in the saddle and Eisenhower became even more determined not to make any major organizational changes at such a late date.[6]

But still the efforts to unseat Lee continued. On May 28 two senior generals presented Lee with a plan to place his command, the ComZ, under the First Army Group, which would eliminate Lee's dual role as deputy theater commander. Predictably Lee was incensed. He formally presented his objections to Eisenhower. In a lengthy, vigorously stated analysis of the whole issue of command he characterized the proposal as "so diametrically opposed" to the views previously expressed by Eisenhower and "so far reaching in its application" that he doubted if Eisenhower and Smith had given it sufficient thought. Invoking the experience of World War I, he said that "control and responsibility for the logistical support of all combat forces must be established at the highest U.S. level."[7]

Lee said logistical effectiveness would be impaired "by various interpolated headquarters which could only contribute unacceptable delays." Two years of experience, he said, pointed to the need to place administration and supply under a single commander "with a complete and experienced staff of sufficient size to insure effective and adequate operations." With the sos, he said, such a commander and staff were already in place. Lee had 21,000 officers and 435,000 troops at his command. "This organization has been preparing for the immediate task for two years," he went on, and "duties have been well defined within the organization."[8]

All of this set off a flurry of meetings that led to more meetings. With the invasion only days away, the issue remained unresolved. Eisenhower dithered, as was his inclination, but he basically defended Lee's position and decided to preserve the existing arrangement. For the umpteenth time he instructed his subordinates to sit down together and work things out. But this was a fractious bunch, disinclined to work things out. They would go into battle fighting each other almost as vigorously as they fought the Germans.

Meanwhile Lee and his staff continued their preparations as the tempo throughout Great Britain revved up in anticipation of the daring adventure ahead. "Even the smallest hamlets and rural lanes did not escape the feverish activity that characterized the operations of every depot and training area as well as the various headquarters," Roland Ruppenthal writes. "A prodigious stocking of supplies and equipment took place in these months, evoking the comment that the British Isles were so weighted down with the munitions of war that they were kept from sinking only by the buoyant action of the barrage balloons which floated above the principal ports and military installations."[9]

"There had never been a supply operation like this one," Geoffrey Perret writes in *There's a War to Be Won*. "The number of separate items Sears Roebuck and Company supplied to its customers was approximately 100,000. Service of Supply had to acquire and distribute nearly 3 million."[10]

London had experienced tremendous growth during the war, much like Washington. U.S. forces had gradually taken over more and more accommodations in the crowded London metropolitan area. In April 1942 they occupied less than one hundred thousand square feet of office space plus an officers' mess, a retail shop, a garage, and several small troop billets. Two years later they had thirty-three officers' billets (including twenty-four hotels) and three hundred buildings used for troop accommodations, plus endless depots, garages, and shops and a variety of installations such as post exchanges, messes, a detention barracks, a gym, and clinics and dispensaries.

This concentration was on vivid display at the consolidated officers' mess at Grosvenor House on Park Lane.[11] Occupying the great ballroom of this large hotel, it was nicknamed "Willow Run" after the massive construction facility in Detroit that was churning out airplanes and tanks by the tens of thousands. Operated cafeteria style, it provided twenty-six servings a minute with a seating capacity of nearly one thousand officers at a time. It eventually was serving up to seven thousand meals a day.

In the five months from January through May 1944 the total number of U.S. personnel in the United Kingdom rose from 774,000 to 1,527,000.[12] A typical soldier stood five feet, eight inches tall and weighed 144 pounds. The diminutive size to some extent reflects the effects of the Great Depression, when these young men grew up. In those grim days food was often hard to come by.

Some 40 percent of all the cargo shipped to Britain between January 1942 and May 1944 was received in the five months preceding D-Day. The limited British port and rail facilities were almost overwhelmed. Almost 160,000 men were arriving each month, creating a massive challenge of providing accommodations. Of the total personnel there were 459,511 in Lee's sos.[13]

There was a massive construction operation under way across Great Britain—storage depots, hospitals, and accommodations. The Americans worked with the British trying to reconcile their diverse building standards. The Americans traditionally built most of their barracks and other buildings with wood, but wood was in short supply in England, which relied more on tile and masonry. But they worked it out. By May there was room for 1.6 million people to lay their heads somewhere. Most of the new hospitals, anticipating a flow of wounded from the battles to come, consisted of 834- and 1,082-bed installations based on standard layouts designed by British experts and approved by American engineers and medical officers. Most of them were Nissen huts, many of them on landed estates miles from the nearest railway and requiring completely new water and sewage disposal systems.[14]

All of those American service members running around Great Britain presented other "issues" that challenged military discipline, not to mention cultural mores. For one thing the Americans were much better paid than the British. A GI private drew triple what his British counterpart drew. The army tried to downplay the difference by paying U.S. troops twice a month instead of the British standard of once a month, but that fooled exactly no one. General Hughes was offended by what he perceived as U.S. arrogance over its wealth, particularly with regard to Lee's private train. "When we are living with the British we should live as the British do," he said. "They cannot afford swank, and neither can we."[15]

The majority of healthy British men were in the service, many of them away from home fighting with Montgomery's forces against the Germans in the Mediterranean, in Asia, or on the ships at sea. The British at the time were living on a shoestring. Basic foodstuffs and goods were rationed. The government was effectively bankrupt. Then suddenly there were all these young Americans running around with money and access to a seemingly endless supply of the basics of normal life. There was a goodly amount of what the military leadership characterized as "fraternization." Soldiers preparing to go into battle, not knowing if they were living their last days, engaged in random romances, and the troops resisted all efforts to restrain their amorous activities. The British certainly appreciated the support of the United States in their struggle against Hitler, but they could have done without much of the socializing. The common complaint against the American soldiers was that they were "over-paid, oversexed, and over here."[16]

An impressive number of the arriving troops came across the Atlantic on lightly armed passenger ships protected mainly by their speed. They were much faster than German submarines. The British luxury liners *Queen Mary* and *Queen Elizabeth* were making three round-trips per month, carrying 15,000 troops on each voyage.[17] These two ships by themselves hauled nearly 425,000 persons from the United States to Great Britain, accounting for nearly a quarter of the total buildup. U.S. liners also brought a large number of troops across the pond. (Back in those days most people making the trip across the Atlantic went by ship.) Had the Germans been able to sink one of these behemoths loaded with thousands of U.S. troops it would have been a major catastrophe, but it never happened.

It was Lee's job to make sure all of this unprecedented traffic in personnel and matériel was efficiently managed—unloaded, tracked, and taken to appropriate locations around the country. One convoy alone in March 1944 consisted of eighteen fully loaded U.S. Army cargo vessels and twenty four-part cargoes loaded on regular commercial ships. It brought about fifteen hundred wheeled vehicles, including tanks and self-propelled guns, two thousand cased vehicles, two hundred aircraft and gliders, and about fifty thousand tons of supplies. The rapid clearance of all this matériel through the overworked British ports required seventy-five special trains with ten thousand loaded cars and highway transport of countless trucks. Other traffic bringing British-made goods and the movement of U.S. matériel from one place to another entailed the work of another twenty-seven trains with eight thousand cars (presumably including Lee's personal train). Each week there were at a minimum one hundred special freight trains with eighteen thousand to twenty thousand cars hauling vital materials on railroads already overburdened with traffic.[18]

With all that there was still a massive backlog of matériel at the New York port, which required the stateside managers in Somervell's command to establish priorities based on what would be needed immediately for the invasion. Lee was deeply involved in this process as he and his people kept track of what they had, what was coming, and how much matériel the overtaxed British ports and inland transportation could handle.

One partial solution that quickly took hold—called "prestowage"—was to ship cargo destined to go ashore in Europe without offloading it in Great Britain.[19] Matériel destined for Britain was loaded on the top decks, from which it would be quickly offloaded, and then the ships loaded belowdecks with landing mats, clothing, and equipage and ordnance supplies to be sent on to the coast. There the ships would disgorge their cargo directly onto the beaches. They were essentially floating depots. This was expensive and inefficient because it took badly needed shipping out of the delivery cycle for an indefinite period of time, but the congestion in Great Britain was so extreme it could not be helped. After the invasion was launched, it was anticipated that the port congestion would be gradually reduced as a growing amount of cargo was sent directly to the beach areas and, it was hoped, to ports after they were captured from the Germans and repaired, since the Germans would likely destroy the facilities before retreating. Lee and his people were expected to keep track of all the stuff on the land plus the stuff on the water.

To the extent possible the U.S. forces procured their basic needs from British sources, but the British were short of labor and raw materials, so much of what they needed had to be imported. Then there was the matter of the language barrier. The British playwright George Bernard Shaw had famously observed years before that the British and Americans were one people separated by a common language. Thousands of basic items had diverse names.[20] While learning to drive on the left side of the road, the Americans had to learn to ask for petrol instead of gas, that trucks to the British were lorries, and elevators were lifts. To the British a hot water boiler was a calorifier, a garbage can was a dustbin, shoe tacks were tingles, burlap was hessian, cheesecloth was butter muslin, and a summer undershirt was a tropical vest. As the two armies worked to process paperwork together, there was a great deal of confusion.

While Lee and his troops were managing soldiers and guns, the U.S. Army Air Force was running its own show and building air bases all over the place to handle the thousands of bombers from the United States joining the British in attacks on Germany's industrial plants and population centers. The idea of bombing cities in order to pressure the Germans into quitting the war was no doubt largely in response to the German bombings of Great Britain, but one would think from that experience that such bombing tends to increase the resolve of citizens, not undermine it. That was the effect on Germany, where the people continued fighting and turning out more war equipment right up until the final weeks of the war.

The air force depended on Lee's sos for handling many of its supplies and was among Lee's most strident critics.[21] It contended that delivery had been slow and that the sos made unnecessary demands for justification of increased deliveries of certain items. It felt that the sos made supply decisions based more on what it had than what the air force needed. But the air force was also at odds with Somervell's operation. It wanted to take control of at least 50 percent of the common items of supply and equipment before they left the United States; it wanted to set up its own supply line external to Lee's sos.

In his review of the situation Lutes for the most part found the air force complaints unfounded. He noted that without exception the air force requisitions for common items had been promptly filled and their delivery expedited. The problem was that the air force wanted more of certain items than were authorized, and for that the sos could not be faulted. Lutes said Lee and his staff were as competent as any combat staff to decide if specific units should receive more supplies than allocated.

But as D-Day loomed the crescendo of criticism of Lee intensified. The various combat commands resented Lee's unprecedented authority and did not believe he and his people appreciated their situation. Somervell thought the sos should do a better job of communicating with the commands and should remember it was there for one purpose—to supply the customers and not tell the customers what they want. He believed that if Lee's sos did a better job of convincing the commands they were doing their level best to serve them, then the friction would disappear. What Somervell failed to grasp was that it was less a matter of communication than one of power.

"What the combat commands really objected to, of course, was the prospect of General Lee's continued authority as deputy theater commander," Ruppenthal writes.[22] The final decision about Lee lay with the supreme commander. While he was fully aware of the criticisms of Lee and the sos, as well as the tensions between his combat commands and the sos, Eisenhower finally decided to abandon any thought of replacing Lee. Instead he put complete faith in him and trusted his organization to support American forces in the upcoming operation.

CHAPTER TWELVE

The Overlord Logistical Plan

Amateurs discuss tactics. Professional
soldiers study logistics.

—TOM CLANCY

Hitler knew an invasion of Europe was coming, but he didn't know where or when. The British and Americans conducted various subterfuges to convince the German dictator that they intended to land far to the north of their actual target. They manufactured a ghost army presumably based in the north of Great Britain and led by Patton, who played his part masterfully.[1] The Germans fell for it, but not to the extent that they neglected other possibilities. When Hitler recalled Rommel from North Africa, he put him in charge of the coastal defenses along the English Channel. The Desert Fox took the assignment seriously and supervised extensive construction of defensive positions, which included barriers to prevent tanks from crossing the beaches, interlocking machine guns to mow down soldiers trying to cross the beaches, and an ample array of artillery to bombard the beaches. Both sides anticipated that the key battle would occur right on the beaches as the Allies sought to move inland and the Germans attempted to drive the invaders back into the sea.

This was an important distinction. In the Pacific theater the Japanese had moved away from trying to defend beaches of contested islands, choosing instead to move inland into mountainous areas where they dug caves and stockpiled food and ordnance. The technique was to prove costly for invading U.S. soldiers and marines, but if the Germans had studied that experience, they took no note of it. They were going to defend Nazi Europe on the beaches.

The backup phase of the operation from both the Allied and German points of view was the importance of ports, of which there were few in the area capable of handling large inflows of military equipment.[2] Without a reliable gateway for massive amounts of supplies, no modern army could stay in the field for very long. There was only one significant port in the area where the main American thrust would come near Omaha Beach—Cherbourg—and it wasn't much of a port. It had been built many years before to accommodate passenger ships, and not many at a time. It was served by only one railroad. The Allies also assumed the Germans would trash the Cherbourg port on their way out (which they did).

The Allies figured they could not long sustain a major military operation bringing supplies across the beaches even if the weather was benign, which one can never assume in the English Channel. They did have some revolutionary new craft specifically designed to bring troops and equipment onto the beaches, in particular the LSTS and DUKWS. The DUKWS (called Ducks) were armored floating vehicles with wheels; they could drive right up onto a beach with their machine guns spitting fire. Both LSTS and Ducks had been employed in the Pacific battles and in North Africa and had proven their worth. They would do it again in Normandy. The Ducks did have their drawbacks. They were small, hard to unload, performed poorly in mud, and were slow in the water, doing about 5 knots at best. Today similar vehicles ferry tourists in cities where there is opportunity to move about on the water as well as on roads.[3]

But these innovative vehicles, as useful as they were, did not solve the problem of bringing in hundreds of tons of supplies and equipment on a daily basis. The Allies needed another plan and settled on the notion of constructing ad hoc port facilities. They estimated that the minimum facilities required for discharge uninterrupted by weather would have a capacity of six thousand tons per day by D-Day plus four to five days, nine thousand tons a day by D-Day plus ten to twelve days, and twelve thousand tons by D-Day plus sixteen to eighteen days. The solution was to build their own ports in England, tow them across the channel, and set them up on the beaches on the day of the assault. They were basically floating ship breakwaters, pierheads, and piers, and the concept was evolving right up until D-Day. There were to be two big ones, one in the

British sector and one in the American—Mulberry B for the British and Mulberry A for the Americans.[4]

But even if the Mulberries worked as planned—and given the unpredictable weather and seas it was by no means certain they would—the invading troops would have to depend on supplies coming across the beaches for at least two weeks, maybe more. The Mulberries were a job for the engineers, not sos, but Lee and his staff were counting on them. They were involved in the planning and keenly interested in how they would work. Without them, and without a major port, they would have precious few supplies to provide the troops. Without food and fuel they could accomplish little.

There were actually several small ports in the area besides Cherbourg—Grandcamp, Isigny, Saint-Vaast, Barfleur, and Granville near Normandy and Saint-Malo and Brest in Brittany, to name a few. But they were dispersed here and there and altogether could handle only a few hundred tons of supplies a day. Cherbourg was the largest and the one of primary concern to the American command. Although it was assumed the Germans would sabotage the port facilities, the Allies planned to open it for limited operations within three days. That plan was more optimistic than realistic.[5]

For reasons still unclear the U.S. Army decided—against the advice of Lee—to invest a great deal of time and effort, not to mention lives, taking the port of Brest on the west coast of Brittany. Brest was a backward area of France where a few people lived along a rugged coastline, deriving modest livings from the sea. Brest was so isolated and its rail and road communications so primitive that Lee and his staff were making plans to build a new port from scratch on the other side of the Brittany peninsula. Brest turned out to be a terrible battle with Germans who refused to surrender and fought to the last bullet. Before it was all over, and the Americans had taken ten thousand casualties, SHAEF had already decided not to put the port back in operation.[6]

To the north the British were to go ashore on beaches designated as Sword, Juno, and Gold. The American beaches to the south were designated Omaha and Utah. In the first three months of the invasion nearly 1,340,000 American troops and 250,000 vehicles were to be engaged in France. The initial assault force was to consist of about 60,000 men and 6,800 vehicles of all types. They would be loaded on ships along the southern coast of England and would land on the first tide on D-Day. A follow-up force of about 26,500 men and 4,400 vehicles was to land on the second tide of D-Day.[7] Of course there was no certainty what day that would be.

The early assault forces comprised primarily combat forces for obvious reasons, but the architects knew supply forces would have to follow quickly. The balance between combat and supply had been a continuing source of controversy during the buildup, and it continued to be so even during the invasion itself. Senior combat officers wanted fighting men, not cooks. But Eisenhower recognized the need for supply troops. In the final plans a force of 340,000 ComZ troops, compared to about 665,000 field troops, was slated to be amassed in the first three months of the invasion. In the early days ComZ troops would constitute only 16 to 18 percent of the overall troop commitment but would reach 21 percent within fifteen days, 26 percent in twenty-five days, and 30 percent within forty days.

Lee and his staff did not consider that allotment of service troops—or "slice"—to be sufficient. They knew the SOS would have to not only support the troops in action but also set up bases and lines of communication to support future operations, develop port facilities, create a large depot system, improve roads, and reconstruct essential railroads that had been bombed repeatedly by Allied air units. Maintenance requirements alone for a division slice were estimated to be nine hundred tons per day in the early stages of the battle. The army expected to have twenty-one divisions in France within ninety days of the invasion. They would need a lot of stuff.[8]

In May Lee issued a set of complex instructions intended to ensure that after the invasion supplies would be moved to ports using the shortest possible rail haul and with the fewest possible bottlenecks. A variety of 126 coastal vessels toting about ninety thousand tons of supplies were to arrive on the second tide of D-Day. After that lift was completed these coastal vessels were expected to deliver up to seventeen thousand tons of stuff per day, recognizing there would be attrition due to enemy action and the usual maritime hazards.

And another 20 five-hundred-ton barges loaded with ammunition, fuel, rations, and engineering materials were to be towed across the channel within the first four days to provide an additional bad-weather reserve.

There were not enough trucks.[9] Lee's staff estimated that, in addition to the vehicles already going with the combat units, he would need 240 truck companies with two drivers for each vehicle to permit around-the-clock operation. He also requested that many of the trucks be large ten-ton flatbed semitrailers and truck tractors.

Truck companies in World War II varied in size and makeup depending on their use. An armored division ordnance/light maintenance company would have seven Jeeps, one small repair truck, a ¾-ton command truck, 4¾-ton weapons carriers, thirteen 2½-ton cargo trucks, two 4-ton wreckers, one 5-ton heavy wrecker, and thirteen 1-ton trailers. That would be forty-two vehicles that came with 10 officers and 137 enlisted men. An armored division signals company would be even larger.

Just before D-Day Lee got word he would have two drivers for each truck but only 160 truck companies and very few of the semitrailers. The sos would have to rely on the smaller 2½-ton trucks. This was a worry, but the overall plan did not depend on trucks in the long term. It was assumed the U.S. engineers would have the French railroads up and running and thus providing more economical and efficient transport over long distances. But Lee and his staff knew that would be a major undertaking. What tracks and trains had not been destroyed by the Allied bombing would likely be sabotaged by the Germans.

An even bigger problem was providing fuel for all the vehicles. The military acronym pol stands for petroleum, oil, and lubricants. pol alone represented one-quarter of all the tonnage that would eventually be transported to the eto. For better or worse gasoline had become the lifeblood of modern armies. There were plans afoot to lay a light pipeline underneath the English Channel, but ship-to-shore pipelines were also part of the scheme. There was a critical shortage of piping and people who knew how to handle it. Officers who had worked for major oil companies were tracked down in other units and pressed into service for this undertaking. Lee's Transportation Corps had a large responsibility for receiving, storing, and issuing all packaged POL products, first in the tankers and finally at the opposite end of the supply line in cans and tank trucks. But the Corps of Engineers had to construct all bulk POL facilities and operate them, which entailed the reception, transportation, and storage of the great bulk of POL products needed by the army.[10]

The cross-channel submarine lines were probably even more novel than the Mulberries. It was an exclusively British project known as PLUTO (pipeline under the ocean). It provided for the laying of ten three-inch pipes from the Isle of Wight to Cherbourg, the first line to arrive on D-Day plus twelve. As the logistics strategy unfolded, Cherbourg assumed an ever greater importance in the Allied plans. This was a very complex operation, and the planners invested tremendous time and effort trying to anticipate problems and the amount of fuel that would be transported. If any aspect of the plan failed, it could create a bottleneck that might compromise all operations on the European mainland. As Patton would famously observe later in the conflict, "My men can eat their belts, but my tanks have to have gas."[11]

A major slice of Lee's supply line was of course food. C rations were the basic unit. They kept people fed but not enough to gain weight. Over time the range of components of C ration containers grew until it was possible to eat for a week without having the same meal twice. They usually offered some kind of meat, instant coffee, lemonade powder (for vitamin C), a chocolate bar, and hard candy. The containers usually also included chewing gum, toilet paper, crackers or canned bread, and cigarettes. Always cigarettes. The nation's addiction to cigarettes had gotten a boost in World War I, and it got an even bigger boost in World War II. The soldiers griped, but they consumed everything but the lemonade powder. They wanted beer.

If a soldier was about to go into combat he got promoted to K rations, which looked like and weighed as much as a brick. Therein he would find a chunk of meat of some kind, maybe chicken or pork, a fruit bar, a chocolate bar, a caramel bar, toilet paper of course, more lemonade powder, and salt tablets.[12] The cigarettes were usually some unheard of brand. The soldiers wanted Lucky Strikes or Camels but rarely got them.

The development of amphibious capability was yet another challenge, and there were continuing debates on whether the navy or the army should have lead responsibility. The first challenge was to get the troops ashore under enemy fire, and the subsequent task was to use amphibious capability to transport fuel and equipment to the beaches. The Allies had gained some experience in the muddled invasion of North Africa, but that was with forces largely transported all the way across the Atlantic Ocean and moving into sparsely defended beaches. The invasion of Sicily, which involved movement across a more narrow water obstacle, offered more pertinent experience. For the first time a naval beach battalion was used to achieve closer coordination between the navy afloat and the army ashore.

The army and the navy had to learn to talk to each other, and so did the British and Americans. Early in the planning stages of Overlord— before it had been given that code name—it became apparent that British and American officers were poorly acquainted with the planning procedures of each other's forces, leading to much confusion. Lee took the lead, in coordination with his British opposite number, Gen. Thomas Riddell-Webster, the British quartermaster general, to set up a joint British-American "Q" school to form a cadre of British and American officers familiar with each other's procedures and thus better able to plan for the invasion. The training covered the waterfront of military issues, but given Lee's priorities it was in particular focused on amphibious operations.

From the beginning the school operated on the assumption that it was preparing for the invasion of France across the English Channel. It became a key training organization for the officers who actually planned the invasion. The program evolved into a series of twelve-day courses, and classes grew in size to about seventy officers, half British and half American. Most of the officers who took the courses held important roles on the staffs of units that were scheduled to assault the beaches and set up supply operations on the other shore. By early 1944 the British and Americans were conducting trial amphibious landings in Great Britain. An operation conducted on March 7 landed nearly seventeen thousand men and nineteen hundred vehicles. As to be expected, there were many screwups, but it was a learning process that would pay dividends on D-Day.[13]

A later practice landing, Exercise Tiger, held April 22–30, 1944, showed improvements but was marred by an unexpected visit from German U-boats that appeared out of nowhere and sank two LSTs and machine-gunned men in the water. That event actually took a greater toll of Allied troops than would occur on Utah Beach on D-Day. Some 749 men were lost, most of them in Lee's supply units. Another set of exercises, called Fabius and held April 23–May 7, was patterned after the projected Overlord invasion and had the same general makeup as the real invasion to come. In fact it had to be postponed a day due to inclement weather—just as D-Day would be. This operation ran relatively smoothly. There were a few screwups here and there, but those lessons learned would get no further practice until the big invasion itself.[14]

As D-Day drew nearer, Lee's people were responsible for locating and constructing concentration and marshaling areas near the coast for the troops preparing to embark, as well as for feeding and housing them, waterproofing vehicles, issuing emergency supplies, planning the movement of troops, locating and, where necessary, constructing new roads to embarkation points, preparing those embarkation points, making certain the requisite supplies were where they were supposed to be, providing collection areas for thousands of vehicles of all types, preparing ports and approaches to the ports, supplying recreational facilities for the troops while they waited to embark (to keep them from going crazy), setting up aid stations and hospital facilities for the sick (and wounded to come), and operating depots and dumps for the storage and last-minute issue of supplies. They would get no relief when the armada set sail. They had to get ready to receive wounded soldiers, refugees, and prisoners of war, while all the time preparing to send over the second wave of troops.

Lee did not have enough people to handle all this activity. As early as February he foresaw it would be necessary to use field forces to perform service functions while the operation was being mounted. He estimated that at least fifteen thousand troops would be needed, in addition to the forty-six thousand SOS troops taken off other jobs to assist with the embarkation. For example, there were never enough cooks, though Lee had ordered an increase in training for them. Soldiers gearing up for combat did not enjoy being ordered to perform housekeeping chores, but there was no way around it.

In the days leading up to the invasion the embarkation area became alive with trucks, combat vehicles, and train after train of troops. For Overlord the U.S. Army had accumulated 301,000 vehicles, 2,700 artillery pieces, 1,800 train locomotives, 20,000 railcars, 2.6 million small arms, 300,000 telephone poles, and 7 million tons of gasoline, oil, and lubricants.[15] The crush shut down virtually all normal travel by British citizens in the area, working some hardship and causing resentment. Movement on all highways was strictly controlled. As the hour loomed soldiers received the critical items, which no doubt impressed them with what they were in for. They received antiseasickness pills, water purification tablets, emergency rations, heating units, vomit bags, dusting powder, and insecticide-treated clothing. They put paste on their shoes to protect them from chemical warfare. And to put the icing on the cake they each received 200 francs in the new French currency issued by the Allied military government.

At the last high-level conference before D-Day, held at General Montgomery's headquarters and attended by King George VI himself, Prime Minister Churchill expressed alarm about "the amount of paraphernalia" and also "an excess of motor cars." But his anxieties aside, he wrote in Montgomery's private journal, "On the verge of the greatest adventure with which these pages have dealt, I record my confidence that all will be well."[16]

Perhaps most frustrating of all to many in the high command was the continuing disagreement between combat commanders and Lee about who would control what in the upcoming battle. Gen. Omar Bradley in particular was emerging as a holdout, refusing to acknowledge Lee's dual role as head of SOS, soon to be the Communications Zone on the continent, and also de facto deputy commander of the ETOUSA. In a last-minute negotiation Eisenhower had sought to forge a compromise. As commander of First Army, Bradley preserved his line command in Normandy, including control of logistics, until such time as he chose to relinquish it to Lee. Lee retained control of all American theater-wide functions inside a rump ETO subordinated within ComZ headquarters. Eisenhower also ceded to Lee any direct control SHAEF would have over supply and services commands.

"The Theater Commander will delegate all possible authority to the Commanding General, Communications Zone, who reports directly to him," Eisenhower decreed. "The Communication Zone will be the agency of the Theater Commander for the administration of all US troops and the channel of communications to the War Department excepting on those matters reserved by the Theater Commander himself. For administrative purposes, ComZ headquarters will be considered Theater Headquarters."[17]

For all intents and purposes Lee enjoyed authority comparable to that of Bradley, head of First Army, and Lt. Gen. Carl Spaatz of the U.S. Army Air Force. This was and would remain a major bone of contention between Lee and the other senior officers. He would lose his formal title as deputy theater commander of ETO, but his role remained unchanged.

The countdown continued. While the troops killed their final hours of peace, assuming they had not been pressed into service functions, they played baseball and poker or watched movies. They received better food than they were used to, and some were even permitted to sleep through breakfast and have an extra-large noon meal. Mobile bakeries provided fresh bread. But they were in a virtual prison. Tight security was imposed all around. Thousands of counterintelligence corps personnel patrolled the perimeter.

There were the usual snafus. Many of the troops did not have their basic gear either because it was late getting to them or because they had just gotten off the boat and it had not caught up with them. These vexing shortages continued even after the first troops had shoved off and even when Lee's people were being taxed to the limit. Much confusion resulted from troops simply not following instructions. The use of troops for service functions undoubtedly contributed to the chaos, and service troops who did know what they were doing were being called upon to work around the clock, leaving many exhausted and

THE OVERLORD LOGISTICAL PLAN

prone to make mistakes. Other units by accident or choice showed up with more gear than they were allowed, for which there was no room on the transport craft. Part of this problem was resolved by the acquisition of extra barges that could be beached on D-Day plus one. Against this backdrop the U.S. Navy was assembling twelve hundred ships and other craft for the landing on Omaha Beach and nearly eight hundred more for Utah Beach, some to move the troops and some to bombard the German defenses.

The craft were assembled and ready to load on May 30. Embarkation of both the assault forces and the follow-up forces was completed on June 3, and the marshaling of the remainder was in full swing. The task force convoys assembled along the southern coast of England. The cross-channel movement now awaited only the signal from the supreme commander.

The night of June 3–4 was clear, but the wind was rising and the channel was choppy. Eisenhower was given an unfavorable forecast that evening, and he decided to postpone the invasion for twenty-four hours. Convoys that had already departed were forced to return to port or mill around at sea while their passengers banged against each other and got seasick. The forecast for the next day wasn't much better, but for various reasons a more lengthy postponement would involve at least two weeks until the next favorable tides. Early in the morning of June 5 Eisenhower gave the order to go ahead.

Montgomery was on hand, having just returned from a hiking and fishing holiday in the Highlands during which he slept each night on his personal train, the Rapier, which suggests that Lee was not the only senior officer who had a train at his disposal.[18] Like Lee, Montgomery had his eccentricities, enough to drive his American counterparts to distraction, but they never seemed to weigh him down in quite the same way.

Eisenhower's boys were headed into harm's way. Despite heavy losses in North Africa and Italy and especially the Soviet Union, the German army had still grown from 5.8 million men in 1942 to 6.5 million by the spring of 1944. It was probably the best army the world has ever seen—highly disciplined, committed, usually well equipped and well led. The Allied forces soon learned that anytime they had a German force on the defensive, it was imperative to keep pounding them because given a few hours of reprieve they would regroup and come back as tough as ever.

To defend the French coast Hitler had sixty divisions and two thousand tanks, most of them superior to U.S. tanks. Some German soldiers were older men assigned to light duty on coastal defenses, but most were among Germany's elite battalions. The ss divisions were the most disciplined and fanatical, but having ss units among the regular army created tension and miscommunication.[19]

There is a bias of history—that in reading of events long past we assume the result. The architects of Overlord enjoyed no such certainty of the outcome. They were undertaking the most ambitious, some said foolhardy, amphibious operation in history, never equaled before or since. The weather was unpredictable, the enemy prepared and resolute, many of the soldiers and seamen unproven, and some aspects of the tactical plan—such as the Mulberries—were far-fetched. Certainly the senior British army commander, Field Marshal Alan Brooke, the stern-faced chief of the imperial general staff, had his doubts. "It may well be the most ghastly disaster of the whole war," he noted the day before the troops went ashore.[20]

At some point in the night Eisenhower sat alone in his headquarters drinking coffee and smoking one cigarette after another. He picked up a piece of scratch paper and drafted a message to be released to the press if the great cross-channel invasion failed: "Our landings in the Cherbourg-Havre area have failed to gain a satisfactory foothold and I have withdrawn the troops. My decision to attack at this time and place was based upon the best information available. The troops, the air, and the Navy did all that bravery and devotion to duty could do. If any blame or fault attaches to the attempt it is mine alone.—June 5."[21]

The original of that short paragraph, which says volumes about the nature of true leadership, hangs in a modest frame on a wall in the excellent National WWII Museum in New Orleans.

1. View of war matériel stored at Blitz Park near Liverpool, England. Henry Utley Milne Collection, U.S. Army Heritage and Education Center, Carlisle, Pennsylvania.

2. Typical U.S. Army depot in England. Henry Utley Milne Collection, U.S. Army Heritage and Education Center, Carlisle, Pennsylvania.

3. Interior of a Nissen hut, the type of structure in which many Americans lived during the buildup for D-Day. All the comforts of home—almost. Henry Utley Milne Collection, U.S. Army Heritage and Education Center, Carlisle, Pennsylvania.

4. (*opposite top*) Sergeant Geisler explains the workings of a donut bakery to Lee and Capt. Harold C. King. Henry Utley Milne Collection, U.S. Army Heritage and Education Center, Carlisle, Pennsylvania.

5. (*opposite bottom*) Lee at his desk. Undated U.S. Army photo, courtesy Dwight D. Eisenhower Presidential Library, Abilene, Kansas.

6. Quartermaster railhead in France. Henry Utley Milne Collection, U.S. Army Heritage and Education Center, Carlisle, Pennsylvania.

7. Fuel cans being decanted in France. Henry Utley Milne Collection, U.S. Army Heritage and Education Center, Carlisle, Pennsylvania.

8. Large U.S. Army supply depot near
Paris. Henry Utley Milne Collection,
U.S. Army Heritage and Education
Center, Carlisle, Pennsylvania.

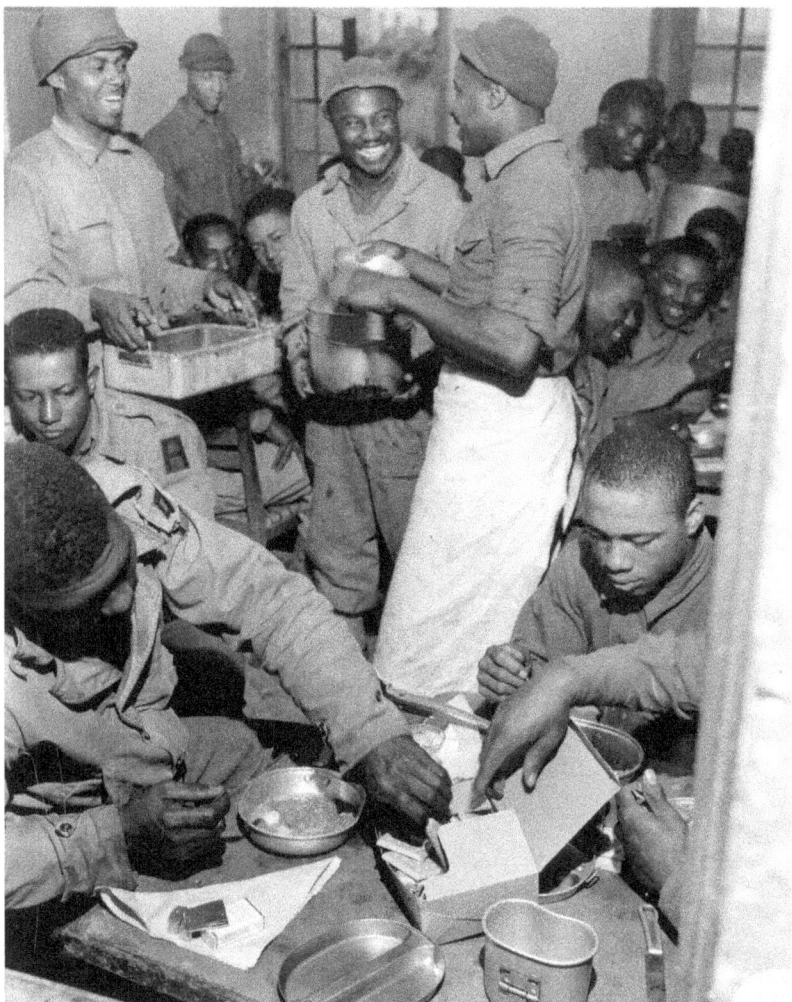

9. Segregated antiaircraft unit members celebrating Fourth of July in France, July 1944. They were among the few black troops engaged in actual combat before Lee issued his integration order. Henry Utley Milne Collection, U.S. Army Heritage and Education Center, Carlisle, Pennsylvania.

10. Drivers pull off a roadway near Alençon, France, to have breakfast. Henry Utley Milne Collection, U.S. Army Heritage and Education Center, Carlisle, Pennsylvania.

11. Chow time for Third Division soldiers in southern France. Henry Utley Milne Collection, U.S. Army Heritage and Education Center, Carlisle, Pennsylvania.

12. (*opposite top*) Lee welcomes Robert P. Patterson, undersecretary of war, on his arrival in France for an inspection tour, August 21, 1944. Patterson sought to have Lee removed from his position. U.S. Army photo, courtesy Dwight D. Eisenhower Presidential Library, Abilene, Kansas.

13. (*opposite bottom*) Eisenhower welcomes labor union leaders on a visit to the combat zone in France, August 1944. (Lee has his back to the camera.) Courtesy Dwight D. Eisenhower Presidential Library, Abilene, Kansas.

14. (*above*) Gen. Brehon Somervell with Lee on an inspection tour. Somervell, who gave Lee his European assignment, was seen as Lee's primary defender when others were trying to have him replaced. James A. Crothers Collection, U.S. Army Heritage and Education Center, Carlisle, Pennsylvania.

15. Eisenhower, Gen. Joseph T. McNarney, Lee, and Gen. Harry J. Collins in Salzburg, Austria, October 1946. U.S. Army photo, courtesy Dwight D. Eisenhower Presidential Library, Abilene, Kansas.

16. (*opposite top*) Lee with Eisenhower on an inspection tour in Canale, Italy, October 16, 1946. Maj. Gen. Bryant E. Moore, commanding general of the Eighty-Eighth Division, is with them. U.S. Army photo, courtesy Dwight D. Eisenhower Presidential Library, Abilene, Kansas.

17. (*opposite bottom*) Eisenhower with Lee driving Jeep in Italy, October 16, 1946. U.S. Army photo, courtesy Dwight D. Eisenhower Presidential Library, Abilene, Kansas.

18. Lt. Gen. John Clifford Hodges Lee, 1944. Personality Collection, U.S. Army Heritage and Education Center, Carlisle, Pennsylvania.

CHAPTER THIRTEEN

The Great Adventure Begins

It was a near run thing, the
nearest run thing you ever saw.
—DUKE OF WELLINGTON, commenting on Waterloo

On the morning of June 5, 1944, seventeen convoys comprising nearly two thousand ships began the trek across the English Channel.[1] The weather was dicey. The routes led through minefields, but they had been well marked. By midnight the convoys were gathering in the final transport area, about twelve miles from the target beaches. The rough water made it difficult to move assault teams from the transports to landing craft. At about midnight Royal Air Force (RAF) bombers began pounding the German batteries along the coast, and soon thereafter paratroopers of the Eighty-Second and 101st Airborne Divisions began dropping behind enemy lines. Right after the RAF came the entire American bomber fleet of 1,635 planes. As the landing craft set out, the U.S. Navy opened a barrage from eight hundred heavy guns on enemy shore batteries along Utah and Omaha Beaches. The air force conducted bombing runs, but the bad weather forced them to unload too far inland to do much damage.

Thousands upon thousands of mostly young men fought seasickness and fear as their transport ships bobbed up and down, side to side, in the rough waves. Aboard the USS *Charles Carroll* Gen. Norman D. Cota, who would be the senior officer on Omaha Beach, said to his officers, "You're going to find confusion. The landing craft aren't going in on schedule, and people are going to be landed in the wrong place. Some won't be landed at all. . . . We must improvise, carry on, not lose our heads. Nor must we add to the confusion."[2]

Of confusion there would be plenty, especially on Omaha Beach. Allied planners from Eisenhower on down had been greatly vexed by the unsettled weather pattern that threatened to compromise the operation, but the weather was a two-sided coin. The Germans were expecting an attack but decided that the weather precluded any serious action for the near future. The German senior commanders, including Rommel, were away from the front visiting family or otherwise taking a rest. The German troops holding the defense positions were likewise relaxed, enjoying what they assumed was a respite from their tedious assignment.

Then they saw the ships.

So many ships. Thousands upon thousands of ships had appeared offshore heading straight toward them. Then the long-range bombardment began with the screaming of the incoming projectiles and the roar of the explosions. Most of the German troops at the concrete emplacements had until this hour escaped the worst of the war experienced by their compatriots in the snowy steppes of the Soviet Union or the sandy wastes of North Africa, but their holiday was at an end. Hell was coming upon them.

Of the five beaches under assault Omaha was to prove the most brutal. The German defenses there were dense and redundant. Some eighty-five machine-gun nests covered Omaha Beach, more than the three British and Canadian beaches combined. Many of the wooden and steel barriers along the shore were mined. The lay of the land favored the defenders, who covered the beach with withering fire and had backup from artillery and mortars. The Germans had concealed these emplacements from air surveillance, so the Allied invasion planners were unaware of them. If that weren't enough, German reinforcements were nearby, ready to move toward the beaches and determined to throw the invaders back into the sea.

Some of the landing craft discharged troops too far from shore, in deep water. Burdened by at least sixty-eight pounds of gear, they sank to the bottom. Some were incinerated as their landing craft were hit by artillery or blown up by mines. Many of those who reached the shore were mowed down like wheat. The waves coming after them stepped over their bodies and continued forward, but there was no place to take cover. For hours it was bloody chaos, and the issue was in serious doubt. On a ship offshore Gen. Omar Bradley, head of First Army, the primary invasion force, paced the deck while trying to see through the smoke and fog and make sense of the discordant reports he was getting from the beach. In his autobiography he recalled that he had at one point seriously considered calling off the whole thing.

But one by one or in small groups of two or three the surviving invaders worked their way around the defensive barriers and took out the German machine-gun nests one at a time. Within a few hours a clearer picture began to emerge. All along the coast Allied forces were securing beachheads and moving inland. The eight assault divisions now ashore had paid a severe price for their success, suffering 12,000 killed, wounded, and missing. At all the beaches a total of 4,414 men had been killed. Most of the casualties were in the missing category, as many had gotten lost in the chaos. Some gradually found their way back to their units. But not all. Along the beaches thousands of the dead lay in rows awaiting hasty burials as soon as adequate ground could be found and cleared of mines and unexploded ordnance.

But the Allies were ashore, and that augured ill for Hitler's Third Reich. There was only one German armored unit close to hand for action on Omaha Beach, and that was the Twenty-First Panzer Division, which had been roughly handled in North Africa and then rebuilt and reequipped in France. Another division farther north almost made it through the gap between the British and Canadian lines and onto the beach. German forces from all over France were converging on Normandy by any means of locomotion available, but these units, like all other German units, were contending with skies filled with Allied aircraft they called "Jabos." These planes strafed and bombed at will, undeterred by the feeble defenses of the once vaunted German Luftwaffe. The same bloody horrors that were being inflicted on the Americans, British, and Canadians coming ashore were being inflicted on the Germans trying to rush to the scene.

By nightfall 156,000 Allied troops were ashore, but their grip was tenuous. They had moved inland barely six miles from Gold and Juno and barely two thousand yards beyond Omaha. Perhaps the most worrisome statistic of all, at least to Lee and his supply organization, was that only one hundred tons of supplies had been brought onto the beach by midnight, significantly less than the twenty-five hundred tons called for in the plan. The troops that made it to shore intact had provisions in their knapsacks sufficient for a day or two. But if they were to hold and strengthen their beachhead, they needed a steady stream of supplies—ammunition, food, plasma, gas for the vehicles—and they needed it by D-Day plus two.[3]

The first men ashore to begin answering this challenge were the first elements of the engineer special brigades, whose job it was to organize the beaches to receive supplies directly from the ships standing off to sea. The first group ashore was a small reconnaissance party that landed within half an hour of the first assault wave in the midst of the frantic battle. Within another half hour eight other groups of engineers reached the beach, but it was immediately clear their task was impossible, at least amid the chaos and carnage. The sand was littered with the bodies of dead and wounded, and the infantry that had reached the seawall or shingle pile on the eastern end of the beach were struggling to offer return fire to the Germans. Thus the supply engineers, practical people, changed their game plan to helping the wounded and adding to the return fire.

Most of the American landings in the first two hours were concentrated in the middle of Omaha Beach and served mainly to increase congestion and offer easy targets for the enemy. One resourceful sergeant in the Thirty-Seventh Engineer Combat Battalion led a mine detector crew into an open area in the face of enemy fire and managed to open the first personnel trail through the hell on the beach. Soon other engineers were clearing areas for transit of supplies, removing mines, cutting through barbed-wire entanglements, and making a road with bulldozers already being offloaded onto the beach. All the time infantry were slipping into the beachhead and gradually silencing the enemy machine guns. Two landing craft unable to find a safe landing place drove full speed through the obstacles up onto the beach while firing all of their weapons at enemy emplacements. About the same time a navy destroyer drew alongside the beach, ignoring the shallow water and pouring broadsides into the enemy positions as it moved along.

The arrival of the destroyer gave impetus to the action across the beach. Without question the engineers played a pivotal role in getting things moving, though certainly not according to plan.[4] By late afternoon, as the tide receded, the engineers returned to the tidal flat to resume the mission they had found impossible in the early stages. With salvaged explosives and bulldozers borrowed from other units they resumed the job of clearing the beach of obstacles and debris. It was by no means a cakewalk even then. They were still under enemy fire, primarily artillery, and the continuous waves of infantry coming ashore complicated the picture. But before long they had five large and six small gaps in the enemy defenses cleared and marked, and the troops were pouring through, eager to get out of the sandy shooting gallery.

By the end of D-Day the prospects for organizing supplies coming into Omaha looked much more favorable.[5] Logistic operations on the first day had been limited and tonnage targets forgotten. Only a handful of supplies had been brought in and put into the improvised dumps. Meanwhile operations on Utah Beach had been going much more smoothly. Routes were cleared relatively easily and quickly. Enemy snipers and artillery continued to vex the invaders throughout the day but not to the degree they had on Omaha Beach. There are no records of actual unloading of supplies on D-Day and D-Day plus one. The chaos of the battle permitted a total discharge of only 26.6 percent, or 6,614 tons, of the planned cumulative 24,850 tons at the two beaches in the first three days.

Thereafter unloading of vital supplies accelerated swiftly as the troops moved inland and enemy resistance faded. There were occasional air raids, but these were directed primarily at the ships moored offshore and in any event did little damage. Troops and vehicles continued to move onto the beach. Landing craft would beach on a falling tide, discharge after the water had receded, and then wait to be refloated on the next tide. Only the smaller craft were doing this at first, but as the discharge of men and equipment fell behind schedule it was decided to try the same technique with the larger LSTs, though the navy was concerned they would suffer debilitating damage. In war caution quickly gives way to audacity. They started running the LSTs up onto the beach. In the first two weeks more than two hundred LSTs were unloaded at Omaha Beach this way without damage. It was a breakthrough that accelerated the process all up and down the beaches.

A variety of craft were used to offload the ships onto the beaches. One of the most effective was the Rhino ferry, a barge made up of pontoon units and propelled by outboard motors. Rhino ferries were towed across the channel, with the crews riding on the open and unprotected decks, and the ferries were then used to unload LSTs and ships. They had large capacity, and their cellular construction made them almost unsinkable.[6]

Of course much of the unloading was done by the popular DUKWs (Ducks). These 2½-ton amphibians bore a major share of the load. Some attempted to go ashore on D-Day but got shot up. A few made it in the early afternoon, but most were held offshore until the next day. The Ducks were popular because they could not only carry cargo to the beach but then continue on land to the dumps being established at some distance, farther and farther with every passing day. Most of the dumps were in small Normandy farm fields, where supplies were stacked along hedgerows, which provided some concealment.[7]

Two days after the landing Lee went to Eisenhower asking for "a little firmer idea of General Eisenhower's personal desires" regarding the delineation of responsibilities in France. As Hughes had noted in an earlier communication, the "mere designation of SOS as a Communications Zone" did not set Lee up as one of the three officers to aid him in his mission. This all came back to Beetle Smith, who was growing weary of the topic. In exasperation he gave up. "Control of theater, administrative, and supply functions shifted to Lee," writes D. K. R. Crosswell, and Lee "remained deputy theater commander in all but name."[8]

By the end of the second week operations on Omaha Beach resembled those of a major port. The discharge and inland movement of cargo and the evacuation of the growing numbers of casualties and prisoners of war were tightly organized. A major gain was the steady increase in trucks, which accelerated the movement of vital cargo inland. The Ducks, designed to travel in water and on land, were by definition inefficient in terms of speed and carrying capability. By that time the daily tonnage discharge at Omaha Beach was averaging nearly nine thousand tons, or about 95 percent of the target, and two thousand vehicles were crossing the beach each day and heading into the war. Movement across Utah Beach also increased, but not to the level of Omaha.[9]

On June 11 the Combined Chiefs of Staff (CCS)—Marshall, Arnold, and King—met in London to review the war plans and resolve a variety of questions, a major one being the relationship between Overlord and the fighting in the Mediterranean. On June 12 Eisenhower took the chiefs on a visit to Bradley at First Army and a tour of the beaches. When Eisenhower returned to England, he sent a memo to Beetle Smith ordering a cut in supply units in favor of more combat troops—a fairly normal if ill-considered act for a combat officer. At the time the troops were suffering a severe shortage of ammunition— particularly artillery and mortar.

Lee was not in on this visit, though he tried to wriggle into it. A few days earlier Marshall, Arnold, and King had arrived in Scotland, but heavy fog prevented their plane from landing at their intended destination—Prestwick. They were diverted to an air transport command base at the northwest tip of Wales, where no preparation had been made to receive them. A Colonel McCarthy had been sent ahead of the delegation to make arrangements. Using Lee's train, McCarthy went ahead to Prestwick. McCarthy had passed along instructions to Lee from Marshall not to meet him, since Lee no doubt had more important things to do as the troops were landing in Normandy. McCarthy delivered the message, but there was no way Lee would pass up a chance to reacquaint himself with Marshall. He was there all decked out as usual, McCarthy recalled, "booted, spurred, and replete with riding crop," waiting for VIPs who never arrived.[10]

On the ground Bradley, who disliked Lee intensely, resented the fact that his estimates on how much ammunition his troops needed were being ignored.[11] He considered the War Department's figures, based on the fighting in the Mediterranean, to be about a third of what was prudent in his totally different situation. The ammunition shortage appeared to confirm his opinion. He believed Lee's people had settled on inadequate levels of support and were incapable of achieving even those. He began a policy of not keeping records of how much war matériel his army received, which meant Lee's sos never knew how much First Army had on hand and in reserve. But this subterfuge served Bradley's purposes. Since sos had no idea what Bradley had, it could not rebut his demands for more. And if Bradley could build up excessive stockpiles, his soldiers would not suffer from lack of sufficient firepower.

Bradley also declined to designate a rear to his force, which enabled him to maintain control of the beaches and to keep Lee out, at least for the time being. Bradley's duplicity was a problem. Without timely and accurate reports to ComZ, Lee did not have the information he needed to inform planners back in Great Britain and the United States, who needed it to regulate production, nor could he adjust the flow of supplies as needed in response to changing conditions.

In a time when coherent communication was vitally needed, everyone was talking past each other. "The same applied to manpower replacements," Crosswell writes. "About 90 percent of the vast communications between the theater and Washington involved routine administration and supply, and much of that entailed harmonizing misunderstandings over requisitioning, shipping and transportation, storage, stock controls, and the levels and distribution of supplies and manpower. Given the complex relationships and overlapping spheres of authority among SHAEF, ComZ, and the commands, the potential for breakdown became very high indeed."[12]

Reports of the shortage of ammunition got Eisenhower's attention, and he called on his chief troubleshooter Hughes to go to Normandy and check it out. On June 13 Hughes flew with Lee to Omaha Beach. Hughes was stunned by what he saw: "The fields were covered with poppies and with huge sticks which the Nazis had put in most of the fields to prevent glider landings," he noted. "However, just as American forces were able to cross the beaches, which were covered with obstacles of every known form, our gliders were able to land and our paratroopers succeeded in getting to the places which they were told to hold. After seeing what our men did, I am convinced there is no such thing as impossible."[13]

Unless of course that something was moving supplies to the troops amid a chaotic command structure in which no one was clearly in

THE GREAT ADVENTURE BEGINS

charge. Hughes believed, as did others, that the success of the venture depended on which side could build up its forces faster and that American supplies were coming in much too slowly. Not only that, but the supplies were still being managed by the Corps of Engineers, not Lee's SOS.[14]

Back in England the next morning Hughes was summoned by Eisenhower. Hughes told Eisenhower that Bradley was not driving supply operations fast enough. At Eisenhower's instruction Smith sent a cable to Bradley telling him to speed up the unloading of supplies, while Eisenhower sent Hughes back to Omaha to take over supervising supplies. When he got to Bradley's headquarters, Hughes was pleased to see that the First Army commander, in response to Smith's cable, was putting pressure on his staff to accelerate the unloading, but he was displeased to learn there had been no mention of him supervising the operation. Hughes thought part of the problem lay with the navy, but he was unable to achieve anything with them. He perceived a lack of communication between the army and navy, as well as between the Americans and the British.

Hughes doubted the wisdom of Bradley's refusal to relinquish control of the beach operations, and he also had doubts about Lee, for whom he had once served as chief of staff. As was his habit, Lee had sent some presents to Bradley ahead of their visit. "When we arrived at General Bradley's headquarters General Lee opened the conversation by asking if the presents had arrived and made a statement to the effect that it was well that the presents had preceded our arrival," Hughes reported to Eisenhower. Hughes later admonished Bradley's G-4 to warn Bradley to be wary of Lee's claims that everything was going well. But after all that, Hughes declined to take a strong stand on Bradley's continued control of the beach area. "In my opinion it is fatal for the First Army to permit any interference with its control at this time," he told Eisenhower.[15]

While the generals bickered, the men on the ground did the work. By June 18 the combined daily discharges at Omaha and Utah were averaging about 14,500 tons, only slightly below expectations. A total of 314,504 men of the planned 358,139 had crossed the American beaches, and eleven of the twelve planned divisions were ashore.

At both beaches the evacuation of wounded and prisoners was proceeding without difficulty. More than 10,000 prisoners had been sent to Great Britain.[16]

Although men and supplies were moving quickly across the beaches, everyone was antsy about the dependence on that conduit because the weather was a variable. On June 16 the first men and matériel began debarking on the Mulberry pierheads, which offered hope of a more stable supply line. And then on June 19 the most savage storm to hit the English Channel in forty years descended. For three days high winds and waves pounded the Normandy coast, wrecking ships and smashing the artificial harbor. When the storm finally subsided, it was clear the U.S. Mulberry was done for. It would never be repaired. The beach was littered again, this time with shattered ships and landing craft. Of the twenty Rhino ferries only one remained operational. The army estimated that eight hundred craft of all types were either beached or destroyed and that the storm had delayed delivery of twenty thousand vehicles and many tons of other supplies.[17]

Predictably there was no unloading of supplies during this period, which threw the schedule out the window. Inability to land supplies became a major problem quickly because there was little reserve on the ground. In particular there was an acute shortage of ammunition, which threatened efforts to take the port of Cherbourg, widely seen as key to the long-term supply challenge. But there was no time for discouragement or lamentations. Everyone went back to work. Discharge operations recovered quickly. On June 23 Omaha brought in ten thousand tons and Utah, sixty-four hundred.

Farther north the British-built pier, Mulberry B, was not hit directly by the storm and, though it had suffered some damage, was quickly brought back into operation. It would serve efficiently for months, providing almost half of the British supplies used on the continent before the port of Antwerp was opened.

For the Americans the key to the supply challenge remained the port of Cherbourg on the Cotentin Peninsula, sometimes called the Cherbourg Peninsula, which had never been all that great a port. As mentioned before, prior to the war it served primarily cruise ships.

There was only one railroad serving the area. Nevertheless a port is a port, and the Americans knew they needed one. As early as June 10, while the armies were still fighting to establish a permanent beachhead, Bradley had ordered an offensive into the peninsula. Within a week his forces had conducted a swift drive across to the western shore, isolating Cherbourg. Hitler ordered his armies to go to Cherbourg's relief, but the generals on the ground knew it was hopeless. The German garrison in Cherbourg was ordered to fight to the last man, a favorite Führer directive. They did put up a fight but surrendered to the Americans on June 27.

That did not mean the port was usable. The Germans had gone to great pains to put the port facilities out of commission. It would take six weeks before it could be brought into use, during which time the troops remained dependent primarily on supplies coming across the beach.[18]

On the same day that Cherbourg fell Eisenhower called Lee. The supreme commander as always was under a lot of stress. There was a bitter, ongoing debate between the Americans and the British about Operation Anvil—a proposed invasion of southern France that would complement the Normandy invasion. The British were opposed to it, contending it would be a wasteful sideshow. The opposition of the British stemmed mainly from Prime Minister Churchill, who was almost hysterical about it. Churchill had actually been lukewarm about Overlord. His preferred strategy was to invade Europe through Italy and Balkans—what he called Europe's soft underbelly. He repeatedly ranted and raved at Eisenhower that Anvil—later redubbed Dragoon—was a great mistake. When he was unable to move Eisenhower, he complained directly to Roosevelt. When he was unable to move either of them, he lapsed into incoherence. "He is becoming more and more unbalanced," Brooke noted in his diary. "He was literally frothing at the corners of his mouth with rage."[19]

But Eisenhower did not call Lee to commiserate about his problems with Churchill. He was livid about the confused supply situation. His armies were making at best grudging progress against determined German opposition, and the nagging shortage of ammunition, especially artillery, was a major sore point. The root cause of the problem was the habitual "selective discharge" of cargo vessels, from which items were unloaded as needed and no record was kept. Many vessels arrived at the beach with their contents unknown. There was a particular need for 81-mm mortar shells to aid in the hedgerow fighting, but no one on shore knew where they were. They had to search the ships one at a time looking for them. This was at least in part the result of unusual demands for certain types of supplies that had not been foreseen by anyone, either in Washington or Great Britain, but such explanations garnered little sympathy from the supreme commander. The alleged shortage of heavy-duty artillery ammunition would remain a matter of dispute throughout the war.

Eisenhower's son John, recently graduated from West Point, happened to be with his father when he called Lee.[20] The call, John recalled, was "blunt and to the point. If Lee wanted to keep his job, Dad said, he had better get over there personally and see to it that things were stepped up. The call took half a minute."[21]

Eisenhower was down on Lee, but he wasn't very happy with Bradley either. Bradley's First Army was the core of the American offensive, and it seemed stuck in a rut. Farther north the British and Canadians under Montgomery also were going nowhere fast. Eisenhower's naval aide Butcher noted that Eisenhower appeared "considerably less exuberant these days. He didn't even seem to get a kick out of the fall of Cherbourg."[22]

Lost amid the frustrations and recriminations was any acknowledgment that the U.S. military had successfully pulled off the most extraordinary amphibious operation in history, across the stormy English Channel, capturing a well-defended shore. It had funneled one and a half million men through the small British nation, loaded down with every conceivable kind of military hardware and stores; it had assembled thousands of ships and landing craft and braved harsh elements to fight its way into Europe. There were many parents of this singular accomplishment, but perhaps none deserved more credit than the guy responsible for pulling it all together—Lt. Gen. John C. H. Lee. And insofar as is known, no one in the senior command ever gave him a medal, a pat on the back, or an "'atta boy"—then or later.

CHAPTER FOURTEEN

The Great Breakout

Victory is the beautiful, bright-colored flower. Transport
is the stem without which it could never have blossomed.
Yet even the military student, in his zeal to master the
fascinating combinations of the actual conflict, often
forgets the far more intricate complications of supply.
—WINSTON CHURCHILL

After securing the beachheads and moving inland a few miles, the
Allied forces were going nowhere fast. The Germans were unable to
push them back into the sea, but they were able to mount stubborn
resistance all along the line, despite constant harassment from Allied
aircraft. The three towns on the east-west lateral road behind the
beach—Carentan, Bayeux, and Caen—remained in German hands.
Montgomery was supposed to take Caen, a key crossroads, but there
too the Germans were digging in and putting up a fight, and Montgomery seemed reluctant to force the issue.

The Germans also were aided by the nature of the landscape, in
particular the notorious Normandy hedgerows in the so-called bocage
country. This was an area of cultivated fields divided by tall, thick
hedgerows that restricted movement and observation. It provided a
natural defensive bulwark that the Germans were not slow to utilize. Sherman tanks could not move through the hedgerows, making them sitting ducks for the German Panzerfausts. The American
troops were under constant fire but could not see where it was coming from. An enemy emplacement might be only a few feet away in
a hedgerow and be invisible until too late. The hedgerows, Bradley
said, "formed a natural line of defense more formidable than any
even Rommel could have contrived."[1]

For weeks the First Army was bogged down as green troops
got accustomed to the rigors of combat and the by now infamous hedgerows took their inexorable toll. They were not only

delaying Bradley's infantry but also the planned breakout to be led by Patton and his yet to be formed Third Army. In this crisis American ingenuity once again came to the rescue. "Previous attempts to force the Normandy hedgerows had failed when our Shermans bellied up over the tops of those mounds instead of crashing through them," Bradley recalled. "There they exposed their soft undersides to the enemy while their own guns pointed helplessly toward the sky."[2]

The solution, conceived by a twenty-nine-year-old sergeant named Curtis G. Culin Jr. from New York City, was a few pieces of sharp scrap steel welded to the front of a Sherman tank. "Four tusk-like prongs protruded from it," Bradley said. "The tank backed off and ran head-on toward a hedgerow at 10 miles per hour. Its tusks bored into the wall, pinned down the belly, and the tank broke through under a canopy of dirt."[3] Almost overnight the ingenious devices were being attached to the Shermans and the hedgerow impediment began to crumble.

The high command also had a plan to circumvent the tough German defenses along the invasion line: Operation Cobra, which also became known as the Normandy Breakout. It was clear a dramatic move was necessary. "By the middle of July we could sense the growing impatience of newsmen who commented critically on the deadlock that seemed to have gripped our beachhead," Bradley said.[4] Bradley hated bad press, but he could not spill the beans on Cobra quite yet. So he just fumed.

In part Cobra was a response to Montgomery's continuing criticism of Eisenhower's emphasis on maintaining a coherent front line against the enemy instead of exploiting weak points and getting behind the enemy's front lines.

Patton had crossed the channel to France with the vanguard of Third Army headquarters on July 6. Patton was the only logical choice to lead such a daring venture, but he came with baggage from North Africa, where his occasional bouts of erratic behavior aroused distrust in certain quarters. "My own feelings about George were mixed," Bradley recalls in his memoirs.

He had not been my choice for Army commander and I was still wary of the grace with which he would accept our reversal in roles. For George was six years my senior and had been my army commander when I fought II Corps in the Sicilian campaign. I was apprehensive in having George join my command, for I feared that too much of my time would probably be spent in curbing his impetuous habits. But at the same time I knew that with Patton there would be no need for my whipping Third Army to keep it on the move. We had only to keep him pointed in the direction we wanted to go.[5]

Patton quickly put Bradley's concerns to rest. "Before many more months had passed, the *new* Patton had totally obliterated my unwarranted apprehensions; we formed as amiable and contented a team as existed in the senior command," Bradley notes.[6] Years later, after Patton was dead, Bradley learned of some of the negative things Patton had said about him and was greatly distressed about it.

On July 20 came word of the assassination attempt on Hitler, which was greeted as good news, but it did not affect the war situation. Soon enough it was learned that the Führer had survived the attempt and was still directing traffic. In terms of the Allied forces in France this was good news because Hitler kept his commanders in a state of confusion with impulsive orders that bore no relationship to actual battlefield conditions. Had a professional military leader been calling the shots, the American situation would have been much more difficult. On that day Eisenhower went to visit Bradley and his staff for final discussions of Cobra.

Cobra took wing on July 26. Bradley launched Gen. J. Lawton Collins's VII Corps against the German line at Saint-Lô, right behind a carpet bombing by twenty-five hundred Allied aircraft. Collins attacked on a narrow seven-thousand-yard front with three veteran divisions abreast and three more following close behind. Within two days they had advanced thirty miles against fading opposition. Patton's soon-to-be-famed Third Army, which had assembled behind Collins's troops, roared through the gap in the German line. In three days Patton covered one hundred miles, cutting deep into the rear of the German forces, which were now endangered largely because of Hitler's insistence that they hold their ground and fight it out to the bitter end.

What had been a breakthrough became a breakout. "The front has, so to speak, burst," Gen. Günther von Kluge informed Berlin. "There is a penetration of two to five kilometers deep on a front seven to eight kilometers wide. It has not yet been possible to seal this off."[7]

Now the Americans were on the move big time. On August 7 Eisenhower moved his advance post across the channel. Lee and his staff were already there, setting up shop near Valognes, just south of Cherbourg. Lee requisitioned a nice chateau for his own personal use. As of that moment the sos became ComZ, and Lee was chomping at the bit to assume control. However, Bradley still controlled the beach from his position as head of First Army, which before long split into First Army and Twelfth Army, with Gen. Courtney Hodges running the First and Bradley, the Twelfth.

With Patton's Third Army off and running it did seem as if the stalemate was broken and the Germans were in deep trouble. What Patton achieved ranked with some of the exploits of Stonewall Jackson in the Civil War. The breakout was made down a two-lane road, hemmed in by water on one side and hills on the other. Patton pushed two hundred thousand men and forty thousand vehicles through what looked like a disaster waiting to happen. One major snafu and the entire exercise would collapse, but Patton and his officers made sure that snafu did not happen. Soon they were roaring across France toward Lorraine. Hodges's First Army was more than twice the size of Patton's and had more tanks, but it was Patton hogging the stage. Hodges measured progress in Germans killed or captured, but Patton measured it in miles. He probably never rode quite as high before or after. "Compared to war, all other forms of human endeavor shrink to insignificance," he said. "God, how I love it."[8]

But what was good for the Third Army was quickly becoming a disaster for Lee and ComZ. "The Allied victory in Normandy was a logistician's worst nightmare," Carlo D'Este writes.

A German general once remarked that the blitzkrieg was paradise for the tactician and hell for quartermasters, but it was Ernie Pyle who described what followed as "a tactician's hell and a quartermaster's purgatory." The Allies had simply outrun their supply lines, and the logisticians were obliged to maintain supply lines stretched to the breaking point, as four Allied armies dashed across France and into Belgium. On D + 100 days (September 14, 1944) the Allies had advanced to where the logisticians thought they would reach only in May 1945. Thus, once beyond the Seine, logistics, not tactics, had become the dominant factor.[9]

The Allies still didn't have a real port that could handle regular shipping, and, perhaps most worrisome of all, Lee still did not have the authority he needed to forge an efficient supply system through the beach area. The farther Patton's forces moved, the harder it was to get fuel and other supplies to them. But Bradley refused to relinquish control of his rear, which is to say the beaches where the supplies were coming in. No one knew who was in charge, which was what the critics of the new system had warned about.

Earlier in July General Hughes had recommended extension of supply and manpower responsibilities to ComZ. "I am convinced," he told Eisenhower, "that more experienced [supply] men should be gotten into the picture."[10] Even Patton, who carried no brief for Lee, agreed. He told Eisenhower that Bradley's people simply did not have the training and experience to handle such a vast load of supplies. Bradley demurred, however, because of his distaste for Lee. "I would have turned it over long ago," he told Eisenhower, "if Everett Hughes had been in command of cz [ComZ]."[11] Eisenhower's response was to send Hughes to Bradley's headquarters to make a deal of some kind. Bradley signed a document of sorts but still made no commitment to fix the rear boundary. Bradley was known as the "GI's general" and made it a point to avoid the fancy trappings acquired by some senior officers, such as Lee, to whom Bradley attributed "an unfortunate pomposity."[12] This difference in style may have been the root cause of Bradley's animosity toward Lee. In any case the confused command structure continued and Lee was left in limbo.

The rapid advance of Third Army glossed over the supply disarray. Somervell happened to be in France when Patton's army began its end run, and even he proved to be more interested in combat operations than supply. "By bold action—no stopping to reorganize or to bring up supplies—we can penetrate Germany by October 1st and finish the war in Europe," he said. "The job is swift pursuit. Patton has the right idea—straight ahead and let the Air Forces take care of the flanks." As for the supply situation, Somervell pronounced it first rate: "Pipe lines being rapidly built; railroads running, Cherbourg to LeMans; motor trucks in fast motion, with good road discipline and no breakdowns. No shortage of weapons, equipment or rations."[13]

Singing from the same hymnal, Lee echoed Somervell's optimism. As if to put the icing on the cake, the Allied armies landed in southern France the next day against light opposition and began moving north. Hitler saw what was happening and was determined that Paris, the hub of transportation in France, should be held. But even he realized, for once in his career, that the task was hopeless. There were too few German troops on hand in Paris and they had no plan. Soon the Germans were packing their bags and heading north.

At a meeting on August 19 Lee had assured Bradley and Eisenhower that ComZ could handle any problems coming its way.[14] But while the Allies were doing their victory dance, the Germans realized the Allies were outrunning their supply lines. The farther Patton's armies moved, the more stretched and vulnerable the supply links to the beaches became.

Despite his optimism, even Somervell detected basic problems. The original plans had called for troops and supplies to be sent directly to France as soon as Cherbourg and other ports were captured and put into use. But it had taken longer to take Cherbourg than planned, and the extensive damage done by the Germans was taking a long time to repair. As September loomed and Patton neared the German border, there was not enough deepwater berthing capacity for all those ships. More than half of Eisenhower's supplies were still coming across the beach. Hughes warned that one more big storm might make a mess of the entire operation. Meanwhile ships were stacked along the coastline, still fully loaded or partially unloaded.[15]

Another problem was that the vaunted pipeline under the channel, intended to provide the armies with fuel, did not work out as planned. It took forty-one days to get it into position, and then after a few weeks of use its couplings gave way. There was no way to repair them from the surface. An entirely new pipeline had to be manufactured and laid across the seabed. It did not become operational until January.

Lee was facing two seemingly insurmountable problems—lack of port capacity and limitations on rail and road transportation. Anticipating a problem, Lee had persuaded the strategic bomber commands not to disable key marshaling yards, rail lines, and other key segments of the east-west railroad corridor. Thus the Atlantic lines were left mostly intact. Actually ComZ found more useful track than expected. But even at the point when Cherbourg would be brought on line, still weeks away, the single line serving the port could initially handle only five thousand tons per day, which was not nearly enough.

The Allied armies were making great progress, and in the process they were rendering moot all the prewar planning to support those armies in the field. The Overlord plan had assumed a steady rate of progress by U.S. forces to specific goals, reaching Le Mans by D plus forty and the overall lodgment area by D plus ninety. The plan was predicated upon an armed force of a specific size reaching prescribed goals. The SHAEF planning staff estimated that a highly mobile force of only six divisions would take part in the exploitation, with an additional six operating at reduced scales of operation. Exploitation across the Seine was almost completely ruled out, as it would not be feasible until ample stocks of supplies had been amassed along the lines of communication.

But war creates its own dynamics, and the U.S. command knew the rapid advances of Patton's Third Army, along with advances by Bradley's forces and the arrival of more Allied forces in the South of France, presented a rare opportunity to administer a killing blow to the enemy. Planners were back at the drawing boards coming up with emergency exigencies. If the U.S. forces could keep four English truck companies it had borrowed, and if British engineers would assist with rail construction, and if the six-inch POL pipeline project could be accelerated, and if a thousand tons of supplies a day were airlifted—lots of ifs—maybe, just maybe an attack across the Seine could be carried out three days earlier than planned, with six divisions instead of four, though other units would be shortchanged.[16]

But there were various contingencies in the scheme. If, for example, Paris were taken, there would be a major shift in the flow of supplies, with more going to aid the civilian population.[17] But reality kept intervening in the planning. Within two weeks U.S. forces had reached the Seine with seven divisions instead of four. By August 24 Operation Overlord was essentially completed, eleven days earlier than planned. In thirty days an area that had been projected to take seventy-five days to uncover was already in Allied control. But by then the forces in the field were beginning to feel the pressure of shortages—fuel, ammunition, food, spare parts—the entire gamut of items required by mobile armies.

There would be no stopping, however, and the supply lines were to be stretched even further. The original plans had contemplated a rest of at least a month at the Seine, so that an adequate administrative organization could be organized and ample supplies brought up. The Allies needed deepwater ports. Supplies were beginning to trickle through Cherbourg, but even when that port was working at full capacity it would not be able to move enough matériel. The port that most likely had the capacity to handle a heavy load was Antwerp, but that lay farther north and was still held by the Germans. The Allies needed something closer, and they needed it now.

By July 25 the supply situation in Normandy was as good as could be expected. The Allies were moving stuff as quickly as possible across the beaches, and discharge at the minor ports and at Cherbourg was being developed as quickly as possible. The supply situation was deemed to be good at the beginning of August, although there were shortages of critical items here and there. In the first days of August deliveries to the armies were substantial, especially to Third Army. But from the beginning of the breakout Lee's ComZ had experienced difficulties in providing Patton's force with fuel. The troops were getting most of their stuff by truck, and the farther the armies went, the longer the journey to and from the beaches became. Lee has been faulted for not establishing sufficient depots near the front lines, but his force never had sufficient capability to provide daily needs, much less be amassing surpluses.

By the end of August 90 to 95 percent of all the supplies on the continent were in the base depots near the beaches, and there were virtually zero stocks between those depots and the armies three hundred miles away.[18] It was a critical situation made more critical by poor bookkeeping, lack of standardized reporting, unauthorized diversion of supplies, and Bradley's policy of deliberately leaving Lee's group in the dark about what his armies had and did not have. Bradley's First Army did not release the rear zone to ComZ until the end of July, and even then it laid claim to stocks not it its own area. There were also sharp disagreements between ComZ and the combat units about how much matériel was being delivered.

But the critical element was the absence of a coherent depot system with ample stocks in strategic places, and that was in part the result of the forces being stuck on the beach much longer than expected, as well as the rapid breakout that exceeded all expectations. ComZ had little time to assume control of the beach after Bradley reluctantly gave it up, and the supply system was about to be tested like never before. By the end of August all hope of establishing supplies in specific service areas was abandoned; it became a matter of moving stuff from the coast to the armies by whatever means could be found.[19]

And a mighty lot of stuff it was, far more than had been anticipated in the prewar planning. The massive quantities required greatly aggravated the supply shortage. The average daily supply needs totaled 66.8 pounds for every Allied soldier: 33.3 pounds of gas, oil, grease, and aircraft fuel; 8 pounds of ammunition, including aerial bombs; 7.3 pounds of engineer construction material; 7.2 pounds of rations; and sundry other stuff. The troops were eating 30 percent more food than the normal ration allocation—or at least that much food was disappearing.

British and German soldiers alike were invariably astounded by how much stuff GIS wasted; it was a luxury they did not share. Eisenhower described his ordnance losses as "extremely high," saying each month he was obliged to replace thirty-six thousand small arms, seven hundred mortars, five hundred tanks, and twenty-four hundred other vehicles. First Army alone used sixty-six thousand miles of field wire each month, stringing almost one hundred miles every hour—double its basic allotment. Of some twenty-two million jerrycans sent to France after D-Day to deliver fuel to the frontline armored units, half had disappeared, and Eisenhower asked for seven million more.[20]

Lee was held responsible for a lot of this, not because he had made mistakes but because he was the officer in charge of supply. His personal eccentricities also played a part. In this context his obsession with reducing waste in mess halls makes good sense. But it was Eisenhower and SHAEF that made the decisions to let Patton race ahead without regard for the supply situation. Lee was left to contend with the ever more severe shortages, especially of fuel.

The answer—the only answer that appeared on Lee's radar screen—was trucks and more trucks, and by now he was wishing the War Department had given him all of the 240 truck companies he had requested. ComZ began sending truckloads of supplies directly from the rear depots to the front lines via the newly constituted Red Ball Express.[21] Seven thousand trucks were pressed into service hauling vital supplies to the combat units, mainly the First and Third Armies, which were farther away from the supplies on the coast with each passing day. The trucks were carting more than four thousand tons of cargo each day on what were typically three-day round-trips to the front.

The Red Ball Express generated lots of press coverage, in part because most of the drivers were African American. At that point in the European war few African Americans were permitted to serve in combat units. Most all of them ended up in service and supply, which meant most of them worked for Lee, which was fine with him. One of the reasons Lee was so unpopular with his fellow officers was his unabashed advocacy of opportunity for African Americans.

There is something uniquely American about the appeal of driving trucks hell for leather along narrow roads through enemy-infested country. The scattered truck convoys delivering matériel and fuel to the advancing armies sometimes got lost and were easy pickings for isolated enemy forces that had been bypassed in the great advance, but that went with the territory. Lee's people tried to keep tabs on the trucks. Military police posted twenty-five thousand road signs in English and French, and small spotter planes tried to monitor the traffic flow. A one-way system of roads was mapped out, creating a huge loop that gradually expanded to keep up with the advancing armies. Only Red Ball trucks were allowed on the circuit.

But the Red Ball Express was burning three hundred thousand gallons of vital gasoline each day, which was roughly equivalent to the consumption of three armored divisions in combat. The trucks were seriously overloaded—sometimes with up to ten tons of cargo on trucks designed to haul two and a half tons. The twenty-five-mile-per-hour speed limit was observed no more closely on the French roads than back in the United States. The Red Ball was tasked to deliver eighty-two thousand tons by September 5, and it delivered eighty-nine thousand, but at a cost. The wrecks came fast and furious. On one notorious stretch of bad road eight gasoline semitrailers in one convoy flipped over, followed by eight more the following day.

Naturally the wear and tear on the vehicles was debilitating. Every day five thousand tires became unusable. Engines broke down continually, but the troops had few mechanics to repair them, insufficient spare parts, and practically no repair facilities. In a short period of time more than nine thousand U.S. military trucks were littering French highways at a time when they were critically needed.

All those trucks laden with goodies invited pilferage, and there was plenty of it, some by the French but probably more by the Americans. Food, cigarettes, and fuel could be bartered with the locals for wine and women. Men in combat facing the prospect of violent death any day are notoriously inclined to seize whatever pleasures they can whenever they can. Some men of course are inclined that way even when there is no war. Much of the pilferage was by Lee's own troops, who by then numbered in the hundreds of thousands. They had the most ready access to the cornucopia of goods being transported. The temptations were irresistible for many.

In an effort to stem the stealing Lee requested thirteen infantry battalions to use as guards. Over Bradley's bitter protest—his disdain for Lee was apparently limitless—Eisenhower gave Lee five battalions, with "shoot-to-kill" authority. Soldiers in that environment did not necessarily need authority to shoot to kill, but in this case they would have been shooting their fellow soldiers and the occasional French citizen.[22]

The Red Ball Express overall moved some four hundred thousand tons of supplies in three months, but at a steep cost. Gradually ComZ was bringing the French railroads back on line, repairing tracks and bridges that had been destroyed in the Allied bombing and bringing in engines and flatcars. Trains were vastly superior to trucks for moving supplies. A single train could haul the same amount as four hundred trucks. Some eighteen thousand men—including five thousand prisoners of war—were rebuilding the rail system.

Rick Atkinson reports in the third volume of his trilogy that thirty-two trains left Cherbourg over a single, reconditioned track on August 15, "creeping across bridges at ten miles per hour, on a two-day trip to Le Mans. A line to Paris opened on September 1, and by the end of the month almost five thousand miles of track had been refurbished."[23]

There were not enough skilled railroad workers, however. Two dozen army railway battalions were brought in from as far away as Persia and Peoria. Atkinson writes that "the Army used 200,000 rail cars in France, of which 31,000 were shipped in pieces from the United States, assembled in Britain, and ferried across the Channel," including freight cars, flatcars, tank cars, gondolas, cabooses, and thirteen hundred muscular American train engines. "By year's end, eleven thousand miles of French and Belgian track had been rebuilt, along with 241 rail bridges," Atkinson notes.[24]

There remained a problem with too few accessible ports, as well as dozens of ships moored in the channel still waiting to be unloaded. More than fifty ports had been studied by Overlord planners for possible use. Lee pared that number down to about thirty-six, of which half, mostly smaller ones, played a small role. The port of Brest was an early objective, but it was too far west of the action and Lee was skeptical it would be of much use.[25]

As it happened, the invasion of southern France, which Churchill had opposed so adamantly, made a major contribution to the shipping and supply problems. In the autumn of 1944 the port in Marseille and other harbors in southern France brought in about one-third of all the Allied supplies.[26] Meanwhile Cherbourg's cargo capacity eventually tripled to a respectable twenty-two thousand tons a day. But even with all that, the SHAEF planners knew that coming operations would still overwhelm the existing capacity. Gradually all eyes were turning toward the great harbor of Antwerp.

But first Lee's eyes were focused on a goal nearer to hand—Paris.

CHAPTER FIFTEEN

Taking the City of Light

Paris is a moveable feast.

—ERNEST HEMINGWAY

Patton's race across France and the steady advance of troops from the south posed the great question: what was to be done about Paris? Eisenhower was skittish about it. He feared if the Allies took Paris he would need four thousand tons of fuel and food a day to support the populace. There was also the fear that the Germans would defend the city, leading to massive violence that would kill thousands of people and wreak tremendous damage. Eisenhower had decided back during Overlord planning that a French division should take the lead in liberating the capital city, presumably assuming responsibility for law and order thereafter and leaving the Allies free to pursue the Germans.

It was imperative that the Allies decide what to do and do it quickly. Hitler had given orders to German troops to burn the city, but the local commander, Gen. Dietrich von Choltitz, for one reason or another failed to follow through. How much credit he deserves for saving the city from destruction is a matter of dispute. With the Allies closing in and most German troops actively fighting with the combat armies, Choltitz lacked the resources to trash such a great metropolis. He had only five thousand men in the city and another twenty thousand at defensive positions outside the city limits. It takes a lot of people to trash a really big city. Choltitz decided to skedaddle instead.

But the Allies had no way of knowing this at the time. They needed to send in the French, and the only French leader with sufficient credibility to pull that off was Charles de Gaulle, leader of the Free French, who was chomping at the bit to do it. But it was a tricky situation. The Paris police had worked closely with the Germans, and their loyalty to de Gaulle was highly questionable. In fact just about everyone's loyalty to de Gaulle was questionable.

There was also a major impediment to the de Gaulle plan—President Roosevelt, who despised de Gaulle and had issued orders to keep him out of the reentry plans. There transpired a spate of communications between Europe and Washington as Eisenhower gradually prevailed upon Marshall and others to dissuade FDR from his anti–de Gaulle vendetta. (It was never exactly clear why FDR despised de Gaulle so much, but it was a fairly common malady of the time. Like Lee, de Gaulle had a way of alienating people.)

On August 24 the French forces entered Paris just as the Germans were pulling out. There was little fighting or destruction. A few days later Eisenhower sent in the Twenty-Eighth Infantry Division, commanded by Gen. Norman Cota, who had distinguished himself at Omaha Beach. The Twenty-Eighth made a big show of marching around the Arc de Triomphe and down the Champs-Élysées. They marched on through town and were soon back at work fighting the Germans.[1]

Eisenhower had promised de Gaulle that the Americans would not commandeer Paris facilities the way the arrogant Germans had done. But somehow Lee never got the memo, or if he did he was unimpressed. The Germans were barely out of sight when Lee began moving his headquarters into the city.[2]

At the time Lee's headquarters was still at Valognes, where about eleven thousand ComZ personnel were living in crude facilities. (Lee himself was ensconced in a chateau—he was never fond of roughing it.) They were all working from hastily erected tents and huts. The actual order to move to Paris was issued by Lee's chief of staff, Brig. Gen. Royal B. Lord, allegedly without Lee's knowledge, but Lord knew his boss. Certainly there is no record of Lee admonishing Lord for his temerity. On September 1 Lord sent a forward echelon to Paris, and within two weeks almost the entire organization was in the French capital, some of its members coming directly from London and the rest from Valognes. The move involved close to thirty thousand people—a total that would grow as the year wore on.

This shift of ComZ sparked an uproar among combat commanders. At a time when fuel and other materials were in short supply, Lee's people were diverting scarce resources to a move that many deemed unnecessary. Even worse, the action distracted Lee's people from their work. Beetle Smith said the move was responsible for delays and difficulties in communications with the War Department back in Washington. SHAEF depended on ComZ for its communications back home.

Eisenhower was slow to find out about Lee's move. He was dealing with other things, including a debilitating knee injury, and logistics always came last on his agenda anyway, but when he did hear about it he went ballistic. He had of course promised the French there would be no Allied takeover of Paris. On September 13 he had Smith write a strong letter of reprimand to Lee in Eisenhower's name, insisting that he stop "the entry into Paris of every individual who is not needed at that spot for an essential duty." Upon reflection he realized he could not order Lee out of Paris because that would consume another two weeks and even more fuel. There was a war to be fought. But he still laid it on Lee. "I regard the influx into Paris of American personnel, including your headquarters, as extremely unwise," he stated, "and I want the whole matter readjusted and corrected as rapidly as it can be without interfering with operations of the fighting troops."[3]

"The personal satisfaction we would have had in throwing them out," Smith said later, "would not have justified the further disruption of service."[4]

By this time Lee had apparently taken his measure of Eisenhower and seemed unfazed by the criticism. For starters he had staked out three suites for his personal use in the Hôtel Majestic and had taken up permanent residence in the Hôtel George V, while his troops spread out across town, taking control of virtually every other hotel. In any event he had perfectly good reasons for the move. Paris was the center of French railways and roads, the historical heart of the nation. One could not travel very far by road or rail in France without going through Paris. It was the obvious place for ComZ headquarters. "In fairness to Lee, Paris was really the only choice for ComZ headquarters," D. K. R. Crosswell writes.[5]

But most of Lee's colleagues were as incensed as Eisenhower. "From rags to riches," Everett Hughes wrote. "From the heat in Valognes to the [Hôtel] King George V—from mud and rain and cold water to beauty, rest and hot water."[6] In retrospect it does appear that Lee's move was the right one. Paris was the center of the country. It made sense for ComZ to be there, but Lee paid a price. His reputation took a severe beating and his relationship with Eisenhower was strained. The army commanders who were already on his case were particularly upset with him over this action. When Bradley, now heading up the Twelfth Army Group, heard about it, he was even more incensed. "No one can compute the cost of that move in lost truck tonnage on the front," Bradley complained. "Field forces in combat have always begrudged the supply services their rear echelon comforts," he said. "But when the infantry learned that ComZ's comforts had been multiplied by the charms of Paris, the injustice rankled all the deeper and festered throughout the war."[7]

Eisenhower was slow to give up his vision of Paris as a leave center for front-line troops who had earned a bit of R&R. He reluctantly authorized Lee to keep his headquarters in Paris but ordered him to cease immediately bringing in personnel who were not expressly needed there and to conduct a survey of all units to see which ones could be put elsewhere. Lee dithered. A few units were moved out, but even more moved in. Lee's headquarters quickly became the nerve center of the ETO's administrative activities.[8] By now ComZ comprised almost five hundred thousand troops—one out of every four GIs on the European continent.[9]

They had no computers in those days, no smartphones or laptops. So Lee's entry into Paris meant the arrival of tens of thousands of clerks with their typewriters and adding machines, a huge telephone exchange, and numerous strange-looking coding devices. U.S. forces, not all of them Lee's, took over 655 hotels in Paris, give or take a few. (After complaints from French officials, Smith did dissuade Lee from taking over the public school buildings.[10]) Rick Atkinson reports that ComZ took over 315 of the hotels for its own use, put 48 others on notice, and laid claim to another 3,000 Paris houses and apartments, with a preference for the more swanky places. Before long many French were complaining that the American takeover of Paris was more extensive than that of the Germans.

Lee was by no means alone in his conquest of Paris. While lambasting Lee for moving into Paris, Eisenhower and SHAEF set up shop just outside the city in Versailles, the famous palace of Louis XIV, the Sun King. Eventually almost two thousand houses in the Versailles area were taken over to house twenty-four thousand Allied garrison troops.

Old Louis had nothing on Lee, who stood at the head of his own empire. It was during this period that Lee's reputation, already outsized, began to take on larger-than-life proportions, as he became the butt of rumors and jokes shared among both senior officers and enlisted men. More people began to notice his curious habit of wearing six stars on his helmet. He always appeared in public dressed to the hilt, with all of his military decorations on display. He was hardly the only general to do this, but there was something about Lee that rubbed people the wrong way. "General Lee continued to be a controversial personality throughout the history of the theater," Roland Ruppenthal writes, "owing in part to the anomalous position which he held. But the controversy over the SOS (now ComZ) was heightened by his personal traits. Heavy on ceremony, somewhat forbidding in manner and appearance, and occasionally tactless in exercising authority which he regarded to be within the province of the SOS, General Lee often aroused suspicions and created opposition where support might have been forthcoming."[11]

In his memoirs Lee recounts that he began every day with prayer at the altar, and he always made sure he was near an altar. He insisted that his retinue of aides and assistants accompany him to church every day and often two or three times on Sunday. Many other senior officers were devout in their faith, but few wore their religion on their sleeves like Lee did. Lee believed Christians were expected by the Lord to witness for their faith, and he was a full-time witness. In retrospect he comes across more as an evangelical than a traditional Episcopalian.

Lee did dwell on ceremony. He expected every subordinate approaching him to salute at ten paces and to be dressed appropriately, which is to say, according to rigorous military decorum. Again, many officers—including Patton—were fastidious about dress and demanded the same among their subordinates, but somehow Lee's devotion to military convention stuck out from all the others. When Lee visited sick and injured troops in a hospital, which he did frequently, the hospital staff quickly learned the rules: dress up, stop all operations, pour liquor down the toilet. One surgeon claimed that even the soldiers in beds were required to lie at attention and those in wheelchairs had to remain at attention until Lee called at ease.[12]

Lee continued his war on waste amid a population of warriors who reveled in waste, while he lived a life of luxury, at least compared to the troops fighting the war. At the Hôtel Majestic, where he kept three suites, he also had a piano and presumably someone to play it at appropriate times. The street that ran by the hotel became known as the Avenue de Salute because military personnel were positioned there to take the names of anyone who failed to exhibit the proper military courtesy. He kept suites at other hotels for his personal use. The Hôtel George V was his official residence, and the front entrance on the street was kept clear for his personal vehicles.

Lee was efficient and well ahead of his time in some areas—in particular race relations. He was honest, circumspect, and free of vices. But he didn't share the common pastimes of his fellow senior officers, such as playing golf or bridge, like Eisenhower. He lacked the common touch and apparently any sense of how his personal habits were compromising his reputation. According to Atkinson, the army's chief surgeon (whom he does not name) in Europe admitted that Lee was "nobody I'd ever want to go fishing with for a week."[13] Unless of course you would enjoy spending a week in prayer and meditation.

But there was little fishing to be done. There was a war to be won, and Lee had a key role to play—getting the supplies to the troops in the field. As soon as he had his people in their new headquarters, it was back to work, trying to move supplies from the beach to the front lines, which were getting ever farther away.

While everyone was dumping on Lee for his move to Paris and all the fuel and time that effort consumed, SHAEF also moved twice in a three-week period in September, ending up in Versailles, while other senior commanders were themselves moving into Paris. Much of the griping about Lee was typical military behavior. "They always gripe about supply people," Beetle Smith, one of Lee's most ardent critics, said. "It is always the contention of the armies that rear echelons keep all the best men and the best supplies. I can't answer whether it was correct or not, but I imagine ComZ ate all right."[14]

Lee had long since abandoned the original supply plans of Overlord made necessary by Bradley's delay in establishing a rear, Patton's breakout, and the unplanned move to Paris. He was basically "winging it" and ended up with demands from the front line driving the war machine, not supply from the rear, as dictated by established military doctrine. By August 30 two main rail lines had extended service into Paris, and by September 18 another line had connected Paris to Liège. The choke point was Paris. Supplies were being moved from Chartres and Dreux to points east of the capital, a process that took five days. Once again Lee's people found themselves moving huge quantities of matériel as quickly as they could, much of it unrequested and unneeded because they often did not know what was in the boxes. The result was masses of matériel and traffic snarls east of Paris.

There remained vast stores of matériel on the ships lingering off the coast. Winter clothing, for example, had a low priority and remained afloat. This would create a major problem as the troops got closer to Germany and farther north as winter rolled around. Suddenly frostbite and trench foot set in, taking badly needed troops out of action. When that happened, ComZ suddenly began shipping winter clothing forward, most of it by air, but staff first had to figure out which ships it was on.[15]

For the time being, however, the focus remained mainly on ammunition.[16] At the end of September Lee appealed to the War Department for faster shipments of heavy artillery ammunition into the ETO. "There is a serious shortage of heavy artillery ammunition for current operations," he noted. "Troops are facing heavily fortified positions and in the opinion of the [field] force commanders concerned only concentrations of heavy artillery fire will reduce these positions without disproportionate loss of life."[17]

Actually there were vast stores of ammunition near Normandy, but nobody knew what was where. ComZ could not easily rectify the problem because according to its records the system was functioning properly. In a practice initiated by Bradley and subsequently copied by others the numbers were being deliberately manipulated.

But there was reason to hope the great supply snafu would soon be unsnarled. On September 4 British forces finally captured Antwerp. On the river Schelde and linked to the North Sea by the Westerschelde estuary, Antwerp is one of the great ports of the world. Unlike other ports wrested from the Germans, Antwerp was virtually undamaged. This was a major disaster for the Germans, and the suddenness of the achievement left them stunned. "You had barely crossed the Somme," Gen. Alfred Jodl said after the war, "and suddenly one or two of your armored divisions were at the gates of Antwerp."[18]

The fall of Antwerp—and in usable condition—lifted the spirits of Lee and ComZ, which suddenly lost interest in rebuilding smaller ports such as the one at Le Havre.[19] Antwerp was only 65 miles from Liège compared to 400 miles for Cherbourg. Even Nancy, the forward depot for the Third Army, was only 250 miles by rail from Antwerp, but it was more than 400 miles from Cherbourg. Unlike other ports on tidal streams, it could receive large seagoing vessels at all stages of the tide, for even the minimum depth along the quays in the river was 27 feet. Furthermore the Schelde was more than 500 yards wide at Antwerp, thus permitting easy maneuvering of the largest ships. Also the extensive rail access to Antwerp meant that the effort to support a division was only about a third of what it was for Cherbourg. On September 14 Lee reported to Eisenhower his opinion that most of the Allied ports would eventually be provided by Antwerp, Rotterdam, and Amsterdam. He suggested that development of other ports henceforward be limited to Cherbourg, Le Havre, and other north coast locations. The beaches were to remain in use, but the total tonnage coming in there was expected to drop substantially.

Lee was unduly optimistic, as he often was. Although the Germans had not trashed Antwerp the way they did Cherbourg, it remained a work in progress. All up and down the river and estuary the Germans had laid mines, which had to be removed slowly. It was a long water access to the port, and the Germans were still getting close enough to disrupt shipping. They were also bombarding the port area with the new buzz bombs, Hitler's much ballyhooed "wonder weapon," that were wreaking havoc in Great Britain. The bombs were inaccurate, but they made a big impression when they hit. Thus the work was progressing under fire.

Meanwhile movement of supplies across the beaches was declining because of inclement weather and also because at Cherbourg the handling of troop convoys and their equipment was putting additional strain on the facilities. The once bright hopes for the port of Brest, finally captured on September 25, were coming to naught. The damage was too severe, and eventually Lee, who had been skeptical about Brest all along, gave up on the port altogether. "The war ended with not a single cargo ship or troopship having berthed at Brest," Atkinson writes.[20]

Everyone pinned their hopes on Antwerp. Eisenhower predicted it would have "the effect of a blood transfusion" on the entire supply operation, but as time went by he became discouraged by slow progress in getting the port working. "As you know," he said in a memo to Smith, "I am terribly anxious about Antwerp, not only the capture of its approaches, but the getting of the port to working instantaneously thereafter."[21]

Thus the beaches continued to provide the main access for the influx of cargo and equipment and would continue to do so well into November. The challenge was exacerbated by bad weather, which turned the roads beyond the beaches into quagmires. Overall use of the beaches had made a major contribution to the supply challenge. In twenty-four weeks of operation they had received about two million tons of cargo (55 percent of the total brought in up to that time), had discharged 287,500 vehicles of all types, and debarked 1,602,000 men.

As previously noted, while the American Mulberry A had been destroyed, the British Mulberry B continued to work well for several weeks, and eventually it was moving more American than British supplies and people. It helped relieve some of the shipping backlog that had continued to develop off the coast. Mulberry B contin-

TAKING THE CITY OF LIGHT

ued to operate until November 19, the same day that discharge over Omaha Beach ceased.[22]

There remained the problem of clearing mines from the waterways to Antwerp and securing access to the waterways from which the Germans were ambushing any and all shipping trying to make the transit. Antwerp did not begin receiving full shiploads until November 28.

CHAPTER SIXTEEN

Lee in the Crosshairs

Gens Lee and Hughes don't get on.

—KAY SUMMERSBY, Eisenhower's driver and companion

The rapid advance of Patton's Third Army coupled with the German reluctance to retreat resulted in an encirclement of the German Seventh Army. Although the Allies were too slow to close the trap completely in the Falaise-Argentan pocket and some German troops escaped, it was still a major debacle for Hitler's troops.[1] The German troops were caught in a pincers, being pummeled simultaneously from the air and from the artillery of Allied troops surrounding them. Three thousand Allied guns ranged the kill zone. With guidance from aerial spotters the gunners walked white phosphorus and high explosives up and down the enemy ranks. Everything the artillery missed the aircraft found. "I saw a truck crew, sitting on the steps of a farmhouse, dejectedly looking at the burning wreckage of their vehicles in the road," a Spitfire pilot said. "So I shot them up as well."[2] A French farmer observing the scene compared it to the last act of the Valkyrie. "We were surrounded by fire," he said.[3] The scene of carnage was one that few who saw it ever forgot. The German Seventh Army was effectively destroyed.

But Hitler had other armies. The American armies were still moving fast, too fast for the supply system to keep up. As a result, they had already used up their operational reserves by the time they reached the Seine. "Since rail lines and pipelines could not be pushed forward quickly enough, motor transport facilities were strained to the breaking point attempting to meet even the barest maintenance needs," Roland Ruppenthal writes. "The Communications Zone consequently found it impossible to establish stocks in advance depots."[4]

The plan called for the armies to pause when they reached the Seine, regroup, and bring up supplies. But the armies crossed the Seine on the run, captured Paris, and kept going after the Germans without pause. The destruction of the German Seventh Army and disintegration of other German units offered opportunities that Eisenhower, Patton, and Bradley were loath to ignore even if they had been inclined to, which they weren't. They were aggressive warriors and were determined to seize every opportunity.

But these decisions carried with them a supply challenge out of proportion to planned capabilities. Supply depots were scattered thinly over northern France and were simply unable to meet the demands being put upon them.[5] Troops in the field, desperate for fuel and food and cigarettes, resorted to hijacking convoys and to other irregular practices that fostered resentment and threatened the integrity of the system.[6]

It wasn't just a matter of having fuel to keep the tanks moving. The Allied forces had entered the fray with masses of brand-new trucks and tanks, but tremendous demands were being put upon them by the Red Ball Express and others, and by September they were beginning to break down.[7] There were insufficient spare parts, maintenance facilities, and trained mechanics. Every decision to let one combat group go forward meant diversion of supplies from other groups. But Eisenhower believed he had the Germans on the defensive, and he and others had learned that when you had the Germans on the run, you dared not let up. Given just a few days to rest and reorganize, they came back at you in full force. It was a disciplined army, and even a disaster like Falaise could not unravel its cohesion.

Britain's General Montgomery continued his demands for a dramatic thrust into Germany and in apparent obedience to that scheme came up with Operation Market Garden, a wild notion that seemed totally out of character for the conservative Brit.[8] His strategic goal was to encircle the heart of German industry, the Ruhr, in a pincer movement. The northern end of the pincer would circumvent the northern end of the Siegfried line, giving easier access into Germany. The aim of Operation Market Garden was to establish the northern end of a pincer ready to project deeper into Germany. Allied forces would project north from Belgium, sixty miles (ninety-seven kilometers) through the Netherlands, cross the Rhine, and consolidate north of Arnhem on the Dutch-German border ready to close the pincer.

The operation employed force concentration, massing airborne forces, whose tactical objectives were to secure the bridges, with armored ground units advancing rapidly thanks to airborne support and then consolidating north of Arnhem. The operation required the seizure of the bridges across the Maas (Meuse) River and two arms of the Rhine (the Waal and the Lower Rhine) together with crossings over several smaller canals and tributaries.

Montgomery was noted for his insistence on adequate supplies before undertaking any operation, but his troops were ill equipped for this one. He asked SHAEF for a thousand tons of supplies a day to be flown into Brussels. Beetle Smith pointed out that such a haul was beyond the capability of U.S. aircraft. After talking to Eisenhower, Smith told Lee "to make every effort to transport by motor truck" at least five hundred tons into the British zone.[9] Shifting supplies to Operation Market Garden meant that three American divisions would be effectively demobilized, at least for a while. Eisenhower was willing to take the risk, but it was a poor decision. The Germans did not cooperate, and Market Garden came to naught.

People up and down the line were growing increasingly frustrated by the lack of symmetry between the combat arms and the supply columns. As Bradley told Patton, the total tonnages that ComZ could guarantee to deliver were sufficient to support the attacks of only one of the American armies if all the other forces reverted to defensive operations. Logistic limitations had imposed a straitjacket on tactical plans. The fighting men in the field were exasperated: they were often reduced to firing a few artillery rounds per day and often had only a few rounds for their rifles. This untenable situation was the result of tactical decisions, made by Eisenhower and SHAEF, that failed to harmonize and prioritize operations and ignored the opinions of the Americans' own logisticians, namely John C. H. Lee. "Preoccupied with operational questions, Eisenhower expected the supply services to run themselves and never grasped the gravity of the potential crisis until the logistical situation had deteriorated to the point where it hamstrung operations," D. K. R. Crosswell writes. "By then it was too late to do much about it."[10]

While Market Garden was getting under way on September 17,

Bradley and Hodges were meeting in secret, bemoaning their lack of supplies, and ranting about Lee.[11] The supply situation was deterring progress all along the line, putting into question the invasion of Germany. The latest crisis concerned an alleged shortage of artillery ammunition. Lee's people promised to deliver three thousand tons of ammunition via emergency airlifts, but the aircraft were grounded by bad weather and could not deliver.

The lack of an adequate supply chain was undermining the entire war effort, causing tremendous anxiety among the senior leadership. Most of this frustration was vented upon Lee and ComZ. Beetle Smith was hearing a steady drumbeat about Lee from Bradley, Patton, Hodges, and others. They were riled up about Lee's move to Paris, which they believed was depriving troops of the full benefits of a dedicated rest center. Echoing an argument that had begun back in Great Britain, they said Lee should not exercise theater-wide control over the allocation of labor and supply because his command, ComZ, had a vested interest in protecting its own domain, to which the combat commands played second fiddle. Smith would have liked to lop off Lee's head, or at least bring him to heel, but without Eisenhower's backing he lacked the authority. A staff officer in the U.S. Army cannot give orders to a lieutenant general in a separate command.

Most of the combat generals hated Lee, but at the same time they were afraid of him; their fear did nothing to ameliorate their animus. On one occasion in October Lee paid a call on Third Army headquarters. Patton rolled out the red carpet as if they were old friends of long standing. Lee was greeted with an honor guard and the Third Army band and then treated to a lavish lunch. The record does not say if Lee took gifts to Patton, but that was his normal mode of operation. If so, he probably took Patton cigars. Old Blood and Guts smoked about twenty cigars each day.

Hughes, who had served early on as Lee's chief of staff, had morphed into one of his fiercest critics. In a meeting with Eisenhower on September 30 Hughes made a compelling case that the supply situation was in tatters, mainly because of the lack of a major port and the wastage of trucks. Yet Hughes said Lee was frittering away his time in Paris worrying about what type of uniform ComZ men should wear. "Gens Lee and Hughes don't get on," Kay Summersby, Eisenhower's comely chauffeur, noted in her diary. It was an astute observation of the obvious.[12] Hughes was advocating removal of the trucks from ComZ and their reassignment to Bradley, an idea unlikely to make a favorable impression on Lee. Eisenhower turned Hughes down on that one.

Despite their differences Hughes and Lee set out together on an inspection trip on October 3. "Lee was on a schedule which, to Hughes' irritation, only allotted thirty minutes for the inspection of U.S. First Army," Alexander Lovelace writes. "However, Lee made the mistake at the end of the short inspection of asking Hughes if he had any questions for the First Army Commander, Courtney Hodges. Seeing the opportunity to start a fight and destroy the inspection schedule, Hughes attempted to get Hodges to demand more transportation. Hodges, however, was passive on the topic, leaving Hughes to note disgustedly that 'We don't command, we collaborate and compromise.'"[13]

Lee and Hughes went on to pay a visit to the advance section (ADSEC) of ComZ. They inspected supply depots, hospitals, and railheads, ending the day with a briefing. Hughes was coming down with a cold or perhaps the flu that would immobilize him for the rest of the month, and standing in the rain with Lee for hours did not improve his temperament. At some point Lee's assistant chief for supplies implied consciously or unconsciously that the service elements belonged to him personally, or at least that was what Hughes thought he said. Hughes stood and asserted that the supply sections answered to the commanding general, not staff officers. Hughes said he "hated to see men in the rear who thought they knew more about what the man at the front needed than the man at the front did," Lovelace writes. "Lee jumped up and tried to laugh off Hughes' remarks by joking that the General was an old Leavenworth instructor who was not acquainted with the Army Service Forces' new methods. Hughes was not amused."[14]

By the end of September the western front had arisen much like the one of the earlier world conflict, though the trenches were not as well developed. The line ran along the eastern border of Belgium and along the western edge of the Ardennes and the western foot-hills of the Vosges Mountains. At this juncture the armies paused for several weeks, gave the troops some badly needed rest, and brought up supplies from the beaches and minor ports. Meanwhile the engineers and logisticians repaired railroads and bridges. October was a frustrating month, but the pause did not mean a cessation of fighting. After weeks of intense pressure from Eisenhower, the Twenty-First Army Group under Montgomery finally got its act together to focus on clearing the water approaches to Antwerp.

Lee of course was deeply committed to Antwerp, which SHAEF had concluded was big enough to handle supply needs for both the American and the British forces. But first it had to be repaired, and it was even more important that the long waterways into the port be cleared of mines and obstructions put there by the Germans. The Germans also had to be driven far enough away that they could not bombard shipping. In anticipation of that effort, on September 19 SHAEF instructed Lee to send a senior planner to the Twenty-First Army Group headquarters to work out plans for the base layout and for sharing the port's facilities. Lee arranged a conference of the Americans and British at Antwerp for September 24–26, and they proceeded to work out an agreement for allocation of storage, for use of rail lines, and for the port's command organization. They also decided which army would be responsible for different reconstruction jobs.

But clearing the waterways and rehabilitation was to take a long time, mainly because Montgomery had given it a low priority and it was in his Twenty-First Army's sector. But by November 7, at long last, Montgomery's armies had cleared the Germans from the banks of the waterways and the many islands in the Schelde estuary. By the end of the month Antwerp would be living up to its promise as the gateway for mountains of supplies, to Lee's great relief. But that was still weeks away.[15]

All of this was still pie in the sky in October, when desultory fighting continued all along the front. Bradley's Twelfth Army Group pounded the German defenders at Aachen and then began a long, bloody siege through the forbidding Hürtgen Forest—a decision that remains controversial to this day.[16] It was hard fighting in a primeval forest seemingly designed for defense. The forest cover was so dense that Allied mastery of the skies was little help. It took months and tens of thousands of casualties. The Allies could just as easily have bypassed that wasteland and left the Germans there to rot, as MacArthur was doing to many Japanese troops on isolated Pacific Islands. But a curious stubbornness was at work among old men wearing the stars, and young men had to pay for it.

One of the unlucky ones sent into the Hürtgen was Capt. Van Mayhall, who had served under Lee in Great Britain as a lieutenant. By October he was serving as G-2, an intelligence officer, on the staff of General Weaver, his favorite "fighting general" in the war zone and the commander of the Eighth Division. "We soon found out that the Hurtgen Forest was a terrible place to fight a battle," he recalls. "It was an area where a reforestation project had been going on for years. Some of the woods were so thick a man could hardly push his way through. It had been fought over, back and forth; mines had been laid all over the place and nobody knew where they were. The incoming artillery would burst in the trees, which was much more effective than bursting on the ground, sending tree limbs crashing down. The patrols that were sent out sometimes couldn't find their way back because of the thick undergrowth."[17]

"Clearing Aachen and the Hürtgen Forest consumed two months of fighting and gutted eight American divisions, to no strategic advantage," Crosswell writes.[18]

In October the most critical struggle of the Allies was logistics. The French rail, canal, and road systems were being put back into operation. American engineers continued to improve and upgrade the ports of Cherbourg and Marseille. And last but not least Lee's ComZ finally began to establish and stock a system of forward depots to support operations along the German border. In the South of France Brig. Gen. Tom Larkin, one of Lee's former chiefs of staff, pushed a gas pipeline north from the coast of Provence all the way to Dijon. Much of this matériel went to the Sixth Army Group, which under General Devers was performing prodigious feats. Most of the Sixth Army Group consisted of French soldiers now fighting to free their own country, but they lacked a credible supply system of their own. Lee had to supply them too. He was making substantive progress against all of his supply challenges, but the "dump Lee" movement continued apace.

As if to underscore Lee's perilous position, October also brought a brief tour of the ETO by the army's chief of staff, George Marshall, who wanted to check on how his armies were doing. (Actually it was Marshall's pending visit that prompted Eisenhower to put serious pressure on Montgomery to clear the approaches to Antwerp.) Eisenhower and Smith met Marshall at Orly Airport on October 6. Eisenhower went with Marshall to Bradley's headquarters in Verdun the next day, stayed with them all day, and then returned to Paris that evening.

Marshall was immediately confronted with the seriousness of the supply situation, in particular the shipping backlog in the English Channel and the shortage of artillery ammunition among the combat groups. There he got an earful about Lee. "Bradley, Patton, Hodges and their staffs provided him with chapter and verse on the many failings of Lee and ComZ—that the movement into Paris had deprived combat soldiers of the full benefits of a rest center in the capital; that Lee should not exercise theater-wide control over the allocation of manpower and supply because ComZ possessed a vested interest in satisfying its own establishment's needs in preference to those of the combat zone; that SHAEF could not superintend the flow of replacements and supply because of the submergence of ETO and the chiefs of services inside ComZ headquarters," Crosswell states. "Marshall proved all too ready to accept the legitimacy of these complaints."[19]

But instead of focusing on Lee, Marshall zeroed in on Beetle Smith. "What made me tired was these things weren't looked into," Crosswell writes. "That was Bedell Smith's great error."[20] Actually Smith had looked into "these things" in some depth and had long since decided that Lee had to go, but he had been unable to persuade Eisenhower. While the generals on the beach fussed and fumed about Lee, there was a more significant threat to Lee in Washington. Robert Patterson, undersecretary of war, had gone over the status of supply in the Mediterranean and Europe with Somervell in August when he had visited. Along with Lee, Patterson and Somervell inspected several sos sites in Great Britain before moving on to Cherbourg.

True to form, Lee entertained the duo in fine style at his chateau near Cherbourg and then took them to meet with Eisenhower and Patton. Lee always orchestrated these meet-and-greet sessions, trying to put his best foot forward. The units to be visited were warned well in advance. Lee made sure his guests saw what he wanted them to see. "Somervell bought the Potemkin village Lee sold him," Crosswell writes, "but Patterson did not. As the civilian head of the mobilization effort, Patterson knew a thing or two about logistics structures and functions. Far from being disposed to swallow Lee's glossy assurances, Patterson saw a supply structure rent by dissension and distrust."[21]

As a result of all this, Lee apparently had both the army chief of staff and the undersecretary of war after his scalp.[22] Patterson suggested to Marshall three officers he believed could replace Lee and do a better job: Lt. Gen. Lucius Clay, Lt. Gen. Leroy Lutes, and Maj. Gen. Henry Aurand. Marshall endorsed this plan, suggesting those three should be permanently attached to the ETO. Somervell was reduced to playing defense. He agreed to "lend" Clay and Lutes, two of his most valuable officers, but was happy to say goodbye to Aurand, who was not an essential cog in Somervell's machine.

Upon Patterson's return to Washington, Marshall cabled Eisenhower that he had gained the "definite impression" that the "assignment of Lutes, Clay and Aurand" would greatly improve SHAEF's supply situation. "Investigation here discloses that I can assign Aurand to you at once, that Clay can be loaned for a 2 or 3 month period beginning next week and that Lutes can be sent for a period of about 1 month."[23] Marshall had made it clear he shared the view that Lee should be replaced, but he made it equally clear that it was Eisenhower's decision. It was an integral part of the military culture, one of the basic traditions of the U.S. Army, that the senior commander should respect the prerogatives of his subordinates. There was nothing sacrosanct about senior officers; they had no job security. During the hard days of battle in 1944 one division commander after another was relieved.

But three-star generals—in Lee's case, make it six stars—were at a different level. Eisenhower was hearing the same complaints about Lee that Marshall heard. He knew there was a problem with ComZ. He could sack Lee, change the system, or do both. He decided to do none of the above. He feared such a dramatic solution might create an even worse problem.

But he had to tread carefully with Marshall. He replied to Marshall that he was sure the three officers mentioned would be a great help: "I sincerely trust that General Clay particularly can start to this theater without delay."[24] The esteemed historian Jean Edward Smith interprets this as a decision by Eisenhower to replace Lee with Clay. Certainly Clay thought so. "But when Clay arrived at SHAEF in early October, Ike had changed his mind about relieving Lee," Smith writes. "Given time to reflect, Eisenhower concluded that the logistics shortfall was not entirely Lee's fault. Ike told Clay he was sorry, but since victory was in sight, he had decided to stick with Lee." Lee did have unquestioned organizing talents, and what was most important was that he had gotten the Allies across the channel—for which Eisenhower was profoundly grateful. He was sorry, Ike told Clay, but since victory was in sight, he had decided to go the rest of the way with Lee. "The supply system might not work perfectly, but at least it worked, and he didn't have to swap horses in the middle of the stream."[25]

But it seems doubtful that was ever Eisenhower's intent, since Somervell had made it clear he could only have Clay for two to three months. More likely Eisenhower was being diplomatic, in an effort to accommodate Marshall without upending his organization. When Clay arrived, Eisenhower asked Clay "to go down and take over the Normandy base section and try to clean up the shipping mess at Cherbourg."[26]

Lucius Clay would have to be on anyone's short list of the most qualified army officers of World War II, and if there was anyone in the system who could probably have done a better job than Lee, despite the incredibly difficult situation, it had to have been Clay.[27] At the time he was Somervell's second in command—the key guy working with domestic industry to channel military supplies across the sea, not only to Europe but to the Pacific theater as well. The son of a former U.S. senator from Georgia, Clay was raised with a keen political sense. He used it to great effect in the Corps of Engineers during the Great Depression, when the corps was engaged in a variety of public works projects. He nourished a long list of useful contacts in Congress. He built a dam and lake in the district of House Speaker Sam Rayburn, who remained forever in his debt. Marshall and Somervell were not oblivious to Clay's political connections. It's hard to believe either of them wanted him to be in Europe, and Somervell had made it clear he was a temporary loan.

After World War II Clay was sent to Germany as high commissioner. Although he had no great love of the Germans and did not speak the language, he recognized that West Germany had to recover economically and politically if it were to remain out of the communist camp. He earned the trust of the Germans, helped them develop a viable democratic government, and eventually rebuilt their economy. He is known as the father of the Berlin airlift, but that was only one of the feathers in his cap. He more than any other single individual is responsible for creating modern Germany.

For such a man a bottleneck at a small port was chump change. "When I got down to Normandy I saw what the problem was," Clay told Jean Edward Smith many years later.

> Patton and Bradley were being held up because they couldn't get supplies, yet there were a hundred ships tied up in Cherbourg and off Omaha and Utah beaches. It was a bottleneck that was slowing down the attack, and it resulted primarily from the fact that we had had to use the port facilities in Normandy far more than we had thought, because Montgomery was way behind in taking Antwerp, and nobody could persuade him to make a frontal assault.
>
> Because of the delay in taking Antwerp, we were having to put pressure on these areas, which were not really designed for this type of traffic. We also found a great deal more destruction at Le Havre than we had anticipated, and we were having difficulty restoring it. Brest we didn't capture until much later. So the only ports we had to support the entire front were Cherbourg, and Omaha and Utah beaches—and the British with their "Mulberry," a floating

dock that was assembled in Britain and floated across the Channel, and really wasn't designed for that much usage.

This tie-up also contributed to our shipping crisis. Obviously, if we could unload the ships sitting off Cherbourg and not use them as floating warehouses, we'd have nothing like the shortage of ships that people in Washington were complaining about. This was one of our troubles. We had literally a hundred ships lying offshore and we were unloading maybe two or three a day.[28]

The essential problem to Clay was too many chefs in the kitchen. After a bit of a tussle with Lee, Clay persuaded the people in Normandy to work for him, not Lee: "We had a very experienced port commander who for years was director of the Port of Philadelphia. The only trouble was that he was being so hounded by higher staffs checking up on what he was doing that the poor fellow was spending all his time explaining why he wasn't doing the job that he was perfectly capable of doing."[29]

Clay asked him if he could run the port. "Yes," he replied, "if you can take all of these other things off my shoulders—and if you can give me control of the port railroad."[30]

Clay agreed to that and said that no staff person under Lee or anyone else for that matter would interfere. He gave the port commander seventy-two hours to resolve the snafu, and that was all he needed. The more serious problem was all the stuff coming across the beaches and being stacked up in muddy farm fields three and a half times faster than ComZ could move it out. "We knew where everything was, but it didn't make a goddamned bit of difference, because we couldn't get to it," Clay said. "Obviously with the front moving forward, our input into those beaches should have been less than our output. But it was just the reverse. All we were doing was transferring the ship bottleneck into a worse bottleneck on the ground. And so I stopped unloading over the beaches. There wasn't a damn bit of sense in unloading ships at Omaha and Utah beaches if you couldn't move the supplies forward."[31]

It took Clay less than a month to resolve the imbroglio, after which he went back to Washington and resumed work for Somervell. All of this of course made Lee look bad or, one might say, even worse, but if he was embarrassed, he gave no sign of it. "Clay has already proved most helpful," Lee wrote Somervell. "He has more than deserved the Bronze Star which we have dignified by awarding one to him—along with Hodges and Huebner for their cracking the Siegfried line. Clay's cracking open the Cherbourg beach situation was no less important."[32]

Eisenhower had promised Clay a division command, but it was not forthcoming. Clay returned to Washington disappointed. "It's very frustrating to have lived through two wars as an Army officer," he said later, "and to have not been, even for a short period of time, on any active military duty during the war."[33]

CHAPTER SEVENTEEN

Stalemate on the Western Front

To get peace, you've got to fight like hell for it.
—GEN. DWIGHT D. EISENHOWER

"The failure to open Antwerp," said Col. William Whipple, chief of the SHAEF Logistical Plans Branch, in early October, "is jeopardizing the administrative soundness of the entire winter campaign."[1] It was with great relief that Eisenhower, Lee, and just about everyone else greeted the news that Montgomery was at long last clearing the way to Antwerp, sending the First Canadian Army to clear the estuary of mines and drive the remaining Germans far enough away that they could not impede shipping. General Marshall warned Eisenhower late in October not to put all of his eggs in one basket— not to rely too much on one port like Antwerp, which because of its size and importance offered a rich target for the enemy.

"General Ike had replied to the Chief of Staff that far from having 'all of our eggs in one basket,' in Antwerp, every other port capable of producing supplies is being developed to the maximum," Eisenhower's aide Butcher noted in his diary. "An explosion of an ammunition ship, which might be caused in several ways, including hits by rockets or flying bombs, would cause a setback in any port."[2]

Lee had negotiated with the British to share control of Antwerp, but Eisenhower overruled him for fear of confusion of responsibility. He decreed the port would be controlled by the British. The long-awaited opening of the port occurred November 28, when a Liberty ship named the *James B. Weaver* pulled in carrying organizational equipment for the port headquarters and a party of war correspondents.

Logistical planners had figured Antwerp could be unloading 15,000 tons a day in December, 21,500 tons per day in January, and 22,500 tons per day by March. Those proved modest goals. By the end of the first week the port had reached the 10,000-ton mark, and by the second week it was averaging 19,000 tons per day, accounting for almost half of the U.S.-origin matériel discharged on the continent, not counting Marseille in the southern sector.[3]

But Marshall's warning to Eisenhower proved prescient. At Antwerp the Allies encountered the same problem they had had in Cherbourg and on the beaches—lack of storage space.[4] It had been the Antwerp port practice in peacetime to clear incoming cargo immediately after it was unloaded. The port lacked facilities for storing large quantities of goods. Within two weeks of the port's opening, about eighty-five thousand tons of cargo had already accumulated in sheds and under tarpaulins behind the quays.[5] A major part of the problem was a shortage of railway cars, which was alleviated by the middle of December. Another part of the problem was the new German V-bombs, the pilotless weapons (anticipating modern drones) that were being launched at Britain. The Germans redirected many of these destructive weapons to Antwerp, but they proved as inaccurate there as they had in Britain. They caused tremendous death and destruction when they did hit, but they rarely struck the intended targets.

Meanwhile Lee's group was making substantive progress using the means at its disposal, which by now included an active port at Cherbourg and the new operation at Marseille. On November 16 the Red Ball Express ceased operations; on that same day the Normandy beaches closed down. In the course of its eighty-one days of operations the Red Ball had carried a total of 412,193 tons of supplies, some initially to the Chartres depot area, some directly to the armies in the field, and in the last stages to the rail transfer points in Paris. With an average of 5,088 tons delivered per day, the total ton mileage came to nearly 122 million. Overall some thirty thousand men had been involved in the Motor Transport Service by the end of 1944, about three-fourths of them African Americans.

But this success got lost in the continuing contretemps between the battle commands and ComZ. According to Bradley's staff, the armies needed 650 tons per division per day to fight effectively but were receiving only 550 tons per division, 400 of which were delivered by ComZ and the remainder by their own transportation. The combat units were particularly incensed by ComZ's practice of shipping them supplies they had not requested and would not need in the immediate future. To them this was an inexcusable waste of time and fuel. But the requisitioned materials were not always available for loading on a particular day, and since ComZ did not want to see empty space on delivery trucks and trains, it shipped things the battle units presumably would need eventually. ComZ was simply filling all the available shipping space.[6]

Despite their carping, the armies were well supplied. In the last ten days of October ComZ reported deliveries of 10,000 tons to the Twelfth Army Group and under 1,000 tons to the Ninth Air Force. But even with these reduced deliveries the armies were able to expand their stockpiles. October was a relatively quiet month on the battlefield, so the combat units were able to accumulate savings. By the end of the month stocks of the Twelfth Army Group totaled more than 155,000 tons—a substantial inventory by any fair reckoning.

The fact that the armies were able to accumulate surpluses at a time when deliveries were sparse seemed to confirm to ComZ that the fighting units were overzealous in their requisitioning. From the first hours on the beaches on D-Day Bradley had made it a practice not to give ComZ an accounting of his supplies, or at least not an accurate accounting. Lee suspected the First Army in particular of taking for granted the advantage in supply that it had enjoyed since D-Day and thought it made a habit of asking for the moon.

Lack of confidence in ComZ was clearly prevalent among senior officers of the combat units, but their complaints often fell on deaf ears at Lee's headquarters. For example, ComZ questioned the urgency of army demands for items listed as "critically short," such as barber kits and handkerchiefs.[7] There was a constant tug-of-war going on between the combat units and ComZ that served no one well. It had become habitual.

The range of complaints varied significantly among the combat units. Patton's Third Army, which had always operated on a shoestring even at the best of times, accepted the shortages of the autumn months with relative equanimity, sometimes even failing to ask for enough.[8] The Ninth Army, under Lt. Gen. William Simpson, had a reputation for consistently efficient staff work, at least where supplies were concerned, and in ComZ's view it could be counted on to limit its requests to actual need.

"At any rate, by late November the Communications Zone was demonstrating its ability to deliver supplies to the combat zone in considerably greater volume than was required for maintenance alone," Roland Ruppenthal writes. By early December it was clear the supply crisis had passed. First Army asked ComZ to stop shipping gasoline, and Third Army actually returned one million gallons.[9]

This progress was not apparent to the senior commanders, who continued to snipe at Lee and lobby for his dismissal. Hughes had observed the episode of Lucius Clay clearing up the backlog at Normandy with bemusement. "I'd hate to be Lee and have Ike pick my men," he recorded. "Ike says Cliff [Lee] has a great faculty of picking poor men and poor organizations. But why shouldn't Ike fire Lee if Lee can't pick proper men."[10]

Conceivably it was because Lee was getting the job done, a possibility discovered by Maj. Gen. Henry Aurand, who had come from Washington with a reputation for being smart but too full of himself for his own good. When Aurand was sent to Europe, no one told him why he was going nor did he ask. He knew only, or thought he knew, that he would be the second-ranking general in ComZ after Lee, but it isn't clear where that notion came from.[11]

Aurand wasn't sure why he was going to Europe, and the people in Europe had no idea why he came. No one met him at the airport; he had to take a taxi to SHAEF headquarters near Versailles. He had a hard time getting past the gate and found himself sitting around a long time waiting to see Beetle Smith. Eisenhower treated him a bit better, recalling that Aurand had written a manual on ammunition stocks, and asked him to try to resolve the nagging shortage of heavy artillery ammunition. Aurand made his way to Paris, where Lee, wondering what he was there for, treated him coolly, possibly because he suspected Aurand was sent to replace him. "I was not asked for by anybody in Europe," Aurand concluded.[12]

As Aurand wandered into the ammunition problem he quickly got caught up in the continuing spat between Lee and the combat commands. In fact the forward areas were crawling with officers trying to resolve the dispute over ammunition.[13] On November 12 Bradley convened a major supply conference at which Aurand produced figures on ammunition production from the War Department showing that it had reduced production in anticipation of reduced need. Brig. Gen. Raymond Moses, the Twelfth Army G-4, had his own numbers, which did not comport with those of Aurand. "These schedules won't meet the demands of the 12th Army Group," Moses said. He added that, if the Twelfth Army's rate of fire was projected over ninety days, "you haven't got that much in France." To Bradley of course it was all just more evidence that Lee's ComZ was stiffing his command, or so he claimed.[14]

Aurand may have been unwanted, but he wasn't gullible. He asked Moses how much ammunition the Twelfth Army Group was holding in reserve. "I don't know," Moses admitted. "We drop that from our records as soon as we get it." Aurand suggested Twelfth Army was sitting on a pile of ammunition "and you're hiding it." Moses denied it.[15]

Aurand went around to the First and Third Armies seeking on-the-ground information about artillery ammunition. He wanted to see the stockpiles for himself. But the officers who should have hosted him either disappeared when he showed up or refused to cooperate. "They weren't going to let anybody else count their reserve stocks," Aurand concluded after a visit to First Army.[16]

But at Ninth Army he found a totally different picture. Ninth Army's Commander Simpson and Aurand had taught together at the War College in Washington. Simpson indicated that supply of ammunition to his Ninth Army was not a problem, saying he and his staff retained "complete confidence in Lee and his ComZ."[17] Everywhere Aurand went he found huge stockpiles of ammunition along the roads "all across the rear area of the First Army," which was "a pretty wide front." Aurand concluded logically enough that First Army was running its own supply operation and accumulating secondary reserves of ammunition "instead of relying on ComZ depots for them."[18]

After the war, Aurand was still amazed by the duplicity he encountered on that tour of combat units: "I had—and still have—the impression that First Army was determined to discredit ComZ, and its secret weapon for this purpose was its concealed assets of ammunition."[19]

Aurand drafted a report of his findings and gave it to Beetle Smith on November 18. He concluded that First, Third, and Twelfth Armies did not keep inventories of ammunition, and their numbers did not correlate with those of ComZ. He said there was a conspicuous discrepancy between Lee's and Bradley's headquarters, implying that one or the other was deliberately gaming the system. This report had the potential to create a major crisis at the senior level of the high command. Predictably the senior staff of the major commands challenged Aurand's findings. He had no friends in that crowd. Smith, knowing how Eisenhower detested such confrontations, chose to believe the preferred fiction that there was a shortage of supplies coming from the United States.

Aurand also was highly critical of the command structure governing relations between the combat divisions and ComZ, as well as the overall organization. In a supposedly confidential dinner with Everett Hughes and others on November 18 Aurand waxed eloquent about his assessment of the overall command situation. He said Eisenhower was wearing too many hats and that ComZ's independent authority was causing friction. He noted that Bradley, Hughes, and Patton had no confidence in Lee, though their complaints about ammunition were devious. Aurand had lots to say about lots of things.[20] He said the "lack of an independently manned national headquarters on the US side was directly responsible for the lack of cooperation—to put it mildly—between 12th Army Group and ComZ. Good personal relationships were difficult enough to achieve without inhibiting them by poor organization." Aurand suggested Eisenhower should "set up at once a separate ETOUSA headquarters, with an adequate staff and its own commander . . . superior to Bradley and Lee."[21] The basic problem, as Aurand saw it—and his view was likely correct—was that absent close supervision, generals at the same level, such as Bradley and Lee, had trouble working together.

Aurand concluded that under the circumstances Lee's ComZ had a "well-nigh impossible job" and had done "everything humanly possible to rectify the situation," but he noted that all three commanders in Twelfth Army Group would hear nothing good about Lee. Aurand said the conflict between Bradley and Lee was deeper than a mere clash of personalities. The real problem was the "historic military mind" that "embraced strategy as the highest goal of its learning, and has despised the logician. This error runs throughout the military of the United States in particular."[22]

The army's historical disdain for logistics, Aurand contended, resulted in a lack of trained supply officers to staff large commands. Before the war Aurand had called for seven hundred officers in supply, an estimate senior command dismissed as wildly excessive. By the summer of 1944 that section of the War Department had a complement of twenty-four hundred supply officers. His fellow supply officers were aware of that history, so they listened when he spoke. Aurand said those responsible for command "lacked knowledge of the logistical art, and the basic principles of organization; or they chose to disregard one or both."[23]

Aurand said the animus and distrust between Bradley and Lee (and there is no evidence that Lee reciprocated Bradley's animus and distrust) would not have occurred had there been sensible, fixed command channels. The confusion of line commands with functional organizations, Aurand said, "was like running wire across two leads."[24] The result was short circuits. Working relationships depended on cooperation more than command, Aurand said, and the framework in the ETO was reflecting precious little cooperation. He noted that everyone there had his own numbers on ammunition, none of which coincided with the numbers in Washington.

This must have been one memorable dinner, and like the others in attendance Aurand was having a few drinks, which apparently loosened his tongue, though there is nothing in the record to suggest he was ever shy about offering his opinions when he was drinking coffee. Aurand placed much of the responsibility for the confusion on Beetle Smith, whom he said "loved power" and "dipped into ETOUSA affairs frequently, particularly on those things about which there was no question and he could seem important." Because of Smith's meddling, Aurand said, "any failure of ComZ can hardly be laid at Lee's door."[25]

Aurand said that "Lee is a soldier" and that Lee took responsibility for an array of problems that Smith could not be bothered with. Actually Smith was in agreement with Aurand about the flawed command structure and had worked on Eisenhower incessantly to change it, without result. Crosswell notes that Aurand got one thing right: the flawed organization "was ideally suited to the purposes of the skilled 'kniver-in-the-back.'"[26]

On November 19 Hughes met with Beetle Smith and suggested Aurand be sent packing. Smith summoned Aurand and told him his rank would be reduced to colonel and he would be sent home.[27] Smith had no authority to do such a thing. Crosswell concludes from this incident that Hughes and Smith were collaborating to protect Eisenhower and other generals from Aurand's criticism of the command structure. This seems unlikely since virtually all of those people had themselves been highly critical of the command structure from the beginning. Nor does Hughes's reputation suggest he would have engaged in a coverup when a solution was at hand. "Poor Henry," Hughes wrote to his wife. "How did a man who causes as much trouble as A[urand] ever get to be a commander?"[28] Smith later relented on Aurand's demotion and exile. It probably occurred to him that if Aurand returned to the War Department, he would be circulating his report about the confused management of ETO. In any event Smith had no authority to break Aurand's rank and send him home.

"Smith and [Everett] Hughes ambushed Aurand because he was another red-headed orphan from out of town," Crosswell writes. "They were not going to allow his critical study to make the rounds in the War Department, given the damage it would do to Eisenhower and all the commands in Europe. What Aurand said might have been poorly timed and ill-considered, but he was not wrong."[29]

Crosswell notes that Smith never gave Lee the benefit of the doubt and kept the heat on Eisenhower to replace Lee with Clay but that he gave up any effort for reorganization. "Lee was a stuffed shirt," Smith said after the war. "I would have liked someone else . . . it would have been so much better with a man like Clay." But Eisenhower "couldn't relieve Lee over a bunch of little things. So we kept him on. That gave him a semi-independent status. One of the crosses we had to bear. There was no other place for him. After all, you have to use the tool you have at the time."[30]

Somervell had sent not only Clay and Aurand but also Maj. Gen. Leroy Lutes of his staff to the ETO. They were all part of Somervell's delegation seeking to resolve the supply crisis, though it was never certain there actually was a supply crisis. Having given up on replacing Lee with Clay and Aurand, Smith had turned to Lutes. "Smith immediately asked me how long I would be in France," Lutes noted in his diary, "and I told him I was on loan for approximately one month to which he replied 'That was not enough.'"[31] But after a chat Lutes intimated he might get free of Somervell and Washington if offered Lee's job. Smith was clearly interested in that but said the only way that could happen would be if a major failure of some kind could be attributed to Lee. Lutes did not rise to the bait. He said he knew of no major failure of ComZ or Lee.

Somervell never wanted Lee's dismissal—if he had Lee would have been gone—but he was concerned about the turmoil among senior commanders and eager for a solution. That is why he sent Clay, Aurand, and Lutes to the ETO. Everywhere Lutes went he found confirmation of what Aurand had found. Bradley and Moses reiterated their complaints about ComZ. Patton also weighed in. Even though he had returned fuel, he insisted he was short of ammunition. Hodges, the First Army commander, was probably the most outspoken about Lee. Of all the commanders, Lutes found him "the most intolerant of any supply deficiency." He impressed Lutes as one who had never really studied the supply challenge and had no interest in doing so. "The importance of proper logistic organization in the theaters of operations was not understood within the Army," Lutes concluded. "The subject received too little attention in peacetime. Lack of doctrine governing logistics activities complicated relationships between theaters and support supply agencies."[32]

Overall Lutes gave ComZ a passing grade, telling Somervell "the supply situation in general is now in good shape at the front and [SHAEF] seem[s] satisfied that the Armies can be supported in the present push." Lutes told Eisenhower, "The machine does not move smoothly but it does run."[33]

As if to provide a distraction from the continuing Lee soap opera, Hughes on November 14 raised out of the blue an issue that no one thought was an issue—the feeding of German prisoners of war.[34] The U.S. Army was circumspect about observing the Geneva Convention in terms of providing for POWs, which included providing them with an ample diet.

For their part the Germans were relatively humane in their treatment of U.S. and British POWs, at least in the sense that they did not work them to death, as they did vast numbers of Soviet prisoners, but no one wanted to do anything that would provoke the Germans into retribution against U.S. POWs. "SHAEF has received information that the condition of Allied prisoners in German hands is definitely not good," Harry Butcher recorded on December 11. "It is feared that with the coming of winter there will be insufficient clothing and bedding. There is said to be no fuel for heat in German prison camps. Many of the Red Cross food packages, on which the Allied prisoners depend so much, have not reached the camps. Since July the German attitude toward Allied prisoners has undergone a marked change for the worse. This change is generally attributed to [SS commander] Himmler."[35]

But Hughes was concerned that the German POWs were doing too well. He had heard complaints from the French that the German POWs were eating better than the French people, which was probably true. Hughes raised the issue with Lee, who evinced no interest in the topic. Hughes persuaded Lt. Gen. Robert Littlejohn, the chief quartermaster of the ETO and the officer responsible for feeding POWs, to discuss the "problem." On December 1 Hughes took it upon himself to inform Littlejohn that the German POWs should be fed less than what was given to the French civilian population and that the Allies should avoid giving the prisoners food not even available in their own country. Littlejohn somehow gave Hughes the impression he was receptive to the complaint and would do something about it.

Hughes also raised the issue with Eisenhower, but whatever response he received is not recorded. Not long after that meeting Hughes was riding with a Col. Charles R. Codman when they passed a POW camp. It was lunchtime, so Hughes figured that was a good time to find out what was on the menu. He and Codman were welcomed by the commandant, "a plump lieutenant colonel," who provided them an excellent meal. Hughes asked what the POWs ate. His host replied that the prisoners' fare "is exactly the same as ours right here."[36] Hughes pointed out to the officer the relevant section of the Geneva Convention that the prisoners should receive perhaps a quarter or at most a third of what they had been getting at that camp.

Hughes's concern was correct. The Geneva Convention stipulated that POWs should receive an amount of food equivalent to what their active forces received. At the time the German soldiers were basically living hand to mouth. In all likelihood most of the German soldiers who found themselves in POW camps safe from flying shrapnel and eating three squares a day thought they had died and gone to heaven. By December 3 the U.S. First, Third, and Ninth Armies alone had captured more than forty thousand POWs. If they were all being fed like the ones Hughes and Codman visited, that was a tremendous food bill, one that was likely to get much larger by the end of the war—as it did. Hughes tried to focus attention on that looming issue but without much success.

His colleagues were more focused on the war. The Germans were on the ropes, or they at least appeared to be down and out. There was growing speculation among senior Allied commanders that the war would soon be over, perhaps by Christmas. But the war continued, and Eisenhower decreed there should be no winter letup. His armies were inflicting thousands of German casualties each day, and he wanted to keep up the pressure. Bradley had a great plan for a November offensive. He hoped to push the First and Ninth Armies to the Rhine and break into the Ruhr valley.

But it was to prove slow going. On November 28 the Ninth Army reached the Roer River, which was as far as it could go. Getting to the Roer had cost Hodges forty-seven thousand casualties and Simpson, ten thousand. The American troops had advanced twenty-two miles into Germany, the Rhine was more than thirty miles away, and the Americans were still bogged down in a slugfest with the Germans in the Hürtgen Forest. In the south Patton's Third Army was fighting what almost seemed like a separate war alongside the Sixth Army under Devers and getting nowhere fast.

Eisenhower remained wedded to his "broad front" plan of maintaining a symmetry all along the western front. This plan, according to the respected military analyst B. H. Liddell Hart, "would have been a good way to strain and crack the resistance of a strong and still unbeaten enemy. But it was far less suited to the actual situation, where the enemy had already collapsed, and the issue depended on exploiting their collapse so deeply and rapidly that they would have no chance to rally. That called for pursuit without a pause."[37]

There was no such pursuit, which the Germans attributed to divine intervention. Germany's Gen. Hans Speidel reported years later that German Army Group B was approaching total collapse and the door to Germany through Belgium was wide open. "Then something unexpected occurred," he wrote. "It was a German variation of the 'miracle on the Marne' for the French in 1914: the furious advance of the Allies suddenly faded away. There could be no supply difficulties with such secure lines of communication. Nor was the 'decreasing strength of the attack' the reason, as new or rested formations were being constantly brought up. The method of the Allied Supreme Command was the main reason."[38]

Speidel's view was widely shared. Germany's Gen. Günther Blumentritt, chief of staff of the entire western front until September 5, said a breakthrough northeast to the Ruhr "would have torn in pieces the weak German front and ended the war."[39] Gen. Siegfried Westphal said not a single bridge over the Rhine had been prepared for demolition: "Until the middle of October the enemy could have broken through at any point he liked with ease, and would then have been able to cross the Rhine and thrust deep into Germany almost unhindered."[40]

Of course the German generals knew their weaknesses much better than did their Allied counterparts, who continued to encounter stiff German resistance, especially in the Hürtgen Forest. What was perhaps more important, had the Allies bet all their marbles on a single thrust into Germany, the obvious candidate to lead it would have been Field Marshal Bernard Montgomery, head of the

Twenty-First Army Group. It was best positioned for such a move, and Montgomery was in fact demanding permission from Eisenhower to launch it. But the thought of a British general taking the lead role was politically untenable.

Years later Bradley put Eisenhower's decision into context: "It would give Monty too large a role in the ground command, in effect upstaging and obscuring Ike. It was a time of extreme jingoism; the American public demanded its own epic-size war heroes, and it wanted them in command at the kill." Historian Stephen Ambrose has echoed that reasoning: "Had Bradley and Patton been on the left, Eisenhower might have given greater consideration to the single-thrust concept, but handling Montgomery was another matter."[41]

Thus the Allies were basically hunkering down for the winter and resolving to finish off the Germans when spring came with rustling shade and apple blossoms filling the air.

CHAPTER EIGHTEEN

Lee's Finest Hour

> Once an army is involved in war, there is a beast in every
> fighting man which begins tugging at its chains. And a
> good officer must learn early on how to keep the beast
> under control, both in his men and in himself.
>
> —GEN. GEORGE C. MARSHALL

On December 16, 1944, there was a wedding at Eisenhower's head-quarters in Paris for a young staff officer and a Red Cross nurse. "It was a sweet ceremony, but everyone shivered," Harry Butcher recorded in his diary. "I sat there in my bridge coat—the heaviest I own—and despite that and my long heavy GI underwear, wool muffler, socks and gloves, I still shivered. General Ike sat just ahead of me in his blouse. After the wedding, the party went to the Supreme Commander's house, where the bride was kissed by the Supreme Commander."[1]

It was bitterly cold—the winter of 1944–45 would prove to be one of the coldest winters in many years—but the mood at SHAEF was upbeat. The Germans were in retreat all up and down the line. The Soviets were pressing in against the Germans from the east. Although Eisenhower warned against undue confidence, even he believed the end of the war was in sight. And it seemed his position was at last secure. The day before the wedding President Roosevelt had nominated Eisenhower to the five-star rank of General of the Army, along with Marshall, Douglas MacArthur in the Pacific, and Hap Arnold of the air force.[2] Also getting multistar treatment were Adms. William Leahy, Ernest King, and Chester Nimitz, who were named to the equivalent five-star rank of Admiral of the Fleet.

This was big stuff to the career military officers, as it represented the pinnacle of professional achievement. Ulysses S. Grant was the first general in American history to wear four stars. George Washington himself had only three as a lieutenant general, though in 1976, in honor of the bicentennial, Congress posthumously awarded him a fourth star, making him General of the Armies.

Unbeknown to the celebrants the Germans were at that moment unleashing a ferocious assault on Allied forces many miles north of Paris.[3] The senior Allied command had become lulled into complacency by the pounding the Germans had been taking and were well aware that they were getting an even worse pounding on the eastern front. But Hitler still had at least one arrow in his quiver. In early December the German army began assembling a large armored force in the Ardennes, a forested area in southeastern Belgium. Because the weather was foul and the skies cloudy, the usual air reconnaissance missed the buildup. There was evidence that something big was afoot—isolated reports of troops moving into the area and the sounds of tanks moving—but it was dismissed by the senior Allied command at SHAEF.

Here lay a critical weakness in Eisenhower's broad-front strategy. Allied troops were spread thin up and down the line but nowhere thinner than in the Ardennes. No one was expecting an attack there.[4] Bradley had deployed only four divisions, two of which were newly arrived and comprised mainly green, untested troops. Little work had been done on defensive positions. No minefields had been laid, and few foxholes had been dug in the frozen ground. The situation was ripe for disaster.

Where Bradley had four weak divisions, the Germans came with four armies—two panzer and two infantry—a total of some twenty-eight divisions with more than three hundred thousand men and close to fifteen hundred tanks. The fragile American front was overwhelmed and gave way. The implications of the assault were lost on Bradley, who at first dismissed it as a limited local incursion. The Ninth Army commander, Simpson, failed to react in any meaningful way, and Hodges at First Army apparently suffered some sort of nervous collapse. While the high command dithered, the Germans plowed forward.

Hitler may have been at the end of his rope, but he had a big plan. He wanted to drive a wedge between the British and Americans, cross the Meuse River, seize supply dumps on the other side, capture Brussels and Antwerp, and, Hitler hoped, force the Allies to sue for peace. Seizing the Allied supply dumps was key to his plan. The German units were awesome, but they were understrength and short of artillery and fuel. Whatever supply problems the Americans and British had, the Germans were in far worse shape. The German commanders had requested 500 gallons of fuel for each tank. They had to make do with 150. They were running their offensive on a shoestring.

But they were running it with determination. Hitler had another ace up his sleeve—a determined army. "Compared to the mass panic which had gripped many of its units on the western front in September, a month later the Wehrmacht presented a very different opponent," Nicholas Stargardt writes. "Allied commanders were shocked by the stiffening resistance of an enemy that they had assumed was on the point of collapse. At Supreme Headquarters of the Allied Expeditionary Force, Eisenhower called a crisis summit in November to ask why nothing had destroyed the 'will of the Wehrmacht to resist.' The psychological war experts, responsible for debriefing German prisoners of war and profiling their beliefs, were at a loss to explain it."[5]

While Eisenhower kissed the bride in Paris, the Germans were moving. "The Battle of the Bulge was Ike's finest hour as a military commander," writes Jean Edward Smith.[6] "While Bradley and Simpson dithered, and Hodges took to his bed, Eisenhower assumed control of the front and moved quickly to shore up the shoulders on either side of the German breakthrough. Patton was ordered to dispatch the 10th Armored Division to hold the line south of the penetration, and the 7th Armored of Ninth Army was given the same task to the north. With the width of the breakthrough restricted, Eisenhower turned to his strategic reserve: Matthew Ridgway's XVIII Airborne Corps, which was refitting near Reims." Smith notes that "James Gavin's 82nd Airborne Division was rushed by truck to hold the vital road junction at Saint-Vith, and the 101st was sent south to hold a similar road junction at Bastogne: two important choke points essential to the German advance."[7]

Eisenhower also told Lee to defend the Meuse crossings with whatever engineers he could scrape together, as well as to prepare the bridges for demolition.[8] Lee did not have to be told; he was already on it.[9] Smith said this was Eisenhower's finest hour, but this event would also prove to be the acid test of Lt. Gen. John "Jesus Christ Himself" Lee.

Lee already had his hands full. The opening of Antwerp brought the usual problem of congestion on the rail lines in the forward areas, with thousands of railcars bottlenecked. The sudden German assault put all of that matériel in jeopardy. The Germans were counting on taking American supplies, particularly fuel, to keep their armored divisions moving, and that goal was obvious to Lee. The German movement also threatened to cut the lines of communication with Antwerp, throwing the entire American supply system into disarray.

ComZ had supply depots and fuel dumps all over the place and directly in the path of the German advance. The most immediate danger was to the logistic stockpiles backing up the First and Ninth Armies, which also lay directly in the path of the German drive and concentrated along the Meuse between Liège and Namur and extending west to Charleroi. The German advance to the Meuse alone promised to overrun many depots and put installations north of the river within range of German artillery. Any advance beyond the Meuse would threaten to cut rail lines from the south or the lines of communication to Antwerp. That would make it virtually impossible for Lee's ComZ to support the First and Ninth Armies for combat.

ComZ was already struggling to manage the surplus of supplies coming into Antwerp, finding room to put stuff wherever it could while still supplying the basic needs of the combat units. Frantic efforts to remove stores from the German line of attack were quickly aggravating the congestion. At this juncture the First Army called on ComZ to replace a substantial loss of combat equipment it needed to continue the fight. So in effect Lee had to move vulnerable stores to the rear, away from the German advance, while still sending critical stores forward to the units in the fight.[10] It was a complex challenge in the midst of a chaotic situation.

Lee was up to the task. "General Lee immediately ordered special defense measures for all vital ComZ installations and for rail bridges, defiles and tunnels, and the chief engineer issued detailed instructions on security measures, including demolitions, for POL, discharge facilities, pipelines, pumping stations and tank farms," Roland Ruppenthal writes.[11]

Within a week some fifty-six hundred railcar loads of supplies were moved to safer locations in conjunction with thirty-seven truck companies in constant motion moving supplies and nearly 250,000 men. The evacuation got under way when ComZ began emptying two of its largest fuel depots near the small town of Malmedy, directly in the path of the German drive. The evacuation of one depot containing about 1,115,000 gallons of gasoline and related products began on December 17. Within forty-eight hours all stocks had been removed except for 124,000 gallons, which were blown up. On two occasions during this shift reconnaissance elements of a German panzer division advanced to within about a thousand yards of this depot. They came close to getting the fuel they needed but no closer. A second installation containing about 2,226,000 gallons was evacuated on the night of December 18 and was completely cleared without loss by December 22.

It was a great melee, and in a few cases the Germans did acquire some stores. Two ammunition supply points, one holding two thousand tons of ammunition and the other about eight hundred tons, were eventually overrun, though U.S. troops continued to draw from one of them at one end while the Germans were taking stuff from the other end. One depot continued to issue rations for three days under sporadic mortar and small-arms fire before it was abandoned, retaken, and drawn down and the remaining supplies burned. Attacks from German V-1 rockets destroyed about twenty-seven hundred tons of supplies of different kinds.

In his biography of Beetle Smith, which is chock-full of accounts of anti-Lee conspiracies in the American high command, D. K. R. Crosswell gives Lee high marks for his performance in this crisis. Lee, he said, "was finally given the opportunity to command in the field and supervised the removal of stores east of the Meuse, including by December 19, the bulk of the dangerously exposed POL stockpiles." Faced with its second great crisis of the campaign in northwestern Europe, "ComZ performed brilliantly this time. Lee pulled back huge stores behind the Meuse, [Gen. Royal] Lord moved the 101st Airborne to Bastogne in record time, and vital supplies went forward in huge quantities. The Bulge proved Aurand's case conclusively: Twelfth Army group and the armies had stockpiled vast reserves of ammunition. Third Army moved up 4,500 tons of ammunition per day during the last half of December—43 percent more than it expended. Time and again the lavish use of American artillery broke up German attacks, inflicting heavy casualties; more vital, it seriously delayed the German penetrations."[12]

Antony Beevor, who otherwise has little good to say about Lee in his book on the Battle of the Bulge, tips his hat to this performance. "On the second day of the offensive, First Army moved 60,000 troops into the Ardennes in just twenty-four hours," he writes. "The despised ComZ of General Lee had achieved miracles. It also managed to transport 85 percent of ordnance stocks out of German reach. Between December 17 and 26, 50,000 trucks and 248,000 men from quartermaster units shifted 2.8 million gallons of gasoline so that panzer spearheads could not refuel from captured dumps."[13]

Third Army's supply installations were not endangered because the German advance did not come that way, and on December 18 Patton was ordered to turn his right-flank corps over to the Seventh Army in the east and to reorient his main battle group to the north. He also was required to take over the VII Corps, which could no longer be controlled or supported by the First Army. "The Third Army thereupon initiated a wholesale redeployment of both combat and service units, a task which called for the closest of coordination of movements and the efficient use of transport," Ruppenthal writes. "Third Army had turned over 25 miles of front to the Seventh Army, withdrawn two corps, and completed administrative preparations for an offensive on the new axis, an accomplishment which Colonel Whipple, chief logistical planner at SHAEF, characterized as one of the most professional performances of the entire war, easily ranking with the more spectacular accomplishments of the preceding August."[14]

The focus of the Third Army move was the little crossroads town of Bastogne, which blocked the German advance.[15] The German high command decreed that the town should be overrun and used as a base of operations. Bastogne and its seven radial roads constituted "an abscess on our line of communications," according to one German commander.[16] But the Americans were determined to thwart that plan if at all possible.

The core of Bastogne's defense was the 101st Airborne Division, which had been rousted out of bed and sent hustling to the fight.[17] It was under the command of Brig. Gen. Anthony McAuliffe, who had parachuted into Normandy and later landed by glider in the Netherlands. The 101st included many green replacement troops, some without helmets or rifles. Along the way to Bastogne they passed GIS retreating from the fray. Many of the newcomers without weapons asked for arms from those retreating, who were more than glad to lighten their loads. It was an interesting picture, captured on film, of U.S. soldiers fleeing to the west and walking down one side of the road while passing the 101st guys heading toward the sound of the guns. They were all soldiers in the same army fighting for the same cause, but one group was beaten and the other wasn't—and each group understood the other.

They were all cold, bitterly cold. Lee sent an emergency convoy hauling five thousand entrenching shovels, two thousand sets of wool underwear, and five thousand pairs of arctic overshoes to Bastogne. Some twelve thousand cold, wet paratroopers and glider pilots arrived in Bastogne, where the situation was described as fluid and obscure. They were up against three divisions from the German Fifth Panzer Army. The fighting was fierce. At one point the Germans politely asked the Americans to surrender, which from their point of view seemed a reasonable course of action. The Americans had fought well and done all that loyal soldiers could do. McAuliffe's reply to the German invitation to surrender—"Nuts!"—has become part of American folklore.

But it must have seemed an empty gesture to the beleaguered troops under his command, at least for a while. Even after the skies cleared briefly on December 23 and the Allied troops began to receive supplies by air, the Germans pressed the attack. With a perimeter of only sixteen miles, every inch was under fire. By Christmas

Eve shivering soldiers were singing "O Little Town of Bethlehem" to the steady drumbeat of incoming artillery fire. Patton sent word that the Third Army was coming to their relief, but the "battling bastards of Bastogne" were running out of ammunition and food. At one point a group of despondent officers shook hands and bade each other goodbye.

But Patton was coming. It was a hard slog along icy roads against determined German opposition, but his troops kept coming. One of the forces moving that way was the Eighth Division, which had managed to survive the Hürtgen Forest, albeit it now had fewer men than before. "It was a terrible move," Mayhall recalls, adding,

It was cold. It snowed most of the time. Everything was iced over. Trucks slipped off the road, tanks broke down, men's feet were cold and sore. Lots of the men had fever—didn't even know they were sick; they just thought they were cold. If contact could have been made with the Germans and fighting could have carried on until somebody had won, it may or may not have been so bad. Oh, the days and hours that I spent trying to keep face, ears and hands warm and still hold back the chills that would run through my chest muscles. Now I know what Valley Forge was like.[18]

Patton well understood the extraordinary demands he had placed on his troops, according to biographer Carlos D'Este. When the Germans counterattacked violently across the III Corps troops' line of advance to Bastogne, resulting in heavy tank losses and in some cases compelling temporary withdrawal, Patton accepted responsibility. "It is probably my fault, because I had been insisting on day and night attacks," Patton said. "This is all right on the first or second day of the battle and when we had the enemy surprised, but after that the men get too tired. Furthermore, in this bad weather, it is very difficult for armored outfits to operate at night."[19]

Patton's decision to move toward Bastogne "doesn't sound like too much of a trick," Mayhall recalls in his autobiography, written many years later. "However, there are a few details involved in making a move like that."[20] Here Mayhall may be reflecting his experience in the sos under Lee.

There are thousands of soldiers to consider; these soldiers had to cover many miles. The infantry is happy to ride, but they are designed to walk. They must be served food; they must be supplied with clothes that can protect them from the winter weather. These are night-and-day clothes, for there are no pajamas out in the snow. There are hundreds of vehicles that have to keep rolling, needing gas, oil, grease and tires. Hundreds of tanks have to be gassed, oiled, maintained, supplied with ammunition. In a corps or army there are a lot of people whose job is to do nothing but keep the movement going in the right direction. Whatever difficulties the 3rd Army had in getting there, they came in walking and rolling and, most important, they came in shooting.[21]

Bastogne was the turning point. The last major German offensive in the west was spent. But the Germans gave ground grudgingly and quickly shifted into defensive mode. No one was predicting an early resolution of the conflict anymore, least of all Lee, who was charged to recoup the situation, supply the armies still fully engaged with the Germans as they retreated, and move the fuel and supplies back to the depots from which they had been so hastily evacuated.

He also had another concern of a more personal nature. His son, John Clifford Lee Jr., had been graduated from West Point in 1941 near the top of his class (fourth among 424) whereupon he, like his father, was assigned to the Corps of Engineers. His first assignment was in Alaska, where he located and supervised construction of airfields on the Aleutian Islands of Attu and Kiska that were to provide defense against Japanese attack.

In November 1943 he joined V Corps in England in preparation for D-Day. At some point Lee pulled rank enough to take John Jr. to personally meet Maj. Gen. Matthew Ridgway, commander of the Eighty-Second Airborne. Later Lee said he had "no regrets over having once taken my dear son to him during active operations in fulfillment of the old tradition of chivalry, to have the young squire serve the best active fighting knight we know."[22]

There was clearly a strong bond between Lee and his son. "Our close father and son relationship is recorded because it has endured," he wrote in his memoirs. "Each time my son has come home or I have visited him, we have been able to pick up where we left off and enjoy what to me has been a most delightful and intimate friendship."[23]

John Jr. landed on Omaha Beach on D-Day, was captured while making a reconnaissance on D-Day plus one, and escaped the following day. For that exploit he won the Silver Star. His father had to have known all this—he was after all in charge of military communications—but whatever anxiety he felt he kept to himself, though he surely shared it with the deity he worshipped every day.

In that conflict the sons of generals neither got preferential treatment nor sought any. The son of Lt. Gen. Alexander Patch, commander of the Seventh Army, was a company commander with the Seventy-Ninth Division, fighting under Devers in northern France, when he was killed in action. Patch and his son, who bore his name, were close. When the young man was killed, Patch took four days off to grieve. He had "recurring moments when it is hard for me to control my grief," he recalled, but his response was to "think clearly and realize" that at least his son's suffering was over.[24]

Patch was one of many senior officers whose sons were killed in action. Maj. Gen. John "Iron Mike" O'Daniel's son was killed in Operation Market Garden in September. Marshall's stepson was killed in Italy in May. Brig. Gen. Cuthbert Stern's son was killed by a land mine in October while serving in Sixth Army Group. Maj. Gen. Donald Stroh's son was killed in September. The generals accepted their losses and soldiered on.

Lee's son John Jr. was fully engaged in the Battle of the Bulge, where he once again distinguished himself. On December 23, when the battle was in full fury, he volunteered for, planned, led, and successfully executed a bridge demolition mission two and a half miles behind German lines. "En route to the objective, Major Lee skillfully bypassed enemy sentries and strongpoints and with utter disregard for his own safety made repeated reconnaissance into possible danger areas," read the commendation for his second Silver Star. "During work upon the bridge, enemy vehicles and foot troops moved constantly back and forth. Major Lee accomplished the task efficiently, silently and speedily. His technical skills and foresightedness in preparatory planning, his courageous and inspiring leadership and cool-headedness during tense moments, assured accomplishment of a mission that greatly hindered enemy movements and materially delayed his advance."[25] Major Lee was clearly a chip off the old block. Father and son survived the war. Lee Jr. later served in Korea as a colonel. In addition to the Silver Stars, he won a Bronze Star, the Legion of Merit, and the Distinguished Service Medal.

Whatever innocence the American soldiers may have still had with them by December 1944 was pretty much used up by the time they fought this terrible battle in the snow. The ferocity of the fighting was perhaps best exemplified during the massacre at Malmedy at the outset of the battle.[26] The First ss Panzer Division was probably the most powerful of all the German units. Its troopers were cocky and well trained—twenty thousand men backed by two hundred tanks and assault guns. The division's spearhead was a battle group of twenty-two hundred men led by a young colonel named Joachim Peiper. Heading west, Peiper's group took the town of Malmedy on December 17, and they gunned down about one hundred American soldiers who had surrendered. This event was of scant interest to the Germans. The ss had been killing people all over Europe for years. It was their specialty. In this case the ss were determined to sow terror in their wake, but the primary effect was to evoke the latent rage of the Americans, who from that point took a special interest in ss troops, few of whom were captured alive.

Peiper's goal was to capture American fuel dumps to keep his tanks running. A gas-guzzling panzer had to be refueled every thirty miles. Not far beyond Malmedy they reached the town of Stavelot, where there was a small fuel dump. But Lee's people got there first. The full dump was released into the road and set ablaze. Eventually Peiper's tanks had to be abandoned when they had used up all of their fuel.

Part of the German offensive was a devious plan to send in English-speaking German troops in American uniforms to sow confusion behind enemy lines. They had some small successes until word got out about it. After that everyone on the road was stopped and interrogated—even General Bradley himself. They were asked questions that presumably only an American would know—about star athletes, movie stars, and so forth. The spies were gradually rounded up and executed. Under the laws of war, such as they are, any soldier wearing the enemy's uniform is a spy and subject to that treatment. After Malmedy there was no hesitation about that business.

There were also rumors of "hit" teams sent to assassinate General Eisenhower. Rumors were rife, and for a while Eisenhower was basically confined to quarters for his own protection. The culprit in this case was likely Lee, who recorded that "proper steps were taken to protect General Eisenhower and his headquarters near Rheims. Especially during the Battle of the Bulge, there were many attempts by the enemy to send assassins through our lines. Providentially, all of them were apprehended."[27]

Lee was diligently going about his business. The partial embargo on forward shipments imposed at the outbreak of the Ardennes fight had naturally caused deliveries to the forward areas to fall off some in the first week, but by the last week of December Lee and ComZ had their machine running full bore again as the American and British armies regrouped and resumed their steady march into Germany.

One conspicuous Allied casualty of the Battle of the Bulge was the fiction that the armies lacked sufficient ammunition, in particular for heavy artillery. General Aurand had effectively punched holes in that story, but his report had been quashed. Suddenly out of the blue the armies seemed to have an abundance of ordnance, and they used it to great effect against the German offensive.

But already in response to the intense pressure the War Department back in Washington was expanding production of heavy ammunition, most of which did not come on line until the war was over. "During the war, American factories produced 408,000 rounds of 240 mm ammunition," Crosswell writes, "and American forces expended less than 30 percent of it in combat."[28]

But the containment of the German offensive left everyone in good spirits and there was little time for recriminations. "In war, one must expect the unexpected," Lee wrote. "We tried and fairly well succeeded in our efforts to predict the difficulties such as meeting the German drive in December. For that effort the Communications Zone was awarded a commendation by General Eisenhower."[29]

Lee's performance in the Ardennes crisis was impeccable and likely can be considered his "finest hour," like the accolade Jean Edward Smith extended to Eisenhower. The record does not show any plaudits for Lee's contributions from his regular tormentors—Bradley, Smith, Hodges, and Patton—but on the other hand the criticism of him subsided, and we hear no more about conspiracies to have him sent home—at least until he conspicuously embraced what was possibly his most unpopular cause.

CHAPTER NINETEEN

Lee's Advocacy of African Americans

He's worse than Ma about church.

—LT. GEN. BENJAMIN O. DAVIS SR.,

writing to his wife about Lee

In the summer of 1925 Brehon Somervell was sent to the U.S. Army War College, then located in Washington DC, where Lee would attend a few years later. It was widely seen as a gateway for promising young officers who would eventually rise to higher rank. Somervell's primary project there was an examination of the use of "Negro manpower" in wartime. He completed this study in cooperation with two other young officers at the request of the school's commandant. "The culmination of [a] year of study by the school's faculty and student body, the report portrayed the Negro as inferior to whites as a technician or fighter, and posited that Negroes, as was the practice, should be largely placed in segregated noncombat units to ensure military efficiency," John Kennedy Ohl writes.[1]

That report generated little interest because it was a fair reflection of racial attitudes in the country at that time—racial attitudes that had not evolved very much since the Reconstruction era. The reality was that African American troops had fought and distinguished themselves in every American conflict, beginning with the American Revolution, but the racist mentality of the country, particularly in the southern states, simply forbade recognition of that reality or any serious effort to upgrade the status of minorities. At every level African Americans were treated as an inferior species—indeed as a distinct species. When the Red Cross collected blood donations for wounded soldiers on the battlefields during World War II, it was careful to keep the blood donated by black troops separate from that of white troops. The National Association for the Advancement of Colored People (NAACP) objected to this practice as having no scientific basis, but science had few votes in Congress. Rep. John Rankin, chair of the House Veterans' Affairs Committee and a racist demagogue from Mississippi, lambasted the "crackpots, communists and parlor pinks in this country . . . trying to browbeat the Red Cross into taking the labels off the blood bank. . . . That seems to be one of the schemes of these fellow travelers to try to mongrelize this nation."[2]

In the nation's capital, filled to overflowing with newly hired government clerks serving the war effort, it became at times impossible to get on a bus to go to work. There was a shortage of drivers, but the private bus company, Capital Transit, refused to hire even a single black driver. In a public hearing the company president, E. D. Merrill, looking thoughtfully at the ceiling, explained that "members of the Negro race have not yet had enough years of cultural growth . . . whereas white people have had generations and generations of experience in this sort of thing."[3]

Black men could drive LSTs onto Omaha Beach and trucks in the Red Ball Express, but in the view of people like Merrill they could not be trusted to drive buses in Washington.[4] It was still the age of Jim Crow. In southern states black residents were relegated to separate water fountains and restroom facilities. Even in Washington, with its large African American population, black people were banned from most restaurants and required to sit in separate sections of theaters. And reports of lynching, usually but not always in southern states, continued to be regular fare of the newspapers, though lynchings weren't really all that newsworthy because they were so commonplace.

But World War II generated powerful forces of change, which had an impact on racial attitudes. There simply were not enough white men to fight two major wars on either side of the globe and at the same time keep the war industries running full tilt. The NAACP and other groups were pressuring the government to integrate the military forces. The Roosevelt administration as always was courting the black vote, which had belonged to the Republicans up until FDR's first election a decade before and was still volatile. The situation was ripe for change.

A division comprising black troops, the Ninety-Second, had made it to France in World War I, but it was not integrated with the American Expeditionary Force even though the senior American general, John Pershing, had received the nickname "Black Jack" allegedly

LEE'S ADVOCACY OF AFRICAN AMERICANS

because of his willingness to command black soldiers.[5] The Ninety-Second fought under French command, and despite rumors to the contrary it fought well. When World War II broke out, there were four regiments of black troops in the U.S. Army—not enough to have an impact on the war. These regiments, like the segregated units that had existed since the Civil War, had mostly white officers. Segregation and racist attitudes were the order of the day, and it was widely reflected in the treatment of black soldiers.

During 1944 the black press offered a growing chorus of criticism of the treatment of black soldiers by the military, particularly where alleged rapes of white women were concerned. "It begins to look like Negro soldiers are getting a thorough rooking in the military courts on 'rape' charges," wrote Roy Wilkins in the *New York Amsterdam News*. "Old southern prejudices which seem to permeate the whole army," opined the *Chicago Defender*, "are almost always present in court-martials to see that the Negro soldiers get sentences out of proportion to the crimes committed." According to the *Pittsburgh Courier*, "The evidence is shockingly skimpy, as it usually is where the accused is black and the judge and jury are white Americans, and the woman is white."[6]

Walter White, president of the NAACP, traveled to Great Britain in 1944 to investigate the treatment of black soldiers in the army.[7] Because Lee was a staunch advocate of African Americans and also because he had a large contingent of them under his command, he was assigned to host White during his visit. Lee gave White his usual VIP treatment, but White was not easily manipulated. After his investigation White made a variety of recommendations to Eisenhower, one of them being the establishment of a biracial, impartial board to review trials of black soldiers. "I came across innumerable instances where Negro soldiers were court-martialed, found guilty, and sentenced to long terms for minor offenses," he said.[8]

Soon after his return to the United States White received a letter from Lee urging him to demonstrate that he was "on the Team," contending that "there is no Negro problem in the European Theater of Operations, United States Army, nor has there ever been a Negro problem."[9] It is difficult to discern whether Lee actually believed this nonsense or was just doing his job, trying to quash criticism of his beloved army and to persuade White to be a team player. Then and later Lee did have a reputation for being something of a Pollyanna, always looking on the bright side of every problem and trying to put a positive spin on difficult situations.

To be sure, there were serious racial problems in the U.S. Army in those days. There were only a few black officers, the senior one being Col. Benjamin O. Davis, a veteran of the Spanish-American War. Davis had been due for retirement in 1941 when he would turn sixty-four, but in 1940—a week before Election Day, with FDR running for his third term—he was promoted to general. "He didn't get his star despite being black," Geoffrey Perret writes. "He got it because he was black."[10] FDR was campaigning for the black vote.

But Davis was carefully chosen for his debut as the nation's first black general. He was an articulate advocate of accommodation and a master of small steps forward. He knew he could not wield a sword like Alexander cutting the Gordian knot to transform the U.S. military into a racial nirvana, but by bits and pieces he could advance the cause.

The rapid expansion of the army that began in earnest in 1941 included the creation of new black regiments. Most of the new army training facilities were being built in southern states, where training could be conducted year round. That meant thousands of northern black men colliding with southern white culture that their ancestors had left behind. There were frequent episodes of violence between white and black soldiers and, more often, between black soldiers and white southern police. Davis spent the first years of his generalship investigating these incidents and trying to serve as mediator. It was a tough slog, but he somehow managed to keep his temper, avoid major disasters, and maintain his credibility.

But he could not keep track of all the relatively minor incidents that besmirched the military, not to mention the country, during those years. One account that appeared in *Yank* magazine recounted the experience of nine black soldiers traveling through the South to a new assignment and being refused service at restaurants, as was commonplace in the South. Finally the lunchroom manager at a railroad depot in Texas told them they could go around back to the kitchen for a sandwich and cup of coffee. As they went, "about two dozen German prisoners of war, with two American guards, came to the station. They entered the lunchroom, sat at the tables, had their meals served, talked, smoked, in fact had quite a swell time. I stood on the outside looking on, and I could not help but ask myself why are they treated better than we are? Why are we pushed around like cattle? If we are fighting for the same thing, if we are to die for our country, then why does the government allow such things to go on?"[11]

Despite such treatment tens of thousands of black Americans volunteered to serve, and many of them distinguished themselves. There were two all-black air units in combat in World War II: the Ninety-Ninth Pursuit Squadron and the 332nd Fighter Group. They both earned credibility and admiration in action in North Africa, Sicily, and the Italian peninsula and fought over Germany in the later stages of the war.

There were also a few all-black units on the ground. The 761st Tank Battalion served under Patton in his Twenty-Sixth Division. Patton had originally been leery of black soldiers, contending they did not have quick enough reflexes to drive tanks in battle. But still he welcomed them warmly when they showed up at the end of October: "Men, you're the first Negro tankers to ever fight in the American army. . . . I don't care what color you are so long as you go up there and kill those Kraut sonsabitches. Everyone has their eyes on you and is expecting great things from you. Most of all, your race is looking to you. Don't let them down, don't let me down."[12]

They didn't let anyone down. The 761st spent 183 days in action—an eternity on the battlefield—and earned commendations from every commander it fought under. The men in the 761st won a Medal of Honor from Congress and several Distinguished Service Crosses.[13]

Patton had actually requested that the 761st be assigned to Third Army. During the hectic great chase across France, the artillery, armored, and tank destroyer units had been intermingled without regard to race because of the desperate nature of the operation. The black soldiers performed well, and there were minimal problems with regard to racial mixing. Indeed half the field artillery battalions at Bastogne consisted of African American soldiers.

But by December 1944 most black combat units were still not integrated, and not every black unit had a sterling record. The reality was that black men who had been denied educational opportunities and decent jobs throughout their lifetimes were simply not as qualified as white soldiers for many assignments, and many of them were understandably less motivated than their white counterparts. They also accounted for a disproportionate share of military discipline problems, for which they usually received more severe punishment than white troops, usually at the hands of white officers from southern states.

But people were needed, and the military draft was remarkably unbiased about who it selected to serve. Tens of thousands of black men joined their white countrymen in the army. By 1944 they constituted about 11 percent of the army—some nine hundred thousand men.[14] The great majority of them were assigned to service units, which means that in the ETO most of them worked for Lee's ComZ. Lee was happy to have them and he kept them busy. "Every DUKW that crossed an invasion beach was driven by blacks," writes Perret. "They unloaded the ships that brought ammo and gasoline. They drove most of the trucks in the Red Ball Express."[15]

But all was not sweetness and light between the races. During the buildup for Bolero there were numerous racial incidents, usually born of resentment among white U.S. soldiers of the casual assimilation of black personnel in Great Britain, where they associated with British women and did not observe the usual protocols of segregation that prevailed in the United States. Eisenhower had been taken aback by the report filed by the NAACP's president, and he expressly requested General Davis to come and look into the causes of the problems, which apparently were a mystery to Eisenhower, and to make recommendations. It wasn't long before Davis was introduced to Lee. Not surprisingly the two of them hit it off. "From the beginning, Davis thought that Lee was sympathetic to the plight of the blacks and that he looked favorably on Davis's efforts," Marvin Fletcher writes. After spending a night in Cheltenham at Lee's headquarters, "Davis began inspection trips to the bases where black and white soldiers were stationed, usually returning to Cheltenham or London in the evening." Fletcher does not mention it, but it is safe to assume Davis was getting around on Lee's famous train.[16]

Not everyone saw that relationship the same way. "I wish you could have heard JC [Lee] with his Kansas 'suh's discussing the future of the black race with the colored apostle," Hughes wrote to his wife Kate. "Between them they had the colored soldier and the white soldiers buddies before we had arrived."[17]

Davis counted it one of his successes that he was able to persuade Lee to admit black soldiers to the officer candidate school Lee had created in England. "Blacks believed that they were not being allowed into the program because of their race," Fletcher writes. "Davis discussed the issue with General Lee, who agreed to create a board of officers, with Davis as its head, and authorized it to admit ten black candidates to the program. Later, Lee increased this number to fifteen."[18]

When Davis returned to the United States, he and Lee frequently exchanged letters. Lee wrote Davis that it had been "a distinct pleasure" to work with him, and he was happy that the two of them "seem to view all these matters with practically a single eye."[19] Davis wrote back that he hoped to find a way to work for Lee. Lee wrote a congratulatory letter to Davis on his son's fine performance flying in the air war over Italy. Lee reiterated his hope that Davis would be able to return, which finally happened in 1944 during the final stages of the Bolero buildup.

Davis ended up working on Lee's staff, and they got along "wonderfully well," according to Fletcher. "The only problem was Lee's devout Episcopalianism. He worshipped often and expected his staff to do the same. ('As bad as Ma about church,' Davis wrote his wife helplessly.)" Like many officers, Davis was a practicing Christian, but few if any were as devout as Lee.[20]

It came to pass that the Battle of the Bulge brought to the fore a critical problem that had been festering for some time—a shortage of manpower. Thanks to Lee, and despite the overwrought criticism of ComZ, the troops had ample supplies, including fuel and ammunition. What the armies did not have was enough men. There was steady attrition from combat, battle fatigue (now called post-traumatic stress), and—perhaps most important of all—trench foot. Trench foot eventually caused more than forty-six thousand men to be hospitalized, and it accounted for 9.25 percent of all casualties on the continent. Trench foot is an injury, not an infection. It is caused by long exposure to cold and wet conditions, resulting in crippling injury to the blood vessels and muscle tissues of the feet. It is characterized by discoloration and painful swelling and requires evacuation and prolonged hospital treatment. A large percentage of those so afflicted were unable to return to combat duty, and many were unable to return to any duty. Trench foot eventually resulted in the loss of approximately the strength of three divisions in the Twelfth Army Group alone.

Eisenhower and his commanders were clamoring for men, but the word from Washington was that the manpower well was running dry. The United States was supporting armies all over the world and running vast industries full bore to supply the troops. There were fewer and fewer men to induct into military service, and a growing number of these were men who had been rejected for one reason or another in earlier calls. The War Department's solution was to lean on the armies to shift more men from non-combat roles into the infantry. This demand fell on support units across the board, but the biggest reservoir of noncombat troops was in Lee's ComZ.

For the better part of a year General Marshall had been leaning on Eisenhower to make more efficient use of manpower in the ETO. He reminded the supreme commander of the experience in North Africa, where replacements had been allowed to accumulate and many of them had been used for noncombat duties. Some one hundred thousand service troops, including port labor battalions and antiaircraft units, had been held indefinitely in readiness for the invasion of southern France, which had been postponed several times. Now Marshall was urging that a single officer be in charge of manpower in the ETO—someone with sufficient rank and staff qualified to control all the casual personnel for recovery, put men coming out of hospitals to proper use, and retrain able-bodied white men in Lee's ComZ for use in the combat zone.

Lee had a better idea—shift African Americans into combat units. "Another reason many officers thought Lee unbalanced derived from his long-standing advocacy of greater rights for African Americans in the U.S. Army," D. K. R. Crosswell writes. "At the height of the Bulge, Lee seized on the opportunity and proposed that SHAEF afford black soldiers the opportunity to volunteer for combat duty."[21]

After discussing it with Eisenhower and consulting with Davis, Lee on the day after Christmas 1944 issued an order to that effect:

> The Supreme Commander desires to destroy the enemy forces and end hostilities in this theater without delay. Every available weapon at our disposal must be brought to bear upon the enemy. To this end the Theater Commander has directed the Communications Zone Commander to make the greatest possible use of limited service men within service units and to survey our entire organization in an effort to produce able bodied men for the front lines. This process of selection has been going on for some time but it is entirely possible that many men themselves, desiring to volunteer for front line service, may be able to point out methods in which they can be replaced in their present jobs. Consequently, Commanders of all grades will receive higher authority with recommendations for appropriate type of replacement. This opportunity to volunteer will be extended to all soldiers without regard to color or race, but preferences will normally be given to individuals who had had some basic training in infantry. Normally, also, transfers will be limited to the grade of Private and Private First Class unless a noncommissioned officer requests a reduction.[22]

Somehow Beetle Smith was left out of the loop on this, but when he finally did see Lee's announcement on January 3 he went ballistic. Smith did not share Lee's enthusiasm for using black soldiers. It is an open question whether anyone in the senior command did. Smith went first to Lee, telling him that using black volunteers as individual replacements in white companies was contrary to War Department policy. He said that he personally had no objection to black troops fighting alongside white soldiers in mixed units, but that they—Smith and Lee—could not presume to alter War Department policy, especially with such a volatile issue.

Predictably Smith got nowhere with Lee, who had cleared his move with Eisenhower, and at any rate this was for Lee a holy cause. "Two years ago I would have considered this the most dangerous thing that I have ever seen in regard to Negro relations," Smith told Lee. "I can't see that at all," Lee replied. "I believe it is right that colored and white soldiers should be mixed in the same company."[23]

"Lee fully understood that the integration of combat units, with the concomitant press coverage, would push the desegregation debate at home," Crosswell writes.[24] That was exactly what worried Smith. The same day Smith heard about Lee's order he sent a note to Eisenhower expressing his concerns. He warned that when the press got onto the story the inevitable "result will be that every Negro organization, pressure group and newspaper will take the attitude that, while the War Department segregates colored troops . . . against the desires of the Negro race, the Army is perfectly willing to put them in the front lines mixed in units with white soldiers, and have them do battle when an emergency arises." Smith said the order would put General Marshall in a bind, and he recommended that Lee not issue any more orders without his (Smith's) concurrence. Smith told Eisenhower that he knew more about the War Department's "difficulties with the Negro question" than any other man in the theater, including Lee and Davis, "and I say this with all due modesty."[25]

Smith had never been noted for modesty, due or undue, but Eisenhower did respond to his complaint. He rewrote Lee's order that called for volunteers "without regard to color or race" with preference for those with some infantry training. Black volunteers would be assigned to existing black tank, tank destroyer, and artillery units with any surplus "incorporated in other organizations," presumably meaning infantry.[26]

Eisenhower agreed with Smith that individual black soldiers should not be put into white units. Instead he called for new African American "units which could be substituted for white units in order that white units could be drawn out of line and rested." Marshall must have bit his lip when he read this missive. It was as if Eisenhower did not know how the replacement system worked. Early in the war Marshall had decided that replacements would be fed into the combat units one at a time or in small groups. This was contrary to established military doctrine that the most effective fighting units were those that went through basic training together and entered combat together. Men in combat form bonds and learn to work with each other. The 761st Tank Battalion, for example, had that sense of identity and unit cohesion. Everyone knew it would perform well. But feeding green recruits piecemeal into combat units was a formula for inefficiency. The new guys were outsiders who did not enjoy the confidence and support of the veterans. They did not know what they were doing, received very little guidance, and tended to get killed very quickly. They did not add much to the units' fighting ability.

But that was the system the army had. It had no facilities in Europe to train new combat units from the ground up. The only way to integrate black soldiers into the armies was through the existing system—one or a few at a time into existing units. Lee's order effectively integrated the army.

It almost defies reason to suggest that black men serving in Lee's supply services would eagerly leave their relatively safe and comfortable jobs to take positions in the shooting gallery, but thousands of them did, and they did it in a hurry, as if concerned the offer would be rescinded (which it soon was).[27] By the time Eisenhower issued his revised order, which wasn't much revised, 4,562 black troops had volunteered, including many noncommissioned officers who surrendered their stripes to take a place in the line. It was a once-in-a-lifetime opportunity for men who had been denied their manhood over a lifetime to assert it loud and clear. Once retrained as riflemen, the black troops were formed into platoons. In the Twelfth Army Group, these platoons were assigned to white infantry companies. There they were—black and white men fighting together. By all accounts the black soldiers performed well and were accepted by their white comrades, who by then would have been thankful for any help they could get. Said an artillery forward observer in the 394th Infantry, "We were short-handed and they were welcome."[28]

Even Lee's acerbic critic Stephen Ambrose gave Lee credit for this bold initiative. "Whatever his faults," Ambrose writes, "he stood tall on this one."[29]

"Among the American soldiers finally crossing the Rhine on March 12 was the 5th Platoon of 'colored' infantry mustered from volunteers to help remedy manpower shortages after the Bulge," Rick Atkinson writes. "Many had surrendered sergeant's stripes earned as cooks, drivers and laborers in black service battalions for the privilege of fighting as privates. 'Hitler was the one that got us out of the white folks' kitchen,'" one black observer wrote later.[30]

Another black soldier quoted by Atkinson got to the heart of the matter. "I am an American negro," he said, "doing my part for the American government to make the world safe for a democracy I have never known."[31] He was given that opportunity by Lt. Gen. John C. H. Lee.

CHAPTER TWENTY

Victory in Europe

Victory at all costs, victory in spite of all terror, victory however long and hard the road may be; for without victory there is no survival.

—WINSTON CHURCHILL

By mid-January the Battle of the Bulge was over and the Germans were pulling back toward their homeland, giving ground grudgingly, offering erratic mini-offensives to keep their enemies off guard. The Allies were pressing toward the last significant barrier, the Rhine River, while the Soviets pressed toward Berlin from the east. It was obvious to all, even the German high command, that the great conflict was winding down. But still the Germans kept fighting, doggedly defending the homeland. They were caught between relentless enemies with overwhelming power and a mad dictator who was determined to fight to the death—everyone's death. Hitler was reconciled to the destruction of Germany. In his view it had proven weak, let him down, and did not deserve to survive.

General Bradley, who still had not recovered from the Battle of the Bulge, was among those who believed the Germans were far from finished. "It is entirely possible," he told a War Department visitor, "for the Germans to fight bitter delaying actions until January 1, 1946."[1]

The American soldiers knew better. They knew the end was not far off, but first they had to survive the bitter, numbing cold. Eisenhower's aide Harry Butcher had been bundled up like an Alaska Native at that wedding in Paris the day of the Ardennes invasion, but he was still shivering. The soldiers on the ground living in the snow and ice were not nearly as well insulated, and they were not indoors. They were outside in the wind.

As a general rule soldiers do not like to fight in the ice and snow. They would rather sit by a fire, sip cognac, and warm their feet. By the winter of 1945 many of the American soldiers were having fantasies about that fire—and the cognac.

On one occasion when Eisenhower visited the troops at the front an antiaircraft gunner offered him 500 francs for his fleece-lined boots. Eisenhower pulled off the boots and offered them to the soldier in exchange for "one dead Kraut."[2] But dead Nazis were relatively easy to come by; fleece-lined boots were not. The soldiers complained that instead of getting trench foot they were susceptible to "trench body." They stuffed newspapers in their underwear and fashioned thick socks from wool blankets. Nothing seemed to help very much in the mind-numbing cold of that unforgettable winter. Without doubt some of the victims of trench foot incurred it deliberately to escape the frozen hell in which they were caught. Such an exigency did not incur the dishonor associated with obviously self-inflicted wounds, which also were fairly common. All of the combatants in the air and on the ground figured it was just a numbers game until they were killed; eventually their numbers would come up.

In fact the American soldiers were poorly equipped for the winter weather. There had long been some meager supplies of winter clothes on ships floating off the Normandy coast, but efforts to retrieve them always took a backseat to demands for more ammunition and artillery shells.[3]

There were reasons for the dearth of winter clothing. It was an unusually severe winter. The soldiers had gone through much more clothing than expected in the summer and fall fighting, requiring the shipment of more regular uniforms. And the soldiers also had some bad habits with regard to the proper fitting of clothing. But the newspapers back home—notably the *Washington Post*—began printing stories about freezing GIs. That got the attention of the ETO high command, which, then as now, really hated bad press.

The primary problems were that the combat commands in the theater were slow to place orders for winter clothing and that they had failed to adopt combat-tested items recommended by the War Department. The high command was aware that winter was coming—it always did, and at about the same time each year. But combat commanders tended to put such considerations on the back burner, along with most logistics concerns.

The Germans suffered from the same mental block.[4] When Hitler first sent his armies into the Soviet Union, he was expecting a quick victory so there was no provision for winter clothing. When the Russian winter set in—and that phenomenon made the European winter look like spring by comparison—the Nazi war machine was totally unprepared. The soldiers lacked winter clothing, and German industry was not geared up to produce it. The Nazi leadership appealed to the German people to donate winter coats and boots, and millions of them responded, but they came too late for many German soldiers, who froze to death in that icy wasteland.

On the American side there had been little preparation for the previous winter, when GIs had suffered terribly in Italy. It became clear the standard U.S. Army uniform was not adequate. In response to reports from the combat units the War Department got involved in developing more insulated clothing for a new uniform. The new uniform comprised such items as the M1943 sateen field jacket, a high-neck wool sweater, combat service boots, shoepacs, and leather gloves with wool inserts.

The shoepac was basically a combination rubber-and-leather boot that gave better protection against water than either a leather boot or the cloth overshoe.[5] It was designed to fit over two pairs of socks, one of them a heavy ski sock, and it had removable insoles. But though the shoepac was probably the best boot the army came up with, it did not protect against trench foot, at least not in the Seventh Army, which was 90 percent equipped with shoepacs and still had many cases of trench foot.

Unfortunately the military bureaucrats could never agree on a final package, and there was much bickering back and forth, which deferred final decisions. Eisenhower weighed in with his concern that whatever they came up with should look smart and military. Clothing that is warm and insulated tends to be bulky. This contradiction would prove a major issue because there was a lead time of several months to design and manufacture hundreds of thousands of new uniforms.

Yet another factor that deterred sensible decision making about winter clothing was optimism that the war would soon be over, a rosy scenario that came to the fore after Patton's August breakout.[6] The Office of the Quartermaster General, which had lead responsibility for clothing, expressed confidence as early as August 15, 1944, that the war would not see another winter.[7] On that same day it submitted a requisition for winter clothing to the War Department to clothe one army of 353,000 men for a severe winter, but it was purely a precautionary measure. The United States had many armies in Europe. That requisition, as inadequate as it was, was already a month late when it got to Washington.

The main guy in the line of fire on the clothing fiasco was Maj. Gen. Robert Littlejohn, the SHAEF quartermaster, who was surely as responsible as anyone for the situation. As late as September he had written to Maj. Gen. Edmund Gregory, the quartermaster general in Washington, that "you and I know that the serious fighting cannot long continue."[8] Even Lee fell for this willful fantasy. That same month ComZ asked all supply services to review their requirements and prepare stop orders in anticipation of the end of hostilities.

As the fighting continued and winter drew nearer, this optimism faded and the senior command began to fret about keeping the troops from freezing. Keeping feet warm and dry was the major challenge in avoiding the debilitating trench foot. Shoes and boots that had been fitted during the summer, when men were wearing light woolen or cotton socks, became too tight when worn with two or more pairs of heavy woolen socks. This led to greater demand for larger sizes, but there simply weren't enough to go around and there weren't nearly enough shoepacs.

As the weeks wore on and soldiers in the field struggled against frostbite and trench foot, the army resorted to improvisation. The most distinct characteristic of the army uniform at this time was its lack of standardization.[9] By late winter some seventy different items had been issued, including six types of jackets and seven types of trousers, creating insurmountable supply problems, which Lee of course was expected to handle. Despite efforts to expedite delivery of clothing, front-line troops fought through a large part of the winter inadequately clothed. The Third Army reported as early as November that 60 percent of its troops lacked sweaters, 50 percent lacked a fourth blanket, and 20 percent lacked overshoes of the proper size.

Clothing was the direct responsibility of Littlejohn as was food, but the quartermaster had to work with ComZ to move stuff from one point to another, and in that he had to wait in line like everyone else. At one point in the Normandy phase Littlejohn had fourteen trains loaded with rations but could not move them without locomotives, which Lee was using elsewhere. At the small port of Le Havre Littlejohn found a million blankets or their equivalent aboard a ship waiting to unloaded. Five times the vessel was refused a berth because priority went to ammunition. That priority of course was set by the supreme commander, but Lee had to take the blame.

When he could get no action from Lee's Transportation Corps, Littlejohn got clever. He also had a sixty-day supply of cigarettes on ships offshore, so he began withholding cigarettes from the ration packs, knowing the GIS would raise a ruckus. They did. He got clearance for the cigarette ships and also brought in the winter gear.[10]

But then he could not get transportation to move the heavy clothing to the forward areas. "Clothing was at the bottom of the priority list until the weather turned real bad at the front," Littlejohn said.[11]

D. K. R. Crosswell reports that in late October Littlejohn met with Bradley and Lee to plead for trucks to move the winter clothing to the front-line troops. He was rebuffed. "The men are tough; we must go forward as long as we can," Bradley said. "This necessitates ammunition and gasoline be given top priority."[12] Throughout October the demand for ammunition, particularly artillery ammunition, drove everything else into its wake. Lee was simply responding to demands from the combat commands. He sent an appeal to the War Department for more bullets. "There is a serious shortage of heavy artillery ammunition in the theater," he wrote. "Troops are facing heavily fortified positions and in the opinion of [the] field force commanders concerned only concentrations of heavy artillery fire will reduce these positions without disproportionate loss of life."[13]

Thus even Lee, who of all people should have known better, got caught up in the loud lament about a nonexistent shortage of artillery ammunition. Tons of artillery ammunition sat in supply dumps near the Normandy beaches, but Lee had no way of knowing that because they were controlled by Bradley and the other combat commands, who were simply not cooperating with Lee or his command. They refused to give an honest accounting of what they had on hand. Lee could not fix the problem of missing ammunition, and by October some units actually were running short because according to his records there should have been no problem.[14]

The situation was a typical army snafu caused by people behaving badly. The War Department had actually shut down production of heavy artillery shells because it believed the combat commands already had more than enough—which they did. The combat commanders continued to claim grave shortages. And Lee's ComZ insisted it had moved forward more than enough stocks. The War Department was right. When the war ended, only about 30 percent of the heavy artillery shells dispatched to the ETO had been fired. Lee was right. ComZ had sent more than enough artillery ammo to the combat units. The problem was that the combat commands, particularly Bradley's, were deliberately fudging the records, when they even bothered to keep records. No one knew how much ammo actually went forward. "If the commands knew," Crosswell writes, "they secreted that fact."[15]

As for the winter clothing, when the winter finally set in with a vengeance and the soldiers were freezing, Lee changed the priorities and started moving winter clothing forward as fast as possible, more than half of it by air. But before it all got there the Germans attacked in the Ardennes, pushing the schedule back. Many of the soldiers defending Bastogne were wearing summer gear.

But the bigger problem—the heart of the matter—was that the senior command under Eisenhower never established priorities to reconcile the needs of combat units with the capacity of supply units. "Eisenhower expected the supply services to run themselves and never grasped the gravity of the potential crisis until the logistical situation had deteriorated to the point where it hamstrung operations," Crosswell writes. "By then it was too late to do much about it."[16]

One would think that given Lee's superb performance in the Battle of the Bulge, the moving of useful supplies out of the path of the German juggernaut, and the increasingly obvious reality that victory was near to hand, the senior officers might have relented a bit in their endless campaign against Lee. Such was not the case. On January 7, 1945, Somervell traveled to Versailles, where he met with Eisenhower, and later he and Lee had dinner with Eisenhower. There is no record of their conversation, but Crosswell speculates that Somervell was there at the behest of Undersecretary of War Robert Patterson and to relieve Lee if he found it necessary.[17] After meeting with several people Somervell concluded that ComZ had failed in some respects, but for political and morale reasons he did not want to relieve Lee or any of his senior staff.

The key criticism against Lee at this juncture seemed to be an unfavorable comparison between ComZ and its counterpart, SOLOC, the supply system supporting Devers's Sixth Army Group, which had landed in southern France and was then fighting at the far right of the Allied advance. SOLOC was under the command of Brig. Gen. Thomas Larkin, who had been Lee's first chief of staff in Great Britain. Lee in fact had been instrumental in helping Larkin get his general's star.

As head of SOLOC, Larkin was actually Lee's deputy and had been since late October, but Lee had done little toward merging SOLOC with ComZ. Larkin's performance had won him favorable attention. Even though Larkin was supporting the French army as well as Devers's troops, he used far fewer people than Lee did and seemed to have fewer bottlenecks. Thus Somervell recommended to Eisenhower that he insert Larkin's people into ComZ headquarters as deputies in control of actual operations.

Even though he had a good relationship with Larkin, Lee regarded this initiative as a comedown for him, which it was, and he did not like it very much. But he knew better than to directly confront Somervell, who met with Lee's staff and told them what was going down. Then Somervell met with Larkin's staff and told them they would have control but without the title. They could not have liked that very much. He warned them they would receive a frosty reception at ComZ, and they did. Somervell stayed around a while to make sure his reorganization took root. He held a mass meeting of most of the senior staff of the new combined organization. He said

ComZ's supply of the ETO "has been one of the most magnificent achievements of the war" but that greater efficiency was needed.[18] Then he went back to Washington and left Lee and Larkin to sort out the mess he had created.

Lee knew when to bend. He said Larkin's organization had "set the standard since coming into this theater . . . doing more with less," which Lee said was the highest tribute of efficiency. "These gentlemen," he said, referring to Larkin's staff, "will leaven the rest of us." Eisenhower signed off on the new structure, which took effect January 29.[19]

While all of this was going on, Marshall sent Maj. Gen. Ben Lear to SHAEF to work on the manpower problem, which remained a major headache for the combat commands. Eisenhower decreed that Lear would serve as deputy theater commander in charge of ComZ, which was yet another comedown for Lee, but Lear's headquarters would be at Versailles, not Paris. Here again Eisenhower had second thoughts and backtracked, possibly after hearing from Lee. Three days later he issued an edict giving Lear responsibility for "coordinating, controlling and directing" the functions of the general inspectorate and theater manpower sections.[20] So Lear became the manpower czar, but that did not address his relationship with Lee.

Ever the diplomat, Lee invited Lear to one of his fancy dinners, no doubt hoping to establish a friendly rapport, but that was something Lee was never very good at.[21] Lear responded by asserting that his mandate made him commander of ComZ. Hughes was there and reported that Lee was "hurt," but maybe hurt was not the correct term. Lee saw that his position was clearly threatened, and he was as skilled an infighter as any officer in the theater. By this time Hughes had taken the measure of Lee. "I am wagering," he said to a friend, "that passive resistance as advocated by Gandhi and practiced by a high ranking friend of ours [Lee] will win."[22]

Lear may have had Lee in his sights, but his real enemy was Beetle Smith, who did not care for Lear's expansive mandate. Smith moved quickly, blocking Lear's efforts to take SHAEF and ComZ personnel. "Between Smith and Lee—two well-schooled practitioners of bureaucratic gamesmanship—Lear did not have a chance,"

Crosswell concludes. Lear later noted that he had never seen "so much politics as in ETO."[23]

Basically Lee continued as before in the absence of anyone looking over his shoulder telling him otherwise. Certainly that was not a role to which Larkin aspired. Without question there were snags in Lee's system that were causing problems. Many commands despaired of getting needed items through channels in a timely manner and fell into the habit of sending personal representatives to ComZ headquarters in Paris in quest of shipments long overdue and perhaps lost. To Somervell this use of "bloodhounds" was perhaps the most conclusive evidence that things were amiss. But Somervell recognized also that much of the problem stemmed from the sudden expansion of the breakout, which had imposed tasks on ComZ that were simply beyond its capabilities.

In any event Lee had a reputation, fair or unfair, for attaching more importance to appearance than to the substance of things. "To the field commands this attitude, plus his personal unpopularity, unfortunately tended to magnify the inefficiencies" of ComZ, Roland Ruppenthal writes.[24]

Unpopular or not, Lee folded Larkin and Lear into his organization and soldiered on. The senior commander and his staff were still at SHAEF deciding overall policies, but the official theater staff worked under Lee at ComZ headquarters in Paris. Although Lee no longer held the title of deputy theater commander for supply and administration, his authority had not really changed because his headquarters handled virtually all supply and administrative matters for the theater, including correspondence with the War Department in Washington. It continued to issue theater-wide instructions on administrative matters. In a strange way Lee had lost direct authority, but his staff was still running the war and answering to him. In practical terms Lee was still the guy in charge.

The direct involvement of Somervell had not clarified the lines of authority between SHAEF and ComZ, nor had it addressed the continuing independence of Bradley's Twelfth Army Group, which continued to exercise supply functions that rightfully belonged under Lee's command. "Officers of General Bradley's staff admitted at the end of the war that the army group's deep involvement in supply matters had been improper," Ruppenthal writes. "But it had been necessary, they explained, because of lack of confidence in the Communications Zone and lack of direction from a true theater headquarters."[25]

To the litany of difficulties besetting Lee and ComZ, including the rapid breakout that made a hash of all logistics planning, must be added the pernicious influence of Bradley and the Twelfth Army Group, the largest of the combat commands, which persistently sought to challenge Lee at every turn and issued distorted reports, such as those alleging shortages of heavy artillery ammunition to undermine his credibility. Bradley is properly regarded as a hero of the war and a great American, but his internecine campaign against Lee and ComZ was unprofessional, disruptive, and counterproductive to the war effort.

By this point in the war the ships were discharging endless streams of war matériel at Antwerp, and Lee's supply lines were running like clockwork. The soldiers had everything they needed, with the exception of warm clothes, and the end of the war was in sight. Whatever failings Lee may have had—and all of the generals had failings—he had managed to get the armies across the channel and to pull critical stocks out of the path of the advancing Germans in the Battle of the Bulge. There is something disturbing about this picture late in the war of senior officers ganging up on Lee yet again to land a few final punches, to what purpose one can only speculate. Lee and ComZ may well have learned a few pointers from Larkin and SOLOC, but by that point they could not have amounted to much. It was a final round of petty bitterness that served no one well and enhanced no one's reputation.

Somehow despite the bickering and backstabbing at headquarters the fighting men in the field pressed the battle home. Crossing the Rhine, which is a huge, fast-flowing river, presented some of the same challenges as crossing the English Channel. The main U.S. Army crossing over the Rhine was a twenty-three-span structure 1,753 feet long. But the man who had fought the great Mississippi flood of 1927 and conquered the channel was not intimidated. Lee

　　　　　　　　　　　　　　　　　　　　VICTORY IN EUROPE

had had his people planning for the invasion of the German homeland well in advance—and had made provision for rapid advances. There would be no repeat of the supply crisis in France the previous summer. Whatever else the critics may have said about Lee, he never made the same mistake twice.

When the Germans surrendered on May 7, Lee and ComZ faced another major challenge—the reverse of what they had been dealing with all along. They had to account for all of the supplies scattered about the European countryside, as well as Great Britain, and begin shipping all of it back to the United States. They found themselves at the same time saddled with hundreds of thousands of POWs and millions of displaced persons, including those liberated from Nazi death camps.

"Profiting by our rather trying experience of World War I, we saw to it that our returning soldiers were well cared for physically and morally," Lee recounted in his memoirs. As he tells it,

> the encampment around Rheims was so well conducted and the time of the men so well occupied that few of them wished to go to Paris or elsewhere for entertainment. Without overstressing, we let them realize the advantages of returning home healthy with their savings. In order to use ship accommodations to the full, we planned to double up en route home about the same way we had while bringing them over. For this decision, I took General Eisenhower to one of the final staging camps and let him ask the men assembled in large groups how they felt, saying substantially, "Would you rather wait here for a few more weeks or perhaps months and get a bunk all by yourself en route back home? Or would you rather cut your waiting time to half or less by doubling up aboard ship?" The response was always unanimously, "Let's go!"[26]

Lee moved ComZ from Paris to Frankfurt, Germany, where it officially became the Theater Service Forces. He visited Great Britain, where he was personally honored on his birthday by King George. He visited Berlin, where his son, Maj. John C. H. Lee Jr., had charge of the honor guard of the Eighty-Second Airborne Division.

But he did not hang around longer than he had to. By fall Lee was back in the States, where he accepted some honors in his hometown of Junction City, Kansas, and sojourned with many officers who had served with him. On September 19 he remarried, to a widow named Eve Ellis who was close to his family. By late December he found himself in Washington gearing up for a new challenge.

CHAPTER TWENTY-ONE

Lee's Excellent Italian Adventure

The Creator made Italy from designs by Michelangelo.
—MARK TWAIN

When World War II finally sputtered out and the guns at last were silent, three American generals were rewarded by being appointed high commissioners of the three main defeated nations.[1] Gen. Douglas MacArthur ruled Japan as a veritable shogun, Gen. Lucius Clay ruled West Germany, which he was largely responsible for creating, and Lt. Gen. John C. H. Lee ruled Italy. Lee was the only three-star general in that crowd. Clay wore four and MacArthur wore five. (The stars on the back of Lee's helmet did not count.)

It appears more than a bit incongruous that a senior officer who less than a year before had been put in the dock by his peers and seen his authority circumscribed (at least superficially) because of alleged ineptitude should be honored with this plum assignment. There were other senior command officers who presumably would have been given consideration ahead of Lee. Gen. Mark Clark had led the U.S. ground war in Italy until its final days. Gen. Matthew Ridgway was in command of U.S. forces in Italy when Lee took over. Gen. Jacob Devers had fought in the Italian theater before taking over the Sixth Army Group in France. Beetle Smith was looking for something to do.

But somehow Lee's appointment apparently did not ruffle anyone's feathers, at least not enough to make an issue of it. He had in fact been on the short list of those considered to serve in Germany.[2] It is almost as if the final victory served to put his work in perspective and sparked at least some reconsideration of his contributions. It was clearly a formal recognition of his ability and exemplary character. For Lee's part he did not regard it as unusual—just another job assignment for a diligent army officer.

There may well have been another factor at work. Lee was widely dismissed as a martinet, which *Webster's Dictionary* defines as "a rigid military disciplinarian" and "one who demands absolute adherence to the rules." The combat commanders were rarely accused of being martinets. When you are leading men into deadly battle and the bullets are flying, it simply isn't possible to demand observance of strict military protocol. Patton may have been the exception to this rule—he wanted his soldiers always to look soldierly—but as a practical matter he looked the other way. Exemplary comportment simply was not possible under battlefield conditions.

But Lee did not command men in battlefield conditions, with the possible exception of his adept handling of the Battle of the Bulge supply operation, getting precious fuel and ammunition out of the path of the advancing Germans. His people were behind the lines, sleeping in warm beds and eating three square meals a day. They were ordinary guys, many of them African Americans, and for some it was the first time in their lives they were on top of the world. They had money and, even more important, endless supplies of food, cigarettes, chocolate, and alcohol under their control—crucial items that assume exceptional value in wartime and that can be bartered for an array of favors and services. In that situation they were exposed to tremendous temptations.

Lee campaigned against that mentality throughout his year in Europe, raising hackles among the rank-and-file, who resented his overbearing ways, but in that situation discipline was called for. Even with Lee cracking the whip there was widespread profiteering and various kinds of corruption. He set a personal example of conduct and imposed strict regulations, but there was no way he could effectively restrict the behavior of hundreds of thousands of young men with money to burn in France in wartime conditions. It is safe to say that without Lee or someone like Lee in command the situation would have been much worse. In Italy with the war over Lee would face an even more rigorous challenge keeping his troops in line. His superiors recognized the problem and apparently figured Lee was just the guy to handle it.

"Late in December I was warned about the coming orders which would place me in command of our Mediterranean Theater of Operations, relieving General Ridgway, who had succeeded General [Joseph] McNarney," Lee noted. "By that time we felt that our ETO redeployment and disposal of surplus property had worked out well."[3] He was also relieved to be able to take his new wife, Eve, with him to Italy rather than to Germany, with its harsh, cold weather.

"General Ridgway was instantly responsive to all my requests for getting settled prior to his departure," Lee recalled. "In several significant ways he was most helpful in regard to relations with the British, the Poles and the Italians."[4] Lee's son, John Jr., had fought under Ridgway during the Battle of the Bulge.

Lee also drew support from another old friend, Gen. Sir William D. Morgan, who had become Supreme Allied Commander Europe. "In Italy, General Bill had negotiated the armistice which determined the frontier between the Allied forces and those of Yugoslavia, known as 'The Morgan Line,'" Lee wrote. "In Italy, I carried on the happy practice I had followed in England of having no secrets to the exclusion of our British partners. I followed our ETO practice of having a British officer in our mess and at all of our conferences."[5]

Under the terms of the armistice agreement between the Allied nations and Italy there was established in the Mediterranean region a supreme commander charged with supervising the execution of the armistice terms. That commander—first Morgan and then Lee—had control of all of the Allied forces and in some respects the Italian government and its forces as well. In that capacity he was also senior representative in Italy of the Allied nations. When General Morgan was ordered to Washington via London to head the British mission there it was decided that Lee should take over. "For my last months in Italy, therefore, I was both a subordinate of the Combined Chiefs of Staff of our Army Chief of Staff with many visits from the British War Office, the Admiralty and the Foreign Office," Lee recalled.[6]

Lee's memoir reports that although he had military forces under his command, security was never in doubt. "We were only concerned along the border or about individual trouble makers during such times as visits from General Eisenhower or General Bradley or other officials." Eisenhower and Bradley came with their wives, so there was a lot of entertaining to do. Lee's new wife apparently took to the hospitality circuit with enthusiasm. "Dear Eve was a model wife for a Commanding General," Lee recalled. "Whatever needed being done well, she did it most graciously. She set a splendid example to other service women from her appearance aboard the Italian liner, *Vulcania*, in Naples, to her departure aboard the U.S. Navy's *Grand Canyon* when she sailed. Our relations with the British families left nothing to be desired."[7]

The reference to Eve's sailing apparently stemmed from her trip back to the States in February 1947 to care for Lee's Aunt Jean, who was near death. Eve had also cared for Lee's mother in her final days while her son was in Great Britain preparing for the invasion of Europe and could not return to her bedside.

Lee was intensely focused on Italy's rebuilding efforts after the war "so that by the time we left, they would be able to stand on their own against the Red menace across the border." He noted that the Italians appreciated the help and "were amazingly rapid in their recovery." They had, he said, "performed extraordinary feats of physical reconstruction of their roads, railroads, bridges, ports, cities and towns, exemplifying the Italians' rare ability and industry."[8]

A major challenge for the Italians in the rebuilding was establishing a reliable source of electricity. "I tried to help them work out some hydro-electric planning that might let them compete with Switzerland," Lee wrote.

> I even suggested the use of wind-driven pumps to take advantage of the very heavy and quite steady winds that seasonally swept across the Mediterranean. I still believe there are possibilities in such a scheme of lifting water for storage to level out the power curve when the winds do not blow, meanwhile using the wind power for the generation of electricity. I had seen power developed by wind mills in Kansas thru my boyhood years and of course in the low lands of Europe. Perhaps like other mechanical means of power, new forms of energy may make such ideas obsolete.[9]

Lee also extended solicitude for "unfortunate soldiers who had gotten into trouble and had been given serious sentences," he noted.

Following the practice I had started in Britain and had continued in France, I took over the Disciplinary Barracks set up in Italy. There I was able to restore better than two thirds of those young men to duty status. As I had learned from General Wood, such men are properly regarded as patients under our care. We should do all we can toward restoring them to healthy, useful activities. In principle, I told them that one should never give up hope, no matter how serious his situation may seem to him. Some of these cases seem to have borne fruit beyond expectation.[10]

Lee said his handling of German prisoners of war in Italy could be called Operation Conversion. "Our treatment of them was fair and indeed considerate as to food, clothing, shelter and work," he noted. "We also provided excellent medical care supplementing their own doctors and nurses. Also spiritual care, detailing German-speaking Chaplains who volunteered for such extra duty. We gave the hard working Germans such financial credit as was permitted under the Geneva Convention and certificates of good behavior to take back home to the Allied Occupation Authorities. Many wanted to join the U.S. Army and go to America, especially those whose homelands had been occupied by the Russians." Lee also visited the soldiers on the front lines. "I wanted to be on hand for prompt action, assuming full responsibility for any drastic action that might be necessary." There was none.[11]

Of course Lee wouldn't have been Lee without kicking up a dust storm of some kind, and he had a big one in Italy courtesy of a writer named Robert Ruark, who at the time was working as a stringer for the Scripps-Howard newspaper syndicate. Ruark was actually a prolific novelist, with more than fifteen novels to his credit. He had served in the navy as a gunnery officer on convoys traversing the Atlantic and Mediterranean. He definitely had a creative bent that attempted to bridge the gap between fiction and news. His obituary in the *New York Times* in 1965 said he was "sometimes glad, sometimes sad and often mad—but almost always provocative."[12]

Ruark spent a few days in Italy, talked to some disgruntled soldiers, and filed a series of five long-winded, blistering reports about

Lee's alleged misuse of power and mistreatment of soldiers under his command. Ruark contended that Lee and his senior staff were living lives of luxury while the enlisted men were being poorly housed, inadequately fed, and subject to mass intimidation. He reported that enlisted men were employed as "flunkies" and were excessively punished for the slightest deviations from strict rules of discipline and military courtesy. He wrote disparagingly of a "Disciplinary Training Camp" that Lee called a hospital where inmates were put in a "sweat box" for making wrong turns on the road. He reported soldiers saying they could be court-martialed for "blinking an eye." He noted that military vehicles were required to travel far out of their way to avoid driving by Lee's headquarters and making noise. He reported that at Lee's headquarters there were only twelve showers, two out of order, for 700 men, while there were ten showers for a Women's Army Corps unit of 121. He said that Lee lived among the Italians like a "mob emperor," keeping fancy houses and maintaining a private train "sumptuously equipped" with sleeping cars, a diner, a lounge car, a moving picture car, and a car to carry automobiles—including a Cadillac, a Buick and a Jeep.[13]

There was more in that vein published in newspapers all across the country. The story generated many complaints in the form of letters to Congress and the White House. It all seemed a replay of the stories that had surrounded Lee in Great Britain and France, and indeed Ruark had to be familiar with those stories. He may have gone to Italy expecting to find more of the same.

In response the Pentagon sent the army's inspector general, Maj. Gen. Ira T. Wyche, who had served ably and well in the European theater with the Seventy-Ninth Division. He had participated in the capture of Cherbourg, and together with the Seventh Army his division took the brunt of the German offensive in Alsace after the Battle of the Bulge. Wyche likewise was surely steeped in Lee stories.

Wyche and his aides spent more time in Italy than Ruark did, from August 16 to September 11, 1947, following up on the allegations and interviewing officers and enlisted men. His most compelling finding, and one that seemed to undergird his entire report, concerned the age and training of the enlisted personnel under Lee's command.

These were not seasoned veterans from the war; those men had long since gone home. Most of his personnel at the time were little more than kids. Sixty percent of them were from 17 to 20 years old. The overall average age was 21.7 years. They had received on average eight weeks of training, which, Wyche noted, "is far too little training for men of this age for duty in a foreign country." Wyche added that "because of the immaturity of these young men, considerable supervision and certain restrictions with regard to their personal conduct are deemed necessary, which supervision and restrictions might not be considered necessary or appropriate for older and more seasoned troops."[14]

Wyche's team found that the majority of complaints they encountered centered on dependents not being brought to Italy, actions taken for contracting venereal disease, restrictive policies regarding marriage to Italian nationals, and restrictions on pass privileges—the standard litany of military complaints.

With regard to dependents, the team found that 671 officers and 457 enlisted men had been joined by dependents and that another 56 officers and 50 enlisted men were expecting their dependents to arrive. A further 196 officers and 268 enlisted men were still applying for dependents to come over, but because the contingent in Italy was being drawn down in anticipation of Italian independence they would have to arrange for dependents to meet them in their next stations. Because of the changing political situation many of them had not been informed about the status of their dependents, but there was little that could be done about that when the situation was in flux.

The action against personnel who contracted venereal disease basically came down to noncommissioned officers being segregated and demoted or reduced to the rank of private on that account. "These reductions were made because, in the opinion of Theater authorities [Lee], noncommissioned officers contracting such diseases were not setting a proper example for the men under their charge," Wyche wrote. "Such a policy is in accord with War Department directives on this subject."[15]

As for marriage to Italian nationals, some personnel who were already married objected that bachelors arriving in the theater could marry Italian nationals and be assigned quarters, thereby reducing the number of accommodations available to men who wanted to bring their families into the theater. According to the Wyche team's report, "It is a well-known fact that in that Theater . . . some Italian women of questionable character have taken, or will take, advantage of the immature soldiers and induce them to contract marriage. After considering the matter from both sides, the Theater authorities decided not to approve marriage of American soldiers to Italian women except under exceptional circumstances, which decision, under the conditions presented, appears to be sound and best for all concerned."[16]

Wyche continued rebutting Ruark's accusations for several pages. For example, Ruark had said that enlisted men were poorly housed and fed and subjected to humiliating treatment and outrageous violations of personal integrity, and also that there were flagrant misuses of government property and waste of taxpayer money. "After a thorough investigation on my part, I have found no evidence which indicates that the broad general allegations made by the columnist gave a true picture of conditions in this Theater," Wyche wrote. "On the contrary, I found no mass intimidation, no brutal degrading and humiliating treatment of enlisted men, and there has been no lavish waste of government funds." Using quotes from Ruark's articles, Wyche said he had found no evidence of enlisted men being used as "flunkies, servants and helpless targets for officer conceit."[17]

Wyche quoted a survey by a group of U.S. Army officers who had recently visited the theater: "Although the survey group mission does not require comment on the subject, the discipline, conduct and appearance of troops in the Theater is so outstanding as to warrant the most favorable comment. Such comment is considered especially apropos in view of the fact that these standards appear to have been maintained during a long period of uncertainty regarding future of the command which was anything but conducive to good morale and spirit."[18]

Wyche also quoted James Clement Dunn, the U.S. ambassador to Italy, who said, "In my observation of the officers and men under

General Lee's command in Italy, I have been struck with the fine soldierly bearing, neatness and good conduct of all the men I have seen, either at the various army headquarters or in the Rome Area Command. My own opinion is that General Lee carries on an efficient, disciplined and well-conducted military organization under his command here in Italy."[19]

Wyche visited the Disciplinary Training Center that Ruark had described in horrific terms. The inmates, Wyche wrote,

> live in shelter tents equipped with wooden floors. They are required to work hard and live under strict disciplinary control. The official records indicate that a large percentage of the personnel who have been sentenced to terms of confinement in the DTC have been rehabilitated into useful citizens and released to continue their service in the Army. This rehabilitation program serves to confirm General Lee's repeated statements that the inmates of the DTC should not be viewed as hardened criminals, but rather as patients whose defects could and should be eradicated by proper treatment in the same manner as a physically ill person can be cured by proper medical treatment.[20]

Even Ruark's report about the shortage of showers was off the mark. "As a result of my inspection and investigation, I found that this company has a total of 36 showers—12 in one location and 24 in another, and it was reported to me that these 36 showers were in use at the time Mr. Ruark visited the company on or about 26 July. Although there are 700 men assigned to this company, only about 410 to 450 actually reside in the company buildings. I consider that these 36 showers are ample for that number of men," Wyche wrote.[21]

With regard to the train—there were always trains around wherever Lee was—Wyche noted that the Italian government did make a train available to Lee's command at its own cost: "General Lee has made only three trips to Nice since he had been in the Theater, and not two trips a week as alleged."[22]

General Wyche concluded with an assessment of Lee's character that bears repeating. "General Lee has completed over 42 years of honorable service to his country," he wrote.[23]

He is a man of deep religious tendencies, which have a great influence on his thoughts and actions. He has a most retentive memory and adheres strictly to the rules and regulations as written. He does not deviate from prescribed methods, nor does he permit others in his command to do so. General Lee is a firm believer in the exchange of military salutes. He frequently salutes a subordinate first, and it is not unusual for him, when saluted by a group, to render each member of that group an individual return instead of the single salute required by regulations. So long as military salutes are prescribed in Army regulations, there is little doubt that General Lee will require such salutations to be meticulously rendered by members of his command. Another characteristic of General Lee is his firm conviction that he is directly responsible for the morals, conduct and personal welfare of all members of his command. He spends a great deal of time seeking out and interviewing individual soldiers of all ranks in an effort to learn the conditions under which they serve, and whether or not they can be helped in any way. He has manifested considerable enthusiasm in rewarding achievements, and he never hesitates to punish violations of law and order. However, it has been forcibly evidenced that the punishments given have conformed to regulations. And it is not believed that anyone having had the slightest personal contact with General Lee could be convinced that he would foster, condone or permit to the slightest degree any system of trial and punishment that was not in strict accordance with Army regulations.[24]

Wyche's report was issued October 3, 1947, by which time Lee was back in the United States preparing to retire from the service. He was incensed by the Ruark smear, but then as now it is impossible to rectify libelous media treatment. "Both General Eisenhower and Secretary Royall felt that altho we had the Scripps-Howard newspaper people out on a precarious limb, no eventual good was to be expected by setting them down hard," Lee wrote.[25] "Moreover," he continued, "such a vengeful treatment might be resented by the entire American press. As Secretary Royall said to me, 'It is better to forget and try to forgive.' As a Christian, one had no choice, nor have there been any regrets since except that for my failure to obtain proper recognition for my very able associates and assistants in Italy. Only one was properly recognized, General Bryant Moore, who was given an Oak Leaf Cluster for his D.S.M."[26]

Lee spent his last few weeks of active duty at the Presidio in San Francisco, where he formally retired on December 31, 1947. Predictably he spent his last years in religious work, serving with the Brotherhood of St. Andrew, an evangelical movement affiliated with the Episcopal Church. His wife, the former Eve Brookie Ellis, died in 1953. John Clifford Hodges Lee passed away August 30, 1958, at the age of seventy-one. He is interred in Arlington National Cemetery.

CHAPTER TWENTY-TWO

An Unsung Hero

General John C. H. Lee, a religious zealot often referred to as "Jesus Christ Himself Lee," . . . proved to be a logistics virtuoso and in many ways was the unsung hero of the Allied victory in Europe.

—JEAN EDWARD SMITH

The litany of criticisms leveled against Lee needs to be put in perspective and each criticism addressed in turn.[1] He was first pilloried for demanding and obtaining use of a private train in Great Britain during the buildup for the invasion of Europe. That act was highly recommended to him by the senior officer who had been in charge of supply during World War I, and it proved to be an essential part of Lee's operation. The train was by all reports a serious work environment that Lee's subordinates dreaded because they knew being taken along on it meant long hours of hard work. They were dealing with vast stores of supplies scattered across the countryside and needed to get a handle on what they had and where it was. When Devers was sent to Great Britain as senior commander to pave the way for Eisenhower's arrival, he challenged Lee about the already infamous train. Lee took him along for one of the work rides, and Devers was quickly convinced that the train was an essential component of Lee's operation. The train was a valuable asset that proved its value many times over.

Lee inherited a crisis when the politicians decided suddenly to conduct an invasion of North Africa in 1943, a move that had not been anticipated, at least not by Lee's operation. At the time this word came down Lee and his understaffed supply brigade were receiving vast amounts of unlabeled stores and scrambling to find places to put it all. Every ship was full of something, but no one knew for sure what. Suddenly Lee was told to forget the invasion of 1944 and prepare for a different one in three months. By his own account this was the low point of his career. And yet as always he pulled the rabbit out of the hat. He had his people all over the English countryside working day and night to identify what was where and move material to the embarkation points. By the time the invasion was launched Lee's troops had everything on board ships and ready to go.

The Normandy invasion was without doubt the most ambitious amphibious operation in military history, involving thousands of ships ferrying hundreds of thousands of men across a treacherous water passage against a hostile shore. There were serious concerns that it would be a disaster, and the logistics were the key element. Lee handled it superbly.

Once the invasion of France was launched there was in fact a huge logjam of supplies piled up around Omaha Beach, and those supplies were not reaching the troops in combat. A major reason for this imbroglio was Bradley's repeated refusal to cede control of the beaches to Lee, as he was supposed to do. This recalcitrance kept the supply situation in flux much longer than should have been the case, to the detriment of the troops. The only reason offered by Bradley for this peculiar action was his personal distaste for Lee. It was unprofessional conduct to say the least.

When the Allied forces drove the Germans out of Paris, Lee took heat for moving his headquarters into Paris, commandeering hundreds of hotels. At the time of the move he was operating from a chateau near Cherbourg and his troops were working from huts and tents. Paris was the historical center of France, where all the primary roads and railroads converged. Lee was in charge of taking advantage of that system and using it effectively to move troops and matériel for the war effort.

"Personally, I have no regrets because it should be clear that, as in combat so also in supporting combat, one should be as far forward as possible," Lee recounted in his memoirs. "Moreover, Paris was as always the center of transportation and indeed government for France. There we had superior communications not only on the ground but thru the atmosphere. Since General Eisenhower held me responsible for communications with the War Department in Washington as well as our ports thru New York City, we tried and succeeded in maintaining promptly and effectively the best of communications. Such could not have been done except in Paris."[2]

Lee was quickly joined in Paris by senior officers of other military units, and Eisenhower himself moved with his headquarters to Versailles, on the outskirts of Paris. Lee was by no means the only luminary to gravitate there.

Lee was widely held responsible for the inability of ComZ to keep supplies moving to forward elements of the army, especially Patton's Third Army, which was soon roaring across France and chasing the Germans back to their fatherland. But Lee was caught up in a dilemma not of his making. He was working from plans, laid down by the Supreme Command (SHAEF), that factored in use of a major port to unload supplies, as well as a systematic advance of the troops in accord with standard military doctrine. In reality they were several weeks late in securing use of the port of Cherbourg, and Patton's breakout made a hash of established doctrine. Lee and his supply organization found themselves scrambling to find ways to get supplies ashore without use of major ports and to get resources to the soldiers hundreds of miles away without use of railroads.

Once again Lee was reduced to scrambling and improvising on the run, and once again he proved up to the task. He created the celebrated Red Ball Express out of nothing, and for several weeks it moved millions of jerrycans of fuel to the troops at the front to keep their tanks and other mechanized vehicles moving, and they delivered other critical supplies as well. The combat units often had to curtail activities for lack of ammo, fuel, and food, and they were always operating with less of a cushion than was comfortable, but overall they kept the war going. Lee was subjected to intense criticism for the vexing supply situation, but the dilemma he was contending with had been hatched by Eisenhower and others at SHAEF who were more focused on tactics than logistics. Given an impossible task, Lee performed superbly.

In the autumn and on into the winter of early 1945, there was a steady drumbeat of complaints from senior generals about an alleged shortage of heavy artillery shells. Lee of course was held responsible. He was hard-pressed to do anything about it because, according to his records, they had more than enough. But the combat commands, led by Bradley, deliberately obfuscated in reporting on how much ammunition they had on hand and in most instances simply refused to give Lee any information at all.

General Aurand came to the theater to review the situation and concluded that the combat commands had more than enough explosives lying around and that they were deliberately concealing that fact while demanding more ammo and blaming Lee for a nonexistent shortage. Aurand gave this report to Beetle Smith, who was perhaps Lee's most ardent critic, and he swept it under the rug.

When the Germans attacked in the Ardennes in December, the combat forces suddenly had all the ammo they needed and then some, which they used to blunt the assault. Lee was not tasked to bring more heavy artillery ammo to the front but rather to get it out of the path of the advancing Germans. Still the top brass clung to the myth of an ammunition shortage. As late as January 1945 Somervell was setting in motion more production of heavy artillery ammunition and reducing Lee's authority in reaction to alleged ineptitude that presumably contributed to the alleged shortage. After the war it was determined that the armies had fired less than 30 percent of the heavy artillery ammunition they had had in hand.

One might reasonably ask why the senior commanders persisted in this farce, and the only credible answer is that it was all part and parcel of their continuing campaign to undermine Lee. Even with victory in sight they continued that campaign. One is left to wonder why they disliked him so intensely.

Part of the reason—probably the main reason—was the force structure imposed by Somervell and the War Department in which an independent supply operation, first sos and then ComZ, was established with its commander on a par with the senior combat commanders. In fact for a while Lee was, as deputy commander under Eisenhower, their superior in rank. This represented a dramatic change in traditional military doctrine and left the commanders dependent upon Lee for their supplies. The old guard resented it to the point that they used every tactic at their disposal to undermine the structure. As head of ComZ, Lee was simply the focal point of that campaign.

In addition there was the timeless animosity of combat troops for supply units—the guys in the rear who slept in warm beds, ate good food, and had access to cool wine and warm women. Combat soldiers knew they could not survive long without the supply troops, but the general resentment was nonetheless on that account. Lee was the most powerful and influential supply officer in the history of the U.S. Army, or perhaps any army, and that served to accentuate this timeless resentment of the faceless, lucky stiffs in the rear.

This resentment of Lee was inflated by his personal demeanor, which for many was off-putting in the extreme. The wearing of six stars—three on the front of his headgear and three on the back—was an affectation that invited ridicule. He did not mention this in his memoirs and insofar as is known never sought to explain it. But other senior officers also had peculiar affectations. Patton wore two pistols into battle and boasted of killing many Germans with them, at best an exaggeration that Eisenhower thought humorous.

Lee's advocacy of better treatment and more opportunity for African Americans was also a red flag for many of his contemporaries who were caught up in the racist attitudes that prevailed in that time and place. Today he seems ahead of his time; then he just seemed weird.

Lee's religious fervor also set him apart. Many senior military officers were religious, or at least professed to be, but few if any wore their faith on their sleeve to the degree that Lee did—before, during, and after his service in World War II. His zeal was that of an evangelist, and he sought at every opportunity to share his convictions with others. Eisenhower said Lee reminded him of Oliver Cromwell, the Puritan zealot who governed Great Britain briefly in the 1650s. Benjamin Davis, the African American general who otherwise thought Lee hung the moon, complained in a letter to his wife that Lee "was worse than Ma" about church.

But that religious faith sustained Lee through a long, dark night of brutal struggle against forces beyond his control among colleagues right and left doing their level best to stab him in the back. Many of his contemporaries suffered from ulcers and other nervous afflictions, some of those officers being immobile at times, but Lee was calm in the eye of the storm. He did not respond in kind, then or later, to the barbs at his expense, nor did he try to blame others for his problems or seek to have anyone broken from command, which was daily fare among his fellow senior officers. In his memoirs he speaks in glowing terms of Eisenhower, Bradley, Smith, and Patton as if they were drinking buddies. Actually Lee had no drinking buddies, which may have been one of his problems. In any case Lee stands out head and shoulders above the rest. He was never small or vindictive.

There is yet another factor that may have diminished Lee, at least in the eyes of historians. Writing about World War II is fascinating but grim. It is one long tragedy of death and destruction. There is little comic relief to be found. Perhaps writing about Lee has provided them with some comic relief from their otherwise dreary business. But he was never the clown they portray him to be. He was a serious military leader contending with a tremendous challenge that had his country, indeed the Western world, hanging in the balance.

One officer said Lee was a "queer duck" and another said memorably that he would not want to go fishing with him. But they were not engaged in a popularity contest in the ETO. They were trying to win a war against a determined enemy. Lt. Gen. John Clifford Hodges Lee got the troops across the English Channel on D-Day, got the fuel and ammo to the armies fighting in the field despite an array of obstacles in his way, and somehow got everything that might have been of use to the Germans out of their path during the Ardennes offensive. No other officer in history was responsible for such a complex, massive supply operation, and it seems unlikely one will ever be again. It was an extraordinary performance by an exemplary officer and gentleman who deserved better treatment from his colleagues at the time, and from historians in our own time.

NOTES

Introduction

1. Bailey, *Home Front*, 77.
2. Eisenhower, *Crusade in Europe*, 290.
3. Crosswell, *Beetle*, 764.
4. Ambrose, *Citizen Soldiers*, 336.
5. Jordan, *Brothers, Rivals, Victors*, 287.
6. Perret, *There's a War to Be Won*, 373.
7. Crosswell, *Beetle*, 297.
8. Beevor, *Ardennes 1944*, 20.
9. Atkinson, *Guns at Last Light*, 237.
10. Smith, *Eisenhower in War and Peace*, 205.

1. Slings and Arrows

1. Goldwyn's guy was apparently not up to the job. Perret, *There's a War to Be Won*, 303–4.
2. Jordan, *Brothers, Rivals, Victors*, 287.
3. Beevor, *Ardennes 1944*, 20.
4. Butcher, *My Three Years with Eisenhower*, 660.
5. Atkinson, *Guns at Last Light*, 238. The Communications Zone was Lee's all-encompassing command in the European theater, where he controlled the flow of all supplies to Allied forces.
6. Atkinson, *Guns at Last Light*, 238.
7. Crosswell, *Beetle*, 297.
8. Ohl, *Supplying the Troops*, 210.
9. D'Este, *Patton*, 647. SHAEF stands for Supreme Headquarters Allied Expeditionary Force.
10. Ambrose, *Citizen Soldiers*, 336–37.
11. Ambrose, *Citizen Soldiers*, 333–38.
12. Ruppenthal, *Logistical Support of the Armies*, 1:267.
13. Smith, *Eisenhower in War and Peace*, 205; Smith, *Lucius D. Clay*, 181.

2. A Woman Named John

1. All of this content about Lee's family and his early life is derived from Lee, "Our Estimate of Our Service," his unpublished memoirs.
2. Lee, "Our Estimate of Our Service," 3.
3. Lee, "Our Estimate of Our Service," 3.
4. Lee, "Our Estimate of Our Service," 4.

5. Lee, "Our Estimate of Our Service," 4.

6. Lee, "Our Estimate of Our Service," 5.

7. Lee, "Our Estimate of Our Service," 6.

8. In his memoirs Lee has an unnerving habit of referring to himself as "we," but not all the time. It is interesting to speculate that he picked up the "royal we" from his contacts with the royal family in Great Britain during the war. I have changed "we" to "I" in several places to avoid confusing the reader.

9. Lee, "Our Estimate of Our Service," 7.

10. Lee, "Our Estimate of Our Service," 9.

11. Lee, "Our Estimate of Our Service," 15.

12. Lee, "Our Estimate of Our Service," 25.

13. Lee, "Our Estimate of Our Service," addendum, O-5.

14. Lee, "Our Estimate of Our Service," 28.

15. Lee, "Our Estimate of Our Service," 28.

16. Lee, "Our Estimate of Our Service," 27.

17. Lee, "Our Estimate of Our Service," 29.

18. Lee, "Our Estimate of Our Service," 29. Lee refers to his mother as Muddie, possibly because he was uncomfortable calling her John in his text.

19. Lee, "Our Estimate of Our Service," 29.

3. Love and War

1. Lee's marriage and embarkation for World War I, including his first encounter with Brehon Somervell, are drawn from his memoirs, Lee, "Our Estimate of Our Service," 10–46. Various details about World War I are drawn from standard sources.

2. Lee, "Our Estimate of Our Service," 30.

3. Lee, "Our Estimate of Our Service," 31.

4. Lee, "Our Estimate of Our Service," 32.

5. Lee, "Our Estimate of Our Service," 35.

6. Lee, "Our Estimate of Our Service," 36.

7. In this famous incident Colonel MacArthur defended the Forty-Second from criticism by General Pershing. Instead of resenting it, Pershing expressed admiration for MacArthur's stance. Lee, "Our Estimate of Our Service," 37.

8. Lee, "Our Estimate of Our Service," 37.

9. Lee, "Our Estimate of Our Service," 37.

10. Lee, "Our Estimate of Our Service," addendum, O-6.

11. Lee, "Our Estimate of Our Service," 38.

12. Lee, "Our Estimate of Our Service," 39.

13. Lee, "Our Estimate of Our Service," 39.

14. Lee, "Our Estimate of Our Service," 40.

15. Lee, "Our Estimate of Our Service," 41.

16. Lee, "Our Estimate of Our Service," 40.

17. Lee, "Our Estimate of Our Service," 42.

18. Lee, "Our Estimate of Our Service," 42.

19. Lee, "Our Estimate of Our Service," 42.

20. Lee, "Our Estimate of Our Service," 43.

21. Lee, "Our Estimate of Our Service," 45.

22. Lee, "Our Estimate of Our Service," 45.

23. Lee would later earn an enduring reputation as a "hard commander." Lee, "Our Estimate of Our Service," 45.

4. The Great Flood of 1927

1. For this chapter I have drawn on Lee's memoirs ("Our Estimate of Our Service," 53–58) with extensive additions from Barry, *Rising Tide*, esp. 157, 182–85, 200–201.

2. Lee, "Our Estimate of Our Service," 49.

3. Lee, "Our Estimate of Our Service," 50.

4. Lee, "Our Estimate of Our Service," 53.

5. Lee, "Our Estimate of Our Service," 53. It was the era of Prohibition, but it is doubtful that his employees "gladly" accepted his ruling.

6. Lee, "Our Estimate of Our Service," 54.

7. Barry, *Rising Tide*, 176.

8. James Buchanan Eads was a legendary figure in the history of the Mississippi River. He built the first steel bridge across the river, at St. Louis, and he salvaged wrecks from the river bottom and also built gunboats for the Union during the Civil War.

9. Barry, *Rising Tide*, 184.

10. Lee, "Our Estimate of Our Service," 54.

11. Lee, "Our Estimate of Our Service," 54.

12. Lee, "Our Estimate of Our Service," 54.

13. Barry, *Rising Tide*, 183.

14. Lee quoted in Barry, *Rising Tide*, 185.

15. Barry, *Rising Tide*, 197.

16. Lee, "Our Estimate of Our Service," 54.

17. Lee, "Our Estimate of Our Service," 55.

18. Lee, "Our Estimate of Our Service," 56.

19. Lee, "Our Estimate of Our Service," 58.

20. Today the U.S. Army War College is in Carlisle, Pennsylvania.

5. Tragedy

1. Information on Lee and Somervell's activities in Great Depression work projects comes from Ohl's biography of Somervell (*Supplying the Troops*, 26–38) and Smith's biography of Franklin D. Roosevelt (*FDR*, 346).

2. Lee, "Our Estimate of Our Service," 64.

3. Lee, "Our Estimate of Our Service," 64.

4. Lee, "Our Estimate of Our Service," 64.

5. Lee, "Our Estimate of Our Service," 65.

6. Lee, "Our Estimate of Our Service," 66.

7. Lee, "Our Estimate of Our Service," 66.

8. Lee, "Our Estimate of Our Service," 66.

9. Information on New Deal programs is from Smith, *FDR*, 333–59.

10. Smith, *Lucius D. Clay*, 61.

11. Quoted in Smith, *Lucius D. Clay*, 62.

12. Quoted in Smith, *Lucius D. Clay*, 50.

13. CWA job creation statistics from Smith, *FDR*, 245–346.

14. Lee, "Our Estimate of Our Service," 66. Lt. Col. Dan Sultan was named engineer commissioner for the District of Columbia in 1934, much to the consternation of Lee's friend Somervell, who had campaigned hard for the posting. In *Supplying the Troops* John Kennedy Ohl reports that it was Somervell's aggressive maneuvering that cost him the appointment.

15. Lee quoted in Smith, *FDR*, 346.

16. Lee, "Our Estimate of Our Service," 68.

17. Lee was referring to Gen. Edward Murphy Markham, chief of engineers, 1933–37.

18. Lee, "Our Estimate of Our Service," 68.

19. Lee, "Our Estimate of Our Service," 72.

20. Lee, "Our Estimate of Our Service," 73.

21. Lee, "Our Estimate of Our Service," 73. It would be difficult to imagine the chief of engineers denying such a request.

22. Lee, "Our Estimate of Our Service," 75.

23. Lee, "Our Estimate of Our Service," 73.

24. Lee, "Our Estimate of Our Service," 74.

25. Lee, "Our Estimate of Our Service," 74.

26. Lee, "Our Estimate of Our Service," 64–75 (quoted text, 74).

6. War Clouds on the Horizon

1. Data on 1939 U.S. military strength are from Perret, *There's a War to Be Won*, 26, as well as Lee's memoirs, "Our Estimate of Our Service," 76–80.

2. Lee, "Our Estimate of Our Service," 76.

3. Lee, "Our Estimate of Our Service," 76.

4. Lee, "Our Estimate of Our Service," 78.

5. Lee, "Our Estimate of Our Service," 78.

6. Lee, "Our Estimate of Our Service," 80.

7. Lee, "Our Estimate of Our Service," 79.

8. Lee, "Our Estimate of Our Service," 79.

9. Lee, "Our Estimate of Our Service," 79.

10. In the army a major outranks a lieutenant, but a lieutenant general outranks a major general. This author has never been able to find a cogent explanation for the discrepancy.

11. Lee, "Our Estimate of Our Service," 81.

12. Ohl, *Supplying the Troops*, 56–71 (quoted text, 185–86).

13. Somervell quoted in Lee, "Our Estimate of Our Service," 81.

14. Crosswell, *Beetle*, 298–99 (quoted text, 298).

15. Lee, "Our Estimate of Our Service," 81.

16. Lee, "Our Estimate of Our Service," 82.

17. Ruppenthal, *Logistical Support of the Armies*, 1:35–36. Also see Lee, "Our Estimate of Our Service," 83.

18. Lee, "Our Estimate of Our Service," 83.

19. Lee, "Our Estimate of Our Service," 82.

7. Bolero

1. Ruppenthal, *Logistical Support of the Armies*, 1:33–37.

2. Ruppenthal, *Logistical Support of the Armies*, 1:38.

3. Lee, "Our Estimate of Our Service," 84.

4. Ruppenthal, *Logistical Support of the Armies*, 2:267.

5. Lee, "Our Estimate of Our Service," 85.

6. Lee, "Our Estimate of Our Service," 84.

7. Ohl, *Supplying the Troops*, 187.

8. Lee, "Our Estimate of Our Service," 85.

9. Lee, "Our Estimate of Our Service," 85.

10. Lovelace, "Hughes' War," 8–11 (quoted text, 8).

11. Ruppenthal, *Logistical Support of the Armies*, 1:39.

12. Ruppenthal, *Logistical Support of the Armies*, 1:81–83 (quoted text, 1:83).

13. Ruppenthal, *Logistical Support of the Armies*, 1:39.

14. Ruppenthal, *Logistical Support of the Armies*, 1:39.

15. Ruppenthal, *Logistical Support of the Armies*, 1:75.

16. Hughes quoted in Lovelace, "Hughes' War," 10.

17. Ruppenthal, *Logistical Support of the Armies*, 1:81.

18. Lee, "Our Estimate of Our Service," 86.

19. Ohl, *Supplying the Troops*, 184; Atkinson, *Guns at Last Light*, 8, 30.

20. Lee, "Our Estimate of Our Service," 87.

8. Lee's Darkest Hour

1. Ruppenthal, *Logistical Support of the Armies*, 1:84–87.

2. Smith, *Eisenhower in War and Peace*, 211–12; Lee, "Our Estimate of Our Service," 87.

3. Lee, "Our Estimate of Our Service," 71.

4. Ohl, *Supplying the Troops*, 18, 190 (quote); Ruppenthal, *Logistical Support of the Armies*, 1:139–41.

5. Ohl, *Supplying the Troops*, 18.

6. Ruppenthal, *Logistical Support of the Armies*, 1:92; Crosswell, *Beetle*, 296.

7. Ruppenthal, *Logistical Support of the Armies*, 1:98.

8. Crosswell, *Beetle*, 616; Butcher, *My Three Years with Eisenhower*, 7.

9. Ruppenthal, *Logistical Support of the Armies*, 1:98.

10. Eisenhower quotes from Crosswell, *Beetle*, 298.

11. Eisenhower quoted in Crosswell, *Beetle*, 300; Butcher, *My Three Years with Eisenhower*, 7.

12. Butcher, *My Three Years with Eisenhower*, 7.

13. Crosswell, *Beetle*, 301.

14. Lutes quoted in Ohl, *Supplying the Troops*, 191.

15. Lee, "Our Estimate of Our Service," 88.

16. Lee quoted in Lovelace, "Hughes' War," 21.

17. Hughes quoted in Lovelace, "Hughes' War," 21.

18. Butcher quoted in Crosswell, *Beetle*, 305.

19. Lee, "Our Estimate of Our Service," 89.

20. Lee, "Our Estimate of Our Service," 88.

21. Lee quoted in Crosswell, *Beetle*, 307.

22. Information on the buildup in North Africa is drawn from several sources but mainly Atkinson, *Army at Dawn*, chaps. 1–2.

9. Torch

1. Ruppenthal, *Logistical Support of the Armies*, 1:87–113; Atkinson, *Army at Dawn*, 22–67 (quoted text, 31).

2. Gent quoted in Mayhall, *Cranking Up a Fine War*, 76.

3. Mayhall's experience from Mayhall, *Cranking Up a Fine War*, 76.

4. Mayhall, *Cranking Up a Fine War*, 76.

5. Mayhall, *Cranking Up a Fine War*, 78–79.

6. Mayhall, *Cranking Up a Fine War*, 79.

7. Ruppenthal, *Logistical Support of the Armies*, 1:104–5.

8. Ruppenthal, *Logistical Support of the Armies*, 1:104.

9. Ruppenthal, *Logistical Support of the Armies*, 1:105.

10. Ruppenthal, *Logistical Support of the Armies*, 1:109.

11. Atkinson, *Army at Dawn*, 164.

12. Eisenhower quoted in Crosswell, *Beetle*, 356.

13. Ruppenthal, *Logistical Support of the Armies*, 1:112.

14. Lee never explained this magnanimity, but he may have been stung by the criticism he had recently endured and thought it best to avoid the limelight.

15. Lee, "Our Estimate of Our Service," 90.

16. Eisenhower quoted in Atkinson, *Army at Dawn*, 246.

17. Lee, "Our Estimate of Our Service," 90.

18. Brooke quoted in Smith, *Eisenhower in War and Peace*, 255; FDR quoted in Ambrose, *Eisenhower*, 89; Butcher quoted in Atkinson, *Army at Dawn*, 286. Lee makes no mention of Eisenhower's humiliation in his memoirs. Virtually

alone among senior American commanders, Lee had a pronounced reluctance to criticize his peers.

19. Hopkins quoted in Pogue, *George C. Marshall*, 180–81.
20. Ruppenthal, *Logistical Support of the Armies*, 1:116.
21. Ruppenthal, *Logistical Support of the Armies*, 1:117.
22. Ruppenthal, *Logistical Support of the Armies*, 1:117–18.
23. Ruppenthal, *Logistical Support of the Armies*, 1:118.

10. Back to Bolero

1. Conclusion of North Africa campaign from Atkinson's *Army at Dawn* (author's summary).
2. Ohl, *Supplying the Troops*, 185.
3. Ohl, *Supplying the Troops*, 210.
4. Overlord, the code name for the Normandy invasion, was coined by Churchill in the late summer of 1943. Lee, "Our Estimate of Our Service," 91.
5. Lee, "Our Estimate of Our Service," 95.
6. Lee, "Our Estimate of Our Service," 95.
7. Lee, "Our Estimate of Our Service," addendum 0-11 (first and second quotes).
8. Lee, "Our Estimate of Our Service," addendum 0-11.
9. Devers quoted in Wheeler, *Jacob L. Devers*, 236–37.
10. Lee, "Our Estimate of Our Service," 91.
11. Lee, "Our Estimate of Our Service," 91–92 (quote).
12. Lee, "Our Estimate of Our Service," 91.
13. Mayhall, *Cranking Up a Fine War*, 87.
14. Mayhall, *Cranking Up a Fine War*, 88.
15. Mayhall, *Cranking Up a Fine War*, 88.
16. Mayhall, *Cranking Up a Fine War*, 90.
17. Mayhall, *Cranking Up a Fine War*, 89–90 (quote).
18. Mayhall, *Cranking Up a Fine War*, 90, 91 (quote).
19. Mayhall, *Cranking Up a Fine War*, 94.
20. Mayhall, *Cranking Up a Fine War*, 95.
21. Ruppenthal, *Logistical Support of the Armies*, 1:121.
22. Ruppenthal, *Logistical Support of the Armies*, 1:127.
23. Ruppenthal, *Logistical Support of the Armies*, 1:128, 130.
24. Ruppenthal, *Logistical Support of the Armies*, 1:132.
25. Pogue, *George C. Marshall*, 362; Crosswell, *Beetle*, 562 (quote).
26. Hughes quoted in Crosswell, *Beetle*, 613.
27. Moses quoted in Crosswell, *Beetle*, 614.
28. Hughes quoted in Crosswell, *Beetle*, 616.
29. Ohl, *Supplying the Troops*, 226–27.
30. Patton quoted in Crosswell, *Beetle*, 616.

31. Ruppenthal, *Logistical Support of the Armies*, 1:139.

32. Ruppenthal, *Logistical Support of the Armies*, 1:67.

11. Countdown to D-Day

1. Mayhall, *Cranking Up a Fine War*, 134.

2. Mayhall, *Cranking Up a Fine War*, 134.

3. Crosswell, *Beetle*, 752.

4. Lutes quoted in Ohl, *Supplying the Troops*, 228.

5. Crosswell, *Beetle*, 614.

6. Crosswell, *Beetle*, 617.

7. Lee quoted in Crosswell, *Beetle*, 164.

8. Lee quoted in Crosswell, *Beetle*, 164.

9. Ruppenthal, *Logistical Support of the Armies*, 1:231.

10. Perret, *There's a War to Be Won*, 304.

11. Ruppenthal, *Logistical Support of the Armies*, 1:227.

12. Ruppenthal, *Logistical Support of the Armies*, 1:231.

13. Ruppenthal, *Logistical Support of the Armies*, 1:108.

14. Ruppenthal, *Logistical Support of the Armies*, 1:246.

15. Lovelace, "Hughes' War," 18, 22 (quote); Atkinson, *Guns at Last Light*, 22.

16. This was a common joke among the British during World War II.

17. Ruppenthal, *Logistical Support of the Armies*, 1:234.

18. Ruppenthal, *Logistical Support of the Armies*, 1:235.

19. Ruppenthal, *Logistical Support of the Armies*, 1:237.

20. Ruppenthal, *Logistical Support of the Armies*, 1:256.

21. Ruppenthal, *Logistical Support of the Armies*, 1:262.

22. Ruppenthal, *Logistical Support of the Armies*, 1:265.

12. The Overlord Logistical Plan

1. D'Este, *Patton*, 593.

2. Ruppenthal, *Logistical Support of the Armies*, 1:270.

3. Information on landing craft—DUKWs, LSTs, LCTs—from Ruppenthal, *Logistical Support of the Armies*, vol. 1; Atkinson, *Day of Battle* and *Guns at Last Light*; and Perret, *There's a War to Be Won*, 110–12.

4. Ruppenthal, *Logistical Support of the Armies* 1:277.

5. Ruppenthal, *Logistical Support of the Armies* 1:288.

6. Atkinson, *Guns at Last Light*, 151–52.

7. Ruppenthal, *Logistical Support of the Armies*, 1:390.

8. Ruppenthal, *Logistical Support of the Armies*, 1:361.

9. Ruppenthal, *Logistical Support of the Armies*, 1:315.

10. Ruppenthal, *Logistical Support of the Armies*, 1:319.

11. This was a well-known quote from World War II.

12. Ruppenthal, *Logistical Support of the Armies*, 1:439–41.

13. Ruppenthal, *Logistical Support of the Armies*, 1:338.

14. Ruppenthal, *Logistical Support of the Armies*, 1:352.

15. Atkinson, *Guns at Last Light*, 23.

16. Churchill quoted in Atkinson, *Guns at Last Light*, 8.

17. Eisenhower quoted in Crosswell, *Beetle*, 624.

18. Atkinson, *Guns at Last Light*, 7.

19. Atkinson, *Guns at Last Light*, 64.

20. Quotation from Brooke's diary, in possession of Prof. Duncan Anderson, Royal Military Academy Sandhurst.

21. Eisenhower note quoted in Smith, *Eisenhower in War and Peace*, 353.

13. The Great Adventure Begins

1. Ruppenthal, *Logistical Support of the Armies*, 1:375.

2. Cota quoted in Atkinson, *Guns at Last Light*, 38.

3. Smith, *Eisenhower in War and Peace*, 358; Atkinson, *Guns at Last Light*, 64–65; Ruppenthal, *Logistical Support of the Armies*, 1:378–79.

4. Ruppenthal, *Logistical Support of the Armies*, 1:380.

5. Ruppenthal, *Logistical Support of the Armies*, 1:390.

6. Ruppenthal, *Logistical Support of the Armies*, 1:394.

7. Ruppenthal, *Logistical Support of the Armies*, 1:394.

8. Crosswell, *Beetle*, 629.

9. Ruppenthal, *Logistical Support of the Armies*, 1:397.

10. McCarthy quoted in Pogue, *George C. Marshall*, 391.

11. Bradley's distaste for Lee, which he expressed frequently, was never explained. Bradley left behind two autobiographies, one co-written with Clay Blair. In neither does he mention Lee by name; see also Crosswell, *Beetle*, 641.

12. Crosswell, *Beetle*, 642.

13. Hughes quoted in Lovelace, "Hughes' War," 90.

14. Hughes indicated that it all depends on which side can build up forces faster. Crosswell, *Beetle*, 643.

15. Hughes quoted in Crosswell, *Beetle*, 642.

16. Ruppenthal, *Logistical Support of the Armies*, 1:404.

17. Ruppenthal, *Logistical Support of the Armies*, 1:406.

18. Ruppenthal, *Logistical Support of the Armies*, 1:427.

19. Atkinson, *Guns at Last Light*, 38 (Brooke quote), 191–200.

20. Crosswell, *Beetle*, 648.

21. Crosswell, *Beetle*, 648 (John Eisenhower quote), 649.

22. Butcher, *My Years with Eisenhower*, 594.

14. The Great Breakout

1. Bradley, *Soldier's Story*, 296.

2. Bradley, *Soldier's Story*, 296.

3. Bradley, *Soldier's Story*, 342.

4. Bradley, *Soldier's Story*, 336.

5. Bradley, *Soldier's Story*, 355.

6. Bradley, *Soldier's Story*, 355–56 (quote, 356).

7. Kluge quoted in D'Este, *Patton*, 145.

8. Patton quoted in D'Este, *Patton*, 647.

9. D'Este, *Patton*, 647.

10. Hughes quoted in Crosswell, *Beetle*, 653.

11. Bradley quoted in Crosswell, *Beetle*, 653.

12. Bradley quoted in Ambrose, *Citizen Soldiers*, 337.

13. Somervell quoted in Ohl, *Supplying the Troops*, 230.

14. Crosswell, *Beetle*, 684.

15. Ohl, *Supplying the Troops*, 230.

16. Ruppenthal, *Logistical Support of the Armies*, 1:481.

17. Ruppenthal. *Logistical Support of the Armies*, 1:488.

18. Ruppenthal, *Logistical Support of the Armies*, 1:491.

19. Ruppenthal, *Logistical Support of the Armies*, 1:493.

20. Atkinson, *Guns at Last Light*, 240.

21. Ruppenthal, *Logistical Support of the Armies*, 1:496; Atkinson, *Guns at Last Light*, 240.

22. Atkinson, *Guns at Last Light*, 241.

23. Atkinson, *Guns at Last Light*, 242.

24. Atkinson, *Guns at Last Light*, 242.

25. Atkinson, *Guns at Last Light*, 152.

26. Atkinson, *Guns at Last Light*, 242.

15. Taking the City of Light

1. Smith, *Eisenhower in War and Peace*, 383–92.

2. Ruppenthal, *Logistical Support of the Armies*, 2:31–32; Smith, *Eisenhower in War and Peace*, 402.

3. Eisenhower quoted in Crosswell, *Beetle*, 738.

4. Crosswell, *Beetle*, 739.

5. Crosswell, *Beetle*, 739.

6. Hughes quoted in Crosswell, *Beetle*, 739.

7. Bradley, *Soldier's Story*, 406.

8. Crosswell, *Beetle*, 738.

9. Atkinson, *Guns at Last Light*, 236–37.

10. Crosswell, *Beetle*, 739.

11. Ruppenthal, *Logistical Support of the Armies*, 1:267.

12. Atkinson, *Guns at Last Light*, 238.

13. Atkinson, *Guns at Last Light*, 237.

14. Smith quoted in Crosswell, *Beetle*, 740.

15. Ruppenthal, *Logistical Support of the Armies*, 2:233.

16. Ruppenthal, *Logistical Support of the Armies*, 2:247–75.

17. Crosswell, *Beetle*, 743.

18. Jodl quoted in Crosswell, *Beetle*, 703.

19. Ruppenthal, *Logistical Support of the Armies*, 2:110–17.

20. Atkinson, *Guns at Last Light*, 152.

21. Eisenhower quoted in Crosswell, *Beetle*, 726.

22. Ruppenthal, *Logistical Support of the Armies*, 2:54–60.

16. Lee in the Crosshairs

1. Atkinson, *Guns at Last Light*, 159–70.

2. Spitfire pilot quoted in Atkinson, *Guns at Last Light*, 167.

3. Atkinson, *Guns at Last Light*, 167.

4. Ruppenthal, *Logistical Support of the Armies*, 2:5.

5. Ruppenthal, *Logistical Support of the Armies*, 2:7.

6. Ruppenthal, *Logistical Support of the Armies*, 1:499.

7. Ruppenthal, *Logistical Support of the Armies*, 2:134–39.

8. Crosswell, *Beetle*, 712–15.

9. Crosswell, *Beetle*, 711.

10. Crosswell, *Beetle*, 747.

11. Crosswell, *Beetle*, 752–53.

12. Summersby quoted in Lovelace, "Hughes' War," 108. Summersby was Eisenhower's driver and constant companion through most of the European campaign. Historians continue to debate whether they had an affair. Jean Edward Smith concludes that they did. Others disagree.

13. Hughes quoted in Lovelace, "Hughes' War," 109.

14. Lovelace, "Hughes' War," 110.

15. Ruppenthal, *Logistical Support of the Armies*, 2:110–11.

16. Atkinson, *Guns at Last Light*, 312–26.

17. Mayhall, *Cranking Up a Fine War*, 198.

18. Crosswell, *Beetle*, 745.

19. Crosswell, *Beetle*, 751.

20. Crosswell, *Beetle*, 752.

21. Crosswell, *Beetle*, 752.

22. Crosswell, *Beetle*, 753.

23. Marshall quoted in Smith, *Lucius D. Clay*, 182.

24. Eisenhower quoted in Smith, *Eisenhower in War and Peace*, 402.

25. Smith, *Eisenhower in War and Peace*, 402.

26. Eisenhower quoted in Crosswell, *Beetle*, 756.

27. Smith, *Lucius D. Clay*, 183–84.

28. Clay quoted in Smith, *Lucius D. Clay*, 183.

29. Clay quoted in Smith, *Lucius D. Clay*, 183.

30. Port commander quoted in Smith, *Lucius D. Clay*, 184.

31. Clay quoted in Smith, *Lucius D. Clay*, 184.

32. Lee quoted in Smith, *Lucius D. Clay*, 185.

33. Smith, *Lucius D. Clay*, 185; Crosswell, *Beetle*, 765.

17. Stalemate on the Western Front

1. Whipple quoted in Ruppenthal, *Logistical Support of the Armies*, 2:107.
2. Butcher, *My Three Years with Eisenhower*, 696.
3. Ruppenthal, *Logistical Support of the Armies*, 2:110–11.
4. Ruppenthal, *Logistical Support of the Armies*, 2:111.
5. Ruppenthal, *Logistical Support of the Armies*, 2:178.
6. Ruppenthal, *Logistical Support of the Armies*, 2:172.
7. Ruppenthal, *Logistical Support of the Armies*, 2:179.
8. Ruppenthal, *Logistical Support of the Armies*, 2:179.
9. Ruppenthal, *Logistical Support of the Armies*, 2:110.
10. Hughes quoted in Crosswell, *Beetle*, 757.
11. Crosswell, *Beetle*, 757.
12. Aurand quoted in Crosswell, *Beetle*, 758.
13. Crosswell, *Beetle*, 759.
14. Moses quoted in Crosswell, *Beetle*, 759.
15. Moses and Aurand quoted in Crosswell, *Beetle*, 759.
16. Aurand quoted in Crosswell, *Beetle*, 759.
17. Simpson quoted in Crosswell, *Beetle*, 759.
18. Aurand quoted in Crosswell, *Beetle*, 760.
19. Aurand quoted in Crosswell, *Beetle*, 760.
20. Crosswell, *Beetle*, 761.
21. Aurand quoted in Crosswell, *Beetle*, 761.
22. Aurand quoted in Crosswell, *Beetle*, 761.
23. Aurand quoted in Crosswell, *Beetle*, 763.
24. Aurand quoted in Crosswell, *Beetle*, 762.
25. Aurand quoted in Crosswell, *Beetle*, 762.
26. Crosswell, *Beetle*, 763.
27. Crosswell, *Beetle*, 763.
28. Hughes letter quoted in Lovelace, "Hughes' War," 114.
29. Crosswell, *Beetle*, 764.
30. Beetle Smith quoted in Crosswell, *Beetle*, 764.
31. Crosswell, *Beetle*, 764 (Lutes quote), 766.
32. Lutes quoted in Crosswell, *Beetle*, 768.
33. Lutes quoted in Ohl, *Supplying the Troops*, 237.
34. Lovelace, "Hughes' War," 113.
35. Butcher quoted in Lovelace, "Hughes' War," 113.
36. Quoted in Lovelace, "Hughes' War," 116.
37. Hart quoted in Smith, *Eisenhower in War and Peace*, 415.
38. Speidel quoted in Smith, *Eisenhower in War and Peace*, 400.
39. Blumentritt quoted in Smith, *Eisenhower in War and Peace*, 400.
40. Westphal quoted in Smith, *Eisenhower in War and Peace*, 401.
41. Bradley and Ambrose quoted in Smith, *Eisenhower in War and Peace*, 401.

18. Lee's Finest Hour

1. Butcher, *My Three Years with Eisenhower*, 723.

2. Butcher, *My Three Years with Eisenhower*, 408.

3. Stargardt, *German War*, 461.

4. Beevor, *Ardennes 1944*, 111–34.

5. Stargardt, *German War*, 461.

6. Smith, *Eisenhower in War and Peace*, 410.

7. Smith, *Eisenhower in War and Peace*, 410.

8. Smith, *Eisenhower in War and Peace*, 410.

9. Ruppenthal, *Logistical Support of the Armies*, 2:184.

10. Ruppenthal, *Logistical Support of the Armies*, 2:183.

11. Ruppenthal, *Logistical Support of the Armies*, 2:184.

12. Crosswell, *Beetle*, 811.

13. Beevor, *Ardennes 1944*, 163, 366.

14. Ruppenthal, *Logistical Support of the Armies*, 2:184.

15. Third Army redeployment, Ruppenthal, *Logistical Support of the Armies*, 2:184.

16. German commander quoted in Atkinson, *Guns at Last Light*, 453.

17. Beevor, *Ardennes 1944*, 262–99.

18. Mayhall, *Cranking Up a Fine War*, 226.

19. Patton quoted in Atkinson, *Guns at Last Light*, 466.

20. Mayhall, *Cranking Up a Fine War*, 226.

21. Mayhall, *Cranking Up a Fine War*, 226.

22. Lee and son, tribute to John Jr.'s service from the *Military Times* Hall of Valor, http://valor.militarytimes.com/recipient.php?recipientid=88141; Lee, "Our Estimate of Our Service," 98.

23. Lee, "Our Estimate of Our Service," 96.

24. Patch quoted in Wheeler, *Jacob L. Devers*, 353.

25. *Military Times* Hall of Valor.

26. Beevor, *Ardennes 1944*, 144–47.

27. Lee, "Our Estimate of Our Service," 95.

28. Crosswell, *Beetle*, 765.

29. Lee, "Our Estimate of Our Service," 95.

19. Lee's Advocacy of African Americans

1. Ohl, *Supplying the Troops*, 16.

2. Rankin quoted in Brinkley, *Washington Goes to War*, 249.

3. Merrill quoted in Brinkley, *Washington Goes to War*, 249.

4. Brinkley, *Washington Goes to War*, 256–61.

5. Perret, *There's a War to Be Won*, 447.

6. Newspaper articles quoted in Roberts, *What Soldiers Do*, 232–33.

7. Roberts, *What Soldiers Do*, 233.

8. White quoted in Roberts, *What Soldiers Do*, 232.

9. Lee letter quoted in Roberts, *What Soldiers Do*, 233.

10. Perret, *There's a War to Be Won*, 448.

11. Soldier's published comment quoted in Ambrose, *Citizen Soldiers*, 245.

12. Patton quoted in Ambrose, *Citizen Soldiers*, 246.

13. Ambrose, *Citizen Soldiers*, 346.

14. Atkinson, *Guns at Last Light*, 554.

15. Perret, *There's a War to Be Won*, 452.

16. Fletcher, *America's First Black General*, 102.

17. Hughes letter quoted in Lovelace, "Hughes' War," 112.

18. Fletcher, *America's First Black General*, 104.

19. Lee letter quoted in Fletcher, *America's First Black General*, 106.

20. Davis quoted in Fletcher, *America's First Black General*, 134.

21. Crosswell, *Beetle*, 840–42.

22. Lee's order quoted in Fletcher, *America's First Black General*, 139.

23. Lee and Smith quoted in Crosswell, *Beetle*, 841.

24. Crosswell, *Beetle*, 841.

25. Smith quoted in Crosswell, *Beetle*, 842.

26. Crosswell, *Beetle*, 842.

27. Perret, *There's a War to Be Won*, 455.

28. Artillery forward observer quoted in Atkinson, *Guns at Last Light*, 554.

29. Ambrose, *Citizen Soldiers*, 348.

30. Atkinson, *Guns at Last Light*, 554 (including quote).

31. Black soldier quoted in Atkinson, *Guns at Last Light*, 554.

20. Victory in Europe

1. Bradley quoted in Atkinson, *Guns at Last Light*, 337.

2. Eisenhower quoted in Atkinson, *Guns at Last Light*, 340.

3. Ruppenthal, *Logistical Support of the Armies*, 2:222–28.

4. Stargardt, *German War*, 225–26.

5. Ruppenthal, *Logistical Support of the Armies*, 2:229.

6. Ruppenthal, *Logistical Support of the Armies*, 2:223.

7. Ruppenthal, *Logistical Support of the Armies*, 2:223.

8. Littlejohn quoted in Ruppenthal, *Logistical Support of the Armies*, 2:223.

9. Ruppenthal, *Logistical Support of the Armies*, 2:224–28.

10. Crosswell, *Beetle*, 742.

11. Littlejohn quoted in Crosswell, *Beetle*, 742.

12. Bradley quoted in Crosswell, *Beetle*, 742.

13. Lee quoted in Crosswell, *Beetle*, 743.

14. Crosswell, *Beetle*, 743.

15. Crosswell, *Beetle*, 743.

16. Crosswell, *Beetle*, 747.

17. Crosswell, *Beetle*, 843.

18. Somervell quoted in Crosswell, *Beetle*, 844.

19. Lee quoted in Crosswell, *Beetle*, 845.

20. Crosswell, *Beetle*, 846.

21. Crosswell, *Beetle*, 846.

22. Hughes quoted in Crosswell, *Beetle*, 846.

23. Crosswell, *Beetle*, 847 (including quote from Lear).

24. Ruppenthal, *Logistical Support of the Armies*, 2:362.

25. Ruppenthal, *Logistical Support of the Armies*, 2:387.

26. Lee, "Our Estimate of Our Service," 95.

21. Lee's Excellent Italian Adventure

1. Virtually all of the material in this chapter is taken from Lee's memoirs and the report by Maj. Gen. Ira T. Wyche, the U.S. Army inspector general, on the charges made against Lee in a series of articles by columnist Robert C. Ruark. The memoirs and Wyche report are in the U.S. Army Heritage and Education Center in Carlisle, Pennsylvania. Background information about Ruark is from Wikipedia.

2. Smith, *Lucius D. Clay*, 206.

3. Lee, "Our Estimate of Our Service," 98.

4. Lee, "Our Estimate of Our Service," 98.

5. Lee, "Our Estimate of Our Service," 98.

6. Lee, "Our Estimate of Our Service," addendum 0-12.

7. Lee, "Our Estimate of Our Service," 99.

8. Lee, "Our Estimate of Our Service," 98.

9. Lee was not only ahead of his time in race relations but also had a keen interest in renewable energy. Lee, "Our Estimate of Our Service," 99.

10. Lee, "Our Estimate of Our Service," 100.

11. Lee, "Our Estimate of Our Service," 101.

12. Ruark obituary, *New York Times*, July 1, 1965.

13. Ruark's descriptions quoted in Maj. Gen. Ira T. Wyche, Office of the Inspector General, Memorandum for the Chief of Staff, United States Army, U.S. Department of the Army, Public Information Division, October 3, 1947 (hereafter, Wyche memorandum).

14. Wyche memorandum, 5.

15. Wyche memorandum, 8.

16. Wyche memorandum, 8.

17. Wyche memorandum, 11.

18. Wyche memorandum, 12.

19. Dunn quoted in Wyche memorandum, 12.

20. Wyche memorandum, 14.

21. Wyche memorandum, 17.

22. Wyche memorandum, 20.

23. The actual figure at this point in time was thirty-seven years.

24. Wyche memorandum, 000

25. Lee, "Our Estimate of Our Service," 99. "Secretary Royall" was Kenneth C. Royall, the last man to serve as secretary of war. The War Department became the Department of Defense, and Royall moved over to serve as secretary of the army.

26. Lee, "Our Estimate of Our Service," 99. "D.S.M." refers to the Distinguished Service Medal.

22. An Unsung Hero

1. The conclusions reached in this chapter are the author's. The quote about Lee by Jean Edward Smith is from a caption with a photo of Lee published in Smith's *Eisenhower in War and Peace*, 205.

2. Lee, "Our Estimate of Our Service," 94.

BIBLIOGRAPHY

Ambrose, Stephen E. *Citizen Soldiers: The U.S. Army from the Normandy Beaches to the Bulge to the Surrender of Germany*. New York: Simon and Schuster, 1997.

———. *Eisenhower: Soldier and President*. New York: Simon and Schuster, 1990.

Atkinson, Rick. *An Army at Dawn: The War in North Africa, 1942–1943*. New York: Henry Holt, 2002.

———. *The Day of Battle: The War in Sicily and Italy, 1943–1944*. New York: Henry Holt, 2007.

———. *The Guns at Last Light: The War in Western Europe, 1944–1945*. New York: Henry Holt, 2013.

Bailey, Ronald H. *The Home Front: U.S.A.* Alexandria VA: Time-Life Books, 1978.

Barry, John M. *Rising Tide: The Great Mississippi Flood of 1927 and How It Changed America*. New York: Simon and Schuster, 1997.

Beevor, Antony. *Ardennes 1944: The Battle of the Bulge*. New York: Viking, 2015.

Bradley, Omar. *A Soldier's Story*. New York: Henry Holt, 1951.

Brinkley, David. *Washington Goes to War: The Extraordinary Story of the Transformation of a City and a Nation*. New York: Knopf, 1988.

Butcher, Harry C. *My Three Years with Eisenhower: The Personal Diary of Captain Harry C. Butcher, USNR, Naval Aide to General Eisenhower, 1942 to 1945*. New York: Simon and Schuster, 1946.

Cohen, Eliot A. *Supreme Command: Soldiers, Statesmen, and Leadership in Wartime*. New York: Free Press, 2002.

Crosswell, D. K. R. *Beetle: The Life of General Walter Bedell Smith*. Lexington: University Press of Kentucky, 2010.

D'Este, Carlo. *Patton: A Genius for War*. New York: HarperCollins, 1995.

Eisenhower, Dwight. *Crusade in Europe*. New York: Doubleday, 1948.

Fletcher, Marvin E. *America's First Black General: Benjamin O. Davis, Sr. 1880–1970*. Lawrence: University Press of Kansas, 1989.

Fussell, Paul. *Wartime: The Experience of War, 1939–1945*. New York: Oxford University Press, 1989.

Hastings, Max. *Inferno: The World at War, 1939–1945*. New York: Alfred A. Knopf, 2011.

Jordan, Jonathan W. *Brothers, Rivals, Victors: Eisenhower, Patton, Bradley, and the Partnership That Drove the Allied Conquest in Europe*. New York: NAL Caliber/Penguin Group, 2011.

Lee, Lt. Gen. John C. H. "Our Estimate of Our Service Reminiscences' Situation." Unpublished memoirs. U.S. Army Heritage and Education Center, Carlisle PA, 1956.

Lovelace, Alexander G. "Hughes' War: The Allied High Command through the Eyes of General Everett S. Hughes." Thesis submitted to Columbian College of Arts and Sciences, George Washington University, 2011.

Mayhall, Col. Van R. *Cranking Up a Fine War: A Louisiana Soldier from Boot Camp to General's Aide.* Austin TX: ByrenLee Press, 1999.

Mayo, Lida. *The Ordnance Department: On Beachhead and Battlefront.* Washington DC: Center of Military History, 1991.

Ohl, John Kennedy. *Supplying the Troops: General Somervell and American Logistics in WWII.* DeKalb: Northern Illinois University Press, 1994.

Perret, Geoffrey. *There's a War to Be Won: The United States Army in World War II.* New York: Random House, 1991.

Pogue, Forrest C. *George C. Marshall: Organizer of Victory, 1943–1945.* New York: Viking, 1973.

Roberts, Mary Louise. *What Soldiers Do: Sex and the American GI in World War II France.* Chicago: University of Chicago Press, 2013.

Ruppenthal, Roland G. *Logistical Support of the Armies: Volume I, May 1941–September 1944.* Washington DC: Center of Military History, United States Army, 1995.

———. *Logistical Support of the Armies: Volume II, September 1944–May 1945.* Washington DC: Center of Military History, United States Army, 1995.

Smith, Jean Edward. *Eisenhower in War and Peace.* New York: Random House, 2012.

———. *FDR.* New York: Random House, 2007.

———. *Lucius D. Clay: An American Life.* New York: Henry Holt, 1990.

Stargardt, Nicholas. *The German War: A Nation under Arms, 1939–1945.* New York: Basic Books, 2015.

Wheeler, James Scott. *Jacob L. Devers: A General's Life.* Lexington: University Press of Kentucky, 2015.

www.ingramcontent.com/pod-product-compliance
Lightning Source LLC
Chambersburg PA
CBHW020348100426
42812CB00035B/3395/J